Blockchain and AI in Shaping the Modern Education System

Editors:

Randhir Kumar
Department of Computer Science and Engineering
SRM University, AP, India

Prabhat Kumar
Department of Software Engineering
LUT University, Finland

Sobin C.C.
Department of Computer Science and Engineering
SRM University, AP, India

N.P. Subheesh
Teaching Learning Centre
SRM University, AP, India

CRC Press
Taylor & Francis Group
Boca Raton London New York

CRC Press is an imprint of the
Taylor & Francis Group, an **informa** business
A SCIENCE PUBLISHERS BOOK

First edition published 2025
by CRC Press
2385 NW Executive Center Drive, Suite 320, Boca Raton FL 33431

and by CRC Press
4 Park Square, Milton Park, Abingdon, Oxon, OX14 4RN

CRC Press is an imprint of Taylor & Francis Group, LLC

Library of Congress Cataloging-in-Publication Data (applied for)

ISBN: 978-1-032-80170-4 (hbk)
ISBN: 978-1-032-82058-3 (pbk)
ISBN: 978-1-003-50273-9 (ebk)

DOI: 10.1201/9781003502739

Typeset in Palatino Linotype
by Prime Publishing Services

Preface

The book aims to systematically collect and present quality research works in recent trends in Blockchain and AI approaches for providing the development of modern education system. Due to traditional education system policy most of the important data are not secured and transparent. To provide a fast and efficient data analytics solution for modern education system is a very fundamental research issue. The integration of Blockchain and AI for education system can enhance the broader side of the system including key features such as global accessibility, credential verification and recognition, data security, privacy of the identity which is really a key issue of traditional system of education. The current centralized education system is heavily restricted with various challenges such as single point of failure, data privacy, security, transparency, adaptive learning, etc. Thus, this book would emphasize and facilitate a greater understanding of various approaches using the advances in modern education system leveraged by Blockchain and AI for data analysis using machine/deep learning, federated learning, edge computing and the countermeasures to overcome these challenges.

Contents

Chapter 1

Blockchain and AI

Enhancing Personalized Learning

Shahabas Banu Jamsheed[1,*] and *Suhailam P*[2]

In the contemporary world of education, the importance of personalized learning has been developing as a transformative paradigm. Understanding the importance of customized learning styles for each student. The traditional one-fits-all approach is outdated and the introduction of AI is helping to develop a personalized learning system for students [1]. With the introduction of AI, students' individualized learning experiences can be improved and tailored to fit the specific demands and preferences of individual talents. The article examines the transformative potential of artificial intelligence (AI) in educational settings, starting with an overview of personalized learning principles. To generate individualized learning pathways, it emphasizes AI's capacity to process enormous volumes of student data, including learning styles, preferences, strengths, and weaknesses [2]. Educators can deliver individualized content, assignments, and assessments by identifying patterns and trends in student performance by using machine learning algorithms and data analytics. The chapter will

1 Elizabeth School of London, Exchange Tower, 1 Harbour Exchange Square, London E14 9GE.
2 National Institute of Technology, Calicut, Kerala-673601, India.
* Corresponding author: shahbas.b@elizabethschool.com

discuss the intersection of Artificial intelligence and personalized learning in contemporary education. It focuses on how AI algorithms are revolutionizing the educational landscape by analyzing vast datasets to tailor learning experiences to the individual needs and preferences of students. These will enable educators to customize the students' learning pathways, customize the materials, provide individual support, and ensure every student receives personalized attention, instruction, and guidance.

Additionally, the paper addresses the advantages of AI-powered customized learning, such as better academic results, higher teacher effectiveness, and increased student engagement [3]. The article's conclusion promotes the use of AI algorithms in personalized learning strategies, highlighting the field's potential for creativity, inclusion, and efficacy in teaching. Teachers can create more relevant, effective, and engaging learning experiences for all students by utilizing AI's capacity to analyses student data and customize lessons to each student's needs and preferences.

1. Introduction

The current educational system is undergoing a significant transformation, driven by the merger of two cutting-edge technologies: Blockchain and artificial intelligence. Blockchain, a decentralized distributed ledger technology, presents a new approach to secure and transparent information management, while artificial intelligence replicates human cognitive functions, providing advanced problem-solving and decision-making capabilities [4]. Together, these technologies are expected to revolutionize the educational landscape by enhancing data protection, streamlining administrative processes, and personalizing experiences. Interestingly, while blockchain and AI each have distinct complexities and potential, their convergence is particularly powerful in cybersecurity within educational institutions, safeguarding sensitive data and promoting efficient resource management [4, 5]. Furthermore, the potential applications of these technologies extend beyond administrative efficiency. They can influence pedagogical methods and the broader societal impact of education, including urban planning and agricultural output. The integration of blockchain and AI technologies is poised to reshape the educational system by providing robust security measures, enhancing operational efficiency, and offering innovative approaches to learning and teaching. As the education sector faces the challenges of the digital age, the adoption of these technologies can lead to a more equitable, efficient, and future-ready educational environment.

Blockchain technology can provide secure and transparent record-keeping for educational institutions [6, 7]. It can transform the traditional education system by addressing challenges such as secure credentialing and decentralized learning networks [8, 9]. AI can personalize and optimize the learning experience for individual students, leading to enhanced learning results. It is also underlined that establishing knowledge management tools, learning algorithms, and decision support systems will boost the educational process [10]. The combination of blockchain and AI can revolutionize the educational system by improving efficiency, fairness, and personalization [6]. This integration can enhance accessibility, efficacy, and security in education [8, 9]. Challenges to overcome include appropriate infrastructure and potential data privacy concerns [6]. Additionally, the exploration of ethical and social implications is highlighted as a future research direction [8].

Blockchain, as a decentralized and immutable distributed ledger, has the potential to transform the traditional education system by addressing inherent challenges [6, 11]. Due to its decentralized nature, it offers advantages such as integrity, anonymity, credibility, and independence of the institution and time [12]. Blockchain technology can provide secure and transparent record-keeping for educational institutions, ensuring the integrity and authenticity of academic credentials [13, 14].

AI can personalize and optimize the learning experience for individual students, enhancing accessibility, efficacy, and security in education [8, 15]. It can be used to create knowledge management tools, learning algorithms, and decision support systems to strengthen the educational process and enhance learning outcomes [10]. AI's potential applications in education include intelligent classroom teaching, improving students' interest in learning, and cultivating high-quality students [15]. Challenges to integrating blockchain and AI in education include the need for appropriate infrastructure, potential data privacy concerns, and the slow rate of adoption of blockchain technology in education [6, 8, 16]. Data privacy, scalability, legal issues, and the lack of tangible incentives for technology maintenance are some of the challenges associated with blockchain technology in education [14, 17].

Blockchain and AI can enhance the modern education system by providing secure credentialing, personalized learning, and decentralized learning networks [8, 18]. The integration of Education 4.0 and the utilization of blockchain Technology has proven to be efficacious in establishing a dynamic and individualized educational encounter for students in higher education [18]. Blockchain technology, coupled with artificial intelligence, can be used in higher education through intelligent contracts that motivate teamwork and student involvement in school activities, fostering a generation ready to work collaboratively and adopt attitudes of sustainability [3].

1.1 Overview of Modern Educational Challenges

Shift towards digital education to address the limitations of traditional education systems, emphasizing the need for modern learning methods to handle rapid transformations and vast information creation. A comprehensive analysis of education digitalization processes highlights the formation of a knowledge society and the digital stage of modern civilization while acknowledging internal contradictions and problems [19]. Various forms of educational and extracurricular activities are explored, including the use of digital educational resources like electronic journals and diaries, which have been implemented in many Russian schools [19]. The influence of globalization on education, noting the institutional organization and the role of digital technologies in shaping future education systems and the classroom environment. It also addresses the challenges and potential problems associated with digitalization [19].

The impact of globalization on education, emphasizing the need for countries to adapt and promote 21st-century skills as essential knowledge, habits, and traits necessary for success in today's world, applicable across various settings [20]. The text acknowledges the reality that many individuals do not have access to formal education, which hinders their ability to learn and compete globally [20]. Alternative Learning System (ALS) in the Philippines, assessing its effectiveness in imparting 21st-century skills to learners outside the formal education system. The importance of skills like problem-solving, collaboration, and adaptability in a rapidly changing global economy. A study focuses on ALS in the Philippines, a program designed to help out-of-school youth and adults gain education through conformal and informal methods. The research reveals that ALS learners in Northern Philippines have a low level of 21st-century skills acquisition, with local connections being the strongest area [20].

The growing trend of mobile learning (M-learning) and its potential to offer greater autonomy and flexibility in education. The challenges experienced in embracing M-learning, such as technological and infrastructure issues, while simultaneously recognizing the considerable benefits it can provide to the education industry [21]. The potential economic advantages of M-learning, include cost savings for educational institutions and increased accessibility for learners. Areas for future research, such as understanding the factors influencing M-learning adoption and developing guidelines for successful implementation [21].

1.2 Emergence of Personalized Learning

Personalized Learning (PL) is seen as a transformative approach that utilizes big data to tailor education to individual student needs, preferences, and interests. It promises to move away from the one-size-fits-all model to a more student-centered approach. The use of big data in education aims to create adaptive learning environments that can respond to the unique learning paths of each student. However, there is a concern that current implementations of PL may not fully align with progressive educational aspirations and instead resemble behaviorist models of learning.

The tension between the ideals of progressive education, which emphasizes student freedom and self-initiated learning, and the reality of PL implementations, which often prioritize control and efficiency over genuine student autonomy. Educational theories of Rousseau and Dewey to understand the implications of PL. Rousseau's model of well-regulated freedom suggests using student freedom as a means to achieve predetermined educational ends, while Dewey's critique advocates for a focus on social interaction and democratic citizenship [22]. Big data could potentially support a Deweyan approach to education, fostering social participation and meaningful democratic engagement, but acknowledges the challenges.

Personalized Education Goal is to adapt instruction to individual learners, aiming to address their specific needs and leverage their unique resources [23]. As dynamic entities that change during the instructional process, requiring adaptations at various timescales. Success in personalization is linked to the continuous measurement of learner characteristics and systematic, data-driven instructional adaptations [23].

The popularity of personalized learning and educational technology has increased in American K-12 schools, leading to the proliferation of technology-driven PL models [24]. The qualitative case study examines the implementation and evolution of a PL model at Binary High School over three years, using Activity Theory to analyze organizational changes. The school faced challenges with digital resources and student autonomy, leading to the adoption of a "No Excuses" model to prioritize accountability before refocusing on PL [24]. The study provides insights for educators and organizations on developing and implementing PL, highlighting the importance of aligning vision with practice and the impact of digital resources on PL execution.

The concept of personalized learning has evolved with technological advancements, from e-learning to smart learning environments (SLE). Personalized Adaptive Learning (PAL) is a new teaching method that combines personalized and adaptive learning, supported by smart technology for real-time adjustments. PAL focuses on individual characteristics, performance, personal development, and adaptive adjustment to cater to learners' unique needs [25]. The framework for PAL includes learner profiles, competency-based progression, personal learning paths, and flexible learning environments.

Traces PL back to early 20th-century educational reforms advocating learner-centered education. Global efforts in the UK, US, Finland, and Canada to tailor education to individual student needs. Examined the impact of varying technologies and contextual factors on PL implementation [26]. The lack of studies on PL's effects as a whole-school initiative calls for interdisciplinary research [26]. The synthesis aims to provide a clearer understanding of PL and encourage further advancement in the field.

1.3 Role of Technology in Education

Millennials have a strong preference for using technology in education, which should not be ignored by lecturers. Digital tools like Padlet.com, Moodle, and online News Forums are used to engage students and enhance knowledge sharing [27]. Technology enables distance learning, allowing for more flexible educational opportunities. Assigning video projects as part of coursework can increase student interest and engagement with the material.

Technology has revolutionized education, making learning more accessible, efficient, and engaging. It simplifies complex concepts through multimedia and interactive tools, fostering a more enjoyable learning experience. Modern tools help students actively engage in classroom activities and overcome the fear of public speaking [28]. Emerging technologies like AI, AR, and holograms are poised to further shape educational experiences.

Emphasizes the need for a culture of information technology (IT) alongside hardware resources in education systems, particularly in developing countries [29]. Discusses how IT has led to significant changes in classrooms, enabling access to external information and increasing student motivation. Highlights the impact of IT on educational methods, shifting from traditional teaching to technology-based learning opportunities. Explores the concept of a 'global village' where IT plays a role in promoting international understanding and educational development.

Technology has transformed education, making it more interactive and enjoyable. It automates tasks and simplifies complex processes, enhancing efficiency. Modern tools and the internet increase student interactivity and learning. Technology aids in knowledge transfer, making education more effective. The digital footprint in education is expanding, with round-the-clock connectivity and various platforms assisting students in their academic pursuits. Teachers face challenges adapting to new technologies, and barriers include lack of time, access, resources, expertise, and support.

2. The Evolution of Personalized Learning

The Evolution of Personalized Learning is a comprehensive resource that explores the concept of personalized learning in contemporary classrooms [30]. Written by respected educators Allison Zmuda, Greg Curtis, and Diane Ullman, the book delves into what personalized learning looks like, how it transforms the roles and responsibilities of stakeholders, and why it inspires innovation. The authors advocate for a student-centered model that emphasizes co-creation, feedback, sharing, and learning by doing. They discuss elements such as academic outcomes, growth outcomes, mindsets, tasks, audience, and feedback, providing a roadmap for educators to reimagine their roles and create effective personalized learning experiences. The book also addresses assessment, time management, and advancement within personalized learning systems. Overall, it advocates for a shift away from traditional, one-size-fits-all schooling toward a more dynamic and individualized approach to education [31].

2.1 Historical Context

The concept of personalized learning has evolved with technological advancements, from early e-learning to current intelligent tutoring systems. This progression through various web generations highlights the shift from knowledge dissemination to interactive and integrated learning experiences. The impact of information and communication technologies (ICT) on personalized learning, noting how these innovations have allowed educational institutions to keep pace with rapid developments in technology, communications, and computing power [30]. A systematic literature review from 2010 to 2021 is conducted to analyze the trends in personalized learning technologies and applications [30]. The review identifies key research themes, the growing number of publications over the years, and the focus areas within personalized learning. Prospective future research directions in personalized learning, emphasize the need for further studies on the development of new personalized learning models and techniques that leverage artificial intelligence and machine learning.

2.2 Traditional vs. Personalized Learning Models

The traditional model is a factory-style education system designed for a pre-20th-century society, which is not suitable for today's Knowledge Age requiring advanced skills. Personalized Learning emphasizes personalized learning as a response to the outdated traditional model, advocating for education that is tailored to individual student needs and characteristics. Various historical educational reform efforts, such as those by David Snedden, and John Dewey, did not focus on individual student learning needs. Shift towards personalized learning, including national initiatives like "Race to the Top" and examples from the UK, to address the need for a more individualized approach in education [32].

Historically, personalized learning existed through apprenticeship and mentoring. With advancements in educational technologies, it transformed into intelligent tutoring systems and now leverages big data and learning analytics [32]. Traditional learning often provides the same content to all students, regardless of their traits and needs, which is increasingly seen as inadequate in the era of personalized learning. Personalized learning models emphasize adapting to individual learners' conditions, abilities, preferences, and goals, and are inspired by educational philosophies like those of John Dewey, focusing on experiential, learner-centered education. The integration of technology in personalized learning is crucial, as it allows for the adaptation of learning paths, instructional methods, and content to meet diverse individual needs and goals [33].

The traditional Intelligent Tutoring System (ITS) model, includes four components: domain model, student model, teaching model, and user interface [34]. Traditional ITS often focuses on one component, such as domain intelligence, to provide new problems for practice. ITS has evolved from the computer-aided instruction model to incorporate various pedagogical paradigms and artificial intelligence techniques [34]. This evolution reflects a shift from content-focused systems to those considering pedagogical strategies and student modeling.

The new generation of ITS, exemplified by ZOSMAT, emphasizes adaptability to individual student needs. It integrates cognitive theories of learning and AI to offer personalized guidance and support, distinguishing it from traditional ITS. ZOSMAT is designed to mimic a human tutor's behavior, providing individualized learning experiences in mathematics education [34]. It adapts to each student's progress, offering equal educational opportunities regardless of location, and centers on student effort and initiative.

Traditional Learning is described as rigid, non-interactive, and non-adaptive, traditional learning models are likened to static HTML web pages or Computer-Assisted Instruction (CAI), which do not cater to individual student needs. BITS represents personalized learning, using Bayesian networks to adapt to each student's knowledge level, recommend learning goals, and generate appropriate learning sequences, thus providing a more effective, one-on-one tutoring experience. Historical advancements in educational technology, highlight the shift from traditional methods to intelligent, adaptive systems that personalize learning experiences. Empirical studies support the effectiveness of individualized tutoring, which BITS aims to replicate in a web-based environment for teaching computer programming [35]. The evolution from traditional classroom education to web-based educational systems that adapt to individual student needs. ITS highlights the use of ITS, which employs artificial intelligence to provide personalized education by considering individual learning styles and preferences. Type-2 Fuzzy Logic introduces a web-based ITS that utilizes type-2 fuzzy logic to handle uncertainties in student modeling and tailor the learning experience. The effectiveness of the ITS with traditional teaching methods shows that the ITS approach can enhance learning outcomes [36].

2.3 *Importance of Individual Learning Styles*

Emphasizes the role of collaborative settings in teacher development, suggesting that individual learning styles are important within group learning contexts. Teachers' learning activities, such as experimenting with new methods and reflecting on experiences, contribute to their professional growth. Individual learning styles impact changes in cognition and/or behavior, highlighting the significance of personalized learning approaches [37]. The reforms in education require teachers to adapt and learn continuously, making individual learning styles crucial for implementing new teaching practices effectively.

Individual learning styles allow for tailored teaching approaches that cater to each student teacher's unique needs, promoting more effective learning. Understanding different learning styles encourages the use of a variety of teaching strategies, which can help student teachers develop a broader range of skills and knowledge. Recognizing one's learning style can lead to better self-regulation of learning, enabling student teachers to manage their learning processes more effectively. Considering the affective aspects of learning, such as emotion regulation, can enhance the overall learning experience by addressing the emotional dimensions of teaching and learning [38].

Individual learning styles greatly influence creativity, as they determine how students prefer to receive and process information, which can either enhance or hinder creative performance. Independent and collaborative learning styles are linked to higher creativity. The independent style's effect on creativity is mediated by self-efficacy, the belief in one's abilities [39]. For collaborative learning styles, the relationship with creativity is partially mediated by the enjoyment of the learning process, suggesting that pleasure in collaborative tasks can boost creative output [40]. Educational institutions should cater to different learning styles to stimulate creativity, balancing individual and collaborative activities to nurture students' creative potential.

Personalization in E-Learning emphasizes the need for personalized content in e-learning courses to cater to individual learning preferences. Utilizes Howard Gardner's multiple intelligence theory to link learning styles with tailored e-learning course creation [40]. Creating several learner profiles to represent different learning preferences, rather than infinite course models [40]. Individuals have unique preferences for how they receive and process information, which can influence their learning effectiveness. Learning styles have gained significant traction in education, prompting the development of assessments and tailored teaching methods. Scientific studies conclude that there is insufficient evidence to support the effectiveness of learning styles in improving educational outcomes. Evidence does not support widespread educational practices based on learning styles, further methodologically sound research could explore their potential benefits [41].

3. Artificial Intelligence in Education

AI technology has rapidly advanced and is increasingly integrated into the educational environment, impacting teaching processes and classroom management. AI applications in education optimize learning environments, enhance student engagement and creativity, and improve classroom management efficiency. The use of AI in education is growing, with significant application advantages leading to profound impacts on teaching and learning methods. The ongoing development of AI promises further applications in education, contributing to teaching reforms and the integration of teaching and learning [42].

Emphasizing the need for innovation in education, akin to replacing horses with automobiles for faster transportation. The evolution of AI in education from the 1950s highlights the shift from manual grading to automated systems that detect plagiarism and facilitate remote teaching. The transition from mechanical teaching methods to the adoption of microcomputers in the 1970s, led to the current use of AI in various educational applications. AI's Impact sets the stage for discussing AI's extensive adoption in education, particularly in administrative tasks, personalized learning, and enhancing the overall quality of education [43].

AI has been widely applied in educational practices, offering new opportunities and challenges [44]. AIEd has evolved over decades, introducing new paradigms for instructional design and research [48]. AIEd aims to personalize learning, challenge traditional instructor roles, and develop complex systems. The integration of AI with educational theories is crucial for effective learning outcomes. Reflects on the past 25 years of AIED, analyzing key strengths and new opportunities for the field. Evolutionary and Revolutionary Paths suggest two research strands, an evolutionary path focusing on current practices and a revolutionary path embedding technologies in students' lives [45]. The introduction highlights a shift in education, emphasizing skills like metacognition and collaboration, and the need for AIED to adapt to these changes. A shift from viewing technology as a tutor to a mentor, supporting learning beyond traditional domains and settings.

AI is often seen as machines or computers mimicking human thought and action [46]. It's considered a key driver of the Fifth Industrial Revolution, potentially revolutionizing economic development and sectors like education. The advancement of AI is expected to significantly transform social structures, education, and school administration, necessitating adaptation to digital advancements and integration of 21st-century skills [46]. Law, business, education, and engineering stakeholders view AI's integration into education and its implications for the future [46]. AI's role in education could lead to personalized learning, enhanced creativity, and reduced teacher workload, but it also raises concerns about the future role of teachers and potential legal issues.

AI is often seen as machines or computers mimicking human thought and action. It's considered a key driver of the Fifth Industrial Revolution, potentially revolutionizing economic development and education. The advancement of AI is expected to significantly affect social structures, education, and school administration, necessitating adaptation to digital advancements and integration of 21st-century skills. Law, business, education, and engineering stakeholders view AI's role in education and its potential implications for the future. AI could enable personalized education, helping differentiate humans from automated systems while preserving emotional and social aspects [47].

AI has significantly advanced in various sectors, including health, military, and education, leading to innovations and developments. AI's contributions to education, examining its necessity, integration, conveniences, advantages, and disadvantages [48]. AI's impact on special education is highlighted, with a focus on how it aids students with disabilities in their educational journey. Global AI applications in education, such as Seeing AI, Virtual Assistants, and Virtual Reality. AI has enabled continued education during the COVID-19 pandemic through online platforms [48]. Education is crucial for society, impacting all other sectors [53]. The education sector faces challenges like access to education, which AI applications aim to solve through technologies like social robots and smart learning. AI is revolutionizing education by enabling personalized learning and overcoming geographical barriers. AI's role in education, addressing questions about AI's impact and benefits in the field [49].

AI technologies like big data, cloud computing, neural networks, and machine learning, enable machines to simulate human intelligence [50]. AI is seen as a disruptive innovation that could revolutionize future workplaces and education, potentially altering teaching and learning practices. The recent integration of AI into education examines how AI techniques and tools are being applied post-AI proliferation. The need to review AI capabilities in education and identify potential research trends and challenges in the field [50]. AIED industry has seen rapid growth, with significant investment from major companies, and is projected to reach USD 20 billion by 2027 [51]. AI has augmented human capabilities across various disciplines, leading to debates about its transformative potential in society. Philosophical discussions on AI's nature and consciousness continue, with some theorists adopting pragmatic approaches to artificial consciousness. AI technology has been applied in diverse fields, including education, healthcare, and public services, driving innovation and personalized services.

3.1 Historical Development and Milestones

The inception of educational robots dates back to the 1960s with the AI laboratory at MIT, leading to the development of intelligent tutoring robots. AI technology has seen significant improvements, particularly in adaptive learning, teaching evaluation, and virtual classrooms [42]. AI's integration into education has led to personalized learning plans, immersive experiences, and efficient classroom management. Presently, AI is utilized for a variety of educational purposes, including adaptive learning systems like ALEKS and BYJU'S, as well as intelligent tutoring robots like Softbank's Pepper. AI also aids in teaching evaluation through automated essay scoring tools like E-rater [42].

The journey began with the use of microcomputers and personal computers in the 1970s, marking a significant transition to electronic computers for the mass market [52]. This era saw the introduction of computer-aided instruction and learning (CAI/L) in classrooms. Advancements in networking, the Internet, and the World Wide Web led to the development of online intelligent education systems [43]. These platforms allowed for more effective administrative functions and higher-quality teaching activities. The field of AI evolved, leading to its integration into various educational areas. AI's adaptability and machine learning capabilities enabled personalized curriculum and content, enhancing the learning experience.

Today, AI applications in education include humanoid robots and web-based chatbots that independently perform instructional duties or assist educators, further improving the efficiency and effectiveness of educational processes. AI also supports the customization of learning materials to individual student needs, promoting better engagement and retention. AI-enabled mobile devices and virtual reality are taking mobile education to new levels, offering interactive and personalized learning experiences. AI-based chatbots and smart tutoring systems provide personalized online learning and assist both instructors and students in educational activities. AI's role in education continues to expand, with researchers applying advanced techniques to address complex issues and tailor teaching methods to individual students. AI's impact on education is profound, improving administrative tasks, instruction quality, and learning experiences [43]. AI's potential in education is vast, with ongoing developments promising even more innovative applications and benefits for all stakeholders in the education sector. AI's influence on education is significant, with its applications leading to improved efficiency, global learning, smarter content, and enhanced effectiveness in education administration [53]. AI's adoption in education has led to major improvements in various areas, including administration, instruction, and learning. AI's application in education has resulted in increased efficiency and quality of teaching, as well as enhanced learning experiences for students. AI's integration into education has transformed the sector, with its ability to personalize and customize content to students' needs and capabilities. AI's impact on education is evident in its ability to improve administrative tasks, enhance instructional quality, and foster effective learning experiences. AI's role in education is transformative, with its applications leading to significant advancements in teaching and learning processes. AI's influence on education is undeniable, with its capabilities leading to more efficient and effective educational practices. AI's contribution to education is substantial, with its applications enhancing the quality and effectiveness of instruction and learning. AI's presence in education is transformative, with its ability to improve administrative functions, instructional quality, and learning experiences. AI's impact on education is profound, with its applications leading to significant improvements in various aspects of the sector [43].

Initially, AI in education focused on directing cognitive learning, with learners as recipients of AI services, following specific learning pathways [44]. This approach was grounded in behaviorism and utilized programmed instructions for knowledge acquisition. The next phase saw AI as a support tool, with learners collaborating with AI systems. This paradigm shift towards cognitive and social constructivism emphasized mutual interactions and personalized learning experiences. The current trend in AIEd empowers learners to take control of their learning, reflecting the complexity theory. AI is viewed as a tool to augment human intelligence, with a focus on learner agency, personalization, and iterative development of learner-centered learning. Numerous studies and frameworks that have contributed to the evolution of AIEd, highlighting the importance of integrating AI with educational theories to enhance learning outcomes [45].

Focus on modeling domains and learners, with limited empirical data and technology used primarily in computers for formal education settings [45]. Shift towards empirical work with an increased focus on system description and evaluation, particularly in STEM fields, reflecting educational trends and technological advancements. Emphasis on empirical studies with rigorous evaluations, broader content coverage, and support for collaboration, aligning with modern educational practices and the need for personalization in learning.

The concept of general artificial intelligence dates back to at least the 14th century, with significant contributions by Alan Turing in 1937 [54]. AI is seen as a powerful factor in economic development, potentially serving as a cornerstone of the Fifth Industrial Revolution [64]. Record investments in AI, such as China's $40 billion in 2017, highlight its global economic impact and potential to transform education [55]. AI's role in education is anticipated to support personalized learning, helping students discover their talents and reducing teachers' workload [46].

In the 1970s, AIED emerged as a specialized area focusing on new technology for teaching and learning, primarily in higher education [47]. The first ITS went beyond Computer-Assisted Instruction by providing direct feedback and engaging in dialogue with students. Developed in the 1970s, was among the first ITS, which included components like expert models, pedagogical models, student models, and user interfaces. The use of AI in education has gained attention for automating tasks, personalizing learning, and providing data-driven insights to enhance educational outcomes.

The journey of AI began with foundational work by Kurt Gödel and Alan Turing, who laid the groundwork for computational logic and machine intelligence. The 1940s and 1950s saw the modeling of neural networks and the development of symbol-processing programs, marking the early stages of AI. The invention of the AI language LISP and the creation of expert systems like MYCIN in the 1970s and 1980s contributed to the growth of AI. Recent years have witnessed significant advancements with IBM's Watson, Google's AlphaGo, and the introduction of service robotics, showcasing the rapid evolution of AI technology [48].

3.2 Present Applications in Education

AI systems automate administrative tasks like grading and plagiarism detection, enhancing efficiency. Machine learning algorithms personalize curriculum and content, improving student engagement and retention. AI-powered tutoring systems adapt to individual student needs, offering personalized instruction and feedback. AI breaks down physical and language barriers, enabling access to educational resources worldwide. Applications demonstrate AI's role in streamlining administrative functions, tailoring learning experiences, providing intelligent instruction, and facilitating global education access [43]. AI continues to evolve, promising further advancements in the educational sector.

Intelligent Computer-Assisted Instruction (ICAI) systems, teach or tutor various subjects using AI advancements [56]. The development of learning environments that encourage student-initiated learning is highlighted. AI is used in expert systems to assist with educational diagnosis and assessment. The positive impact of AI research on educational applications and the need for further research to address current limitations [56].

Intelligent Tutoring Systems in AI systems provide personalized learning experiences, adapt to students' needs, and offer real-time feedback [57]. Tools that assist in data analysis and promote higher-order thinking skills by focusing on critical aspects of learning. AI technologies that help policymakers understand educational trends and challenges for effective policy formulation [57]. Exploring the roles of AI in supporting teachers and preparing learners for a future where AI may automate many jobs. AI can augment human cognition and offer new perspectives on learning and teaching.

AI enables personalized education by tailoring content to individual student needs, pace, and knowledge levels [58]. ITS provides targeted feedback and adapts to student responses, enhancing the learning experience. AI-powered assessment tools offer efficient, consistent evaluation and immediate feedback on student performance [59]. Robots serve as innovative educational tools, aiding in subjects like programming and science, and supporting students with special needs.

Personalized Learning in AI facilitates tailored educational experiences, adapting content to meet individual student needs for improved engagement and comprehension. ITS addresses the global shortage of qualified teachers, ITS systems support and enhance traditional curricula, utilizing knowledge-based domain information for personalized instruction. AI technologies optimize classroom attendance and utilization while respecting student privacy [60]. AI plays a crucial role in analyzing data to predict and prevent student dropouts, especially in online learning platforms [61]. AI techniques develop accurate models to predict student behavior and performance, aiding in the identification of students requiring additional support. Integrated with Learning Management Systems (LMS), AI helps recommend remedial actions to improve academic learning quality. AI platforms predict future student performance, enabling timely educational interventions [61]. Analyzing student feedback, sentiment analysis enhances the learning process by adjusting content and teaching methods based on student opinions.

Intelligent Tutoring Systems (ITS) systems offer personalized tutorials on subjects like mathematics or physics, adapting to each learner's misconceptions and progress. Educational Data Mining (EDM) involves applying data mining methods to educational systems to analyze large data collections and improve understanding of learners and learning contexts [62]. Learning Analytics (LA) measures and analyzes data about learners and their environments to optimize learning and educational settings [63]. Decision Support Tools use educational data to inform decisions made by stakeholders such as educators, institutions, and learners, aiming to improve learning and teaching through technology [43].

Profiling and Prediction in AI are used to create student models for predicting academic performance, aiding in admissions, and preventing dropouts [64]. Intelligent Tutoring Systems systems offer personalized content, feedback, and support for students, simulating one-on-one tutoring. Assessment and Evaluation in AI automates grading and feedback, evaluates student understanding and engagement, and assesses teaching quality [64]. Adaptive Systems and Personalization in AI tailor learning experiences to individual needs, monitor student progress, and assist in learning design.

3.3 *The Potential Impact of AI on Education*

3.4 *Enhancing Teachers' Roles: Augmentation and Automation*

The incorporation of AI in education presents significant potential for enhancing and automating teachers' responsibilities, thereby improving their overall educational experience. By harnessing the power of AI, educators can streamline administrative tasks, enabling them to dedicate more time to instruction and foster student engagement. AI-driven tools can assist with grading, attendance tracking, and managing classroom activities, thereby alleviating the burden of repetitive tasks. Furthermore, AI can offer real-time insights into student performance, allowing teachers to identify learning gaps and accordingly adjust their teaching strategies. Automation of routine tasks enables educators to focus on individualized instruction, thereby creating a more personalized learning environment. AI can also support teachers' professional development by offering valuable insights into teaching practices and suggesting areas for improvement. By embracing AI, educators can enhance their effectiveness, improve classroom management, and create more dynamic and responsive educational experiences for their students.

3.5 *Improving Assessment and Decision-Making in Education*

The impact of AI on the refinement of assessment and decision-making processes in education is transformative. Conventional assessment methods often fail to capture the complete range of student abilities and learning progress. AI-driven assessment tools offer a more comprehensive and continuous evaluation of student performance and provide insights that extend beyond standard tests and quizzes. These tools can analyze vast amounts of data to identify trends, patterns, and areas in which students may require additional support. In addition, AI can assist in the creation of personalized learning plans by considering each student's strengths, weaknesses, and learning styles. AI's data-driven insights can significantly enhance decision-making in education, from classroom interventions to the formulation of policies. Educators and administrators can make well-informed decisions, allocate resources more effectively, and implement strategies that lead to improved educational outcomes. By harnessing the power of AI, assessment and decision-making processes in education can become more precise, equitable, and responsive to the needs of all learners.

3.6 *Promoting AI and Digital Literacy*

In the contemporary digital era, it is paramount to impart AI and digital literacy to students to ensure their future success. By incorporating this literacy into the curriculum, students acquire the necessary competencies and knowledge to navigate and excel in a technology-driven society. Digital literacy involves the effective and ethical utilization of technology, while AI literacy encompasses an understanding of AI's functioning, applications, and implications of AI. Teachers play a pivotal role in fostering these competencies by integrating pertinent content and practical experiences into their instruction. Through these endeavors, students learn to critically evaluate digital content, comprehend the ethical considerations of AI, and develop problem-solving skills. Furthermore, promoting AI and digital literacy helps bridge the digital divide, ensuring that all students have equal opportunities to succeed in a technology-rich environment. Prioritizing this literacy enables education systems to prepare students to be informed, responsible, and innovative participants in the digital age.

3.7 Personalizing Learning Content and Experiences

The utilization of artificial intelligence in education represents a significant advancement in personalizing learning content and experiences. One-size-fits-all approaches often fail to address learners' multifarious needs and preferences. AI empowers the creation of personalized learning pathways by analyzing student performance data, learning styles, and interests. Adaptive learning technologies allow AI to deliver tailored content, recommend resources, and adjust the pace of instruction to suit the unique requirements of each student. This personalization fosters a more engaging and effective learning experience as students receive support and challenges that align with their abilities. Moreover, AI can facilitate personalized feedback, enabling students to comprehend their progress and areas of improvement. The ability to customize learning experiences according to individual students' needs promotes better outcomes, higher motivation, and enhanced knowledge retention. By leveraging AI for personalization, educational systems can create more inclusive and learner-centered environments that cater to the diverse needs of all students.

4. Challenges and Ethical Considerations

Algorithm Irrationality of algorithms can lead to problems in AI education. This includes issues like bias in data or algorithms that can affect fairness and inclusivity. Data Incompleteness or biased data can result in inaccurate AI systems. Ensuring the accuracy and relevance of training data is crucial for effective AI education. The potential inaccuracy of content used in AI systems can mislead learners. It's important to verify the accuracy and appropriateness of the content provided by AI educational tools. AI in education can raise ethical issues, such as the potential for AI to perpetuate biases or make erroneous associations, which can negatively impact educational outcomes and fairness [65].

AI systems may unintentionally reflect biases present in their training data, leading to unfair treatment of students. It's crucial to actively address and mitigate these biases to ensure equitable learning experiences. The vast amounts of student data processed by AI raise significant privacy concerns. Strong safeguards are necessary to protect sensitive information and maintain trust. AI should support, not replace, human educators [65]. The irreplaceable value of teacher-student interaction must be preserved for comprehensive student development. Implementing AI requires substantial investment in technology, training, and support services, which can be challenging for resource-limited institutions. Ensuring AI is used responsibly involves careful consideration of ethical issues, including data privacy, algorithmic bias, and the potential to exacerbate existing disparities [65].

The integration of AI in education raises significant ethical concerns, particularly regarding data privacy, learner autonomy, and potential biases in AI decisions. The extensive data collection by AI tools necessitates careful consideration of data ownership, access, and retention, aligning with regulations [66]. AI systems must be designed to avoid bias and ensure equitable treatment of all students, avoiding the perpetuation of existing inequalities. Research is needed to address the ethical management of learner data and to develop AI systems that are transparent, just, and beneficial to all stakeholders in education [66].

AI systems in education raise significant privacy issues. Personal data may be exposed excessively online, and despite protective legislation, tech companies' data practices heighten these concerns [67]. The use of AI for monitoring can lead to surveillance, affecting students' and teachers' autonomy. Predictive systems may infringe on individuals' ability to act independently, raising fairness questions [68]. AI platforms can perpetuate societal biases. For instance, language translation models may reflect gender stereotypes and facial recognition systems have misidentified individuals based on race. Automated assessment algorithms, like those used during the pandemic for student evaluations, have been shown to favor certain demographics, leading to unfair and inconsistent outcomes [69].

AI's intricate nature makes it difficult to understand and predict its decisions, leading to ethical dilemmas. The lack of transparency in AI algorithms, known as the "black box" issue, poses significant ethical challenges. AI's influence extends to critical societal domains like autonomous driving and military applications, raising ethical questions about life and death decisions. The ethical Management of Artificial Intelligence (EMAI) framework addresses the ethical management of AI, integrating managerial decision-making, ethical considerations, and environmental dimensions to guide organizations in ethically charged AI projects [70].

The moral implications of AI as moral agents and patients suggest that AI could be considered for moral considerations similar to humans and animals. AI's Moral Impact emphasizes the need for AI to have moral decision-making mechanisms, especially in roles such as teaching, in which AI's decisions can significantly affect human well-being [71]. The moral attributes of tools and technologies highlight the challenges that autonomous technology poses to traditional moral frameworks. The application of moral AI in education emphasizes the importance of aligning AI's moral theoretical basis with that of teachers and students for effective integration [71].

The integration of AI in education requires the handling of vast amounts of sensitive student data, which raises significant concerns about privacy and security [72]. Ensuring the protection of these data against unauthorized access or misuse is crucial [73]. AI systems can inadvertently perpetuate the existing biases found in their training data, leading to discrimination. It is essential to design AI tools that minimize bias and promote fairness. Using AI in education, particularly for personalized learning, could lead to plagiarism and academic dishonesty. Establishing clear guidelines and guardrails is necessary to maintain integrity [73].

The adoption of Artificial Intelligence in Education (AIED) presents challenges, such as systemic bias, discrimination, and privacy concerns. The complexity of AI technology necessitates risk-intensive procedures to ensure quality delivery and acknowledge human values [74]. Ethical issues in AIED include the potential for privacy breaches, biased data collection, and the impact on learner autonomy. The need for ethical guidelines is emphasized to address these concerns and ensure the responsible use of AI in educational settings [74]. The massive amount of data collection involved in AIED raises privacy risks. It is crucial to manage this data responsibly, ensure informed consent, and protect learners' personal information from misuse or violation. The development and deployment of AIED must consider environmental sustainability, minimize ecological impact, and address economic and societal implications such as labor market effects and cultural considerations [74].

5. Conclusion

This chapter discusses the transformative potential of blockchain and AI in shaping modern educational systems. Blockchain provides secure and transparent record-keeping, whereas AI personalizes and optimizes the learning experience of individual students. The integration of these technologies can enhance accessibility, efficacy, and security in education, thereby leading to improved learning outcomes. However, challenges, such as the need for appropriate infrastructure, data privacy concerns, and slow adoption rates, must be addressed. This study highlights the potential of blockchain and AI to revolutionize education by providing secure credentialing, personalized learning, and decentralized learning networks. The integration of Education 4.0 and blockchain technology has proven effective in creating dynamic and individualized educational experiences for higher education students.

Abbreviation

AI	Artificial Intelligence
AIED	Artificial Intelligence in Education
ALS	Alternative Learning Systems
CAI	Computer Assisted Instruction
EDM	Educational Data Mining
EMAI	Ethical Management of Artificial Intelligence
ICAI	Intelligent Computer Assisted Instruction
ICT	Information and Communication Technologies
IT	Information Technology
ITS	Intelligent Tutoring Systems
LA	Learning Analytics
LMS	Integrated with Learning Management Systems
PAL	Personalized Adaptive Learning
PL	Personalized Learning
SLE	Smart Learning Environments

References

[1] Tapalova, O. and Zhiyenbayeva, N. (2022). Artificial Intelligence in Education: AIEd for personalised learning pathways. *Electronic Journal of E-Learning*, 20(5): 639–653.

[2] Essa, S.G., Celik, T. and Human-Hendricks, N.E. (2023). Personalized adaptive learning technologies based on machine learning techniques to identify learning styles: A systematic literature review. *IEEE Access*, 11: 48392–48409.

[3] Li, K.C. and Wong, B.T.-M. (2023). Artificial intelligence in personalised learning: A bibliometric analysis. *Interactive Technology and Smart Education*, 20(3): 422–445 .

[4] BK, A. and Gomathy, B. (2023). Blockchain Integration in Artificial Intelligence: Benefits, applications, research challenges. *IJFMR—International Journal for Multidisciplinary Research*, 5(6): 1–18.

[5] M. Vc and S. (2024). Unifying forces, harnessing blockchain and Artificial Intelligence integration for enhanced innovation. *IJIRCCE*, 12(05): 6103–6109.

[6] Salama, R. and Al-Turjman, F. (2024). Using artificial intelligence in education applications. *Morgan Kaufmann*, pp. 77–84 .

[7] Fedorova, E.P. and Skobleva, E.I. (2020). Application of blockchain technology in higher education. *European Journal of Contemporary Education*, 9(3): 552–571 .

[8] Islam, M.A. and Rihan, N.M. (2024). AI and blockchain as sustainable teaching and learning tools to cope with the 4IR. In *Blockchain and AI*, CRC Press.
[9] Ma, Y. and Fang, Y. (2020). Current status, issues, and challenges of blockchain applications in education. *International Journal of Emerging Technologies in Learning (iJET)* 15(12): Art. no. 12.
[10] Kaul, N., Deshpande, A., Mittal, A. and Raut, R. (2023). The intersection of AI and blockchain in education: A bibliometric and thematic analysis. In *2023 7th International Conference on Computing, Communication, Control and Automation (ICCUBEA)*, pp. 1–6.
[11] Swathi, T., Raj, P.R., Srilakshmi, P. and Padma, M. (2023). Exploring the synergy of machine learning and blockchain in the education sector. In *2023 3rd International Conference on Smart Generation Computing, Communication and Networking (SMART GENCON)*, pp. 1–3.
[12] Juričić, V., Radošević, M. and Fuzul, E. (2019). Creating student's profile using blockchain technology. In *2019 42nd International Convention on Information and Communication Technology, Electronics and Microelectronics (MIPRO)*, pp. 521–525.
[13] Rustemi, A., Dalipi, F., Atanasovski, V. and Risteski, A. (2023). A systematic literature review on blockchain-based systems for academic certificate verification. *IEEE Access*, 11: 64679–64696.
[14] Chae, Y. (2023). Blockchain technology in education: A comprehensive review in transparency. In *2023 Congress in Computer Science, Computer Engineering, & Applied Computing (CSCE)*, pp. 850–857.
[15] Chen, Y. (2022). The impact of Artificial Intelligence and blockchain technology on the development of modern educational technology. *Mobile Information Systems*, 2022(1): 3231698.
[16] Dwivedi, S. and Vig, S. (2023). Institutional readiness to adopt block chain technology in higher education. In *2023 14th International Conference on Computing Communication and Networking Technologies (ICCCNT)*, pp. 1–7.
[17] Dymek, D. and Stal, J. (2023). Blockchain's impact on education: Current landscape and prospects for the future. In *Supporting Higher Education 4.0 with Blockchain*, Routledge.
[18] Aliane, N. and Salim, A.S. (2023). Revolutionising higher education: Case studies on education 4.0 integration and blockchain-enhanced education management. *Eurasian Journal of Educational Research*, 105(105): Art. no. 105.
[19] Grevtsov, K., Kadeeva, O., Syritsyna, V., Ilchenko, O. and Belov, A. (2021). Digitalization of environmental education is the trend of its modernization and reform. *E3S Web Conf.*, 258: 10011.
[20] Tindowen, D.J.C., Bassig, J.M. and Cagurangan, J.-A. (2017). Twenty-first-century skills of alternative learning system learners. *Sage Open*, 7(3): 1–8.
[21] Sarrab, M., Al-Shihi, H. and Rehman, O.M.H. (2013). Exploring major challenges and benefits of m-learning adoption. *British Journal of Applied Science & Technology*, 3(4): Art. no. 4.
[22] Dishon, G. (2017). New data, old tensions: Big data, personalized learning, and the challenges of progressive education. *Theory and Research in Education*, 15(3): 272–289.
[23] Tetzlaff, L., Schmiedek, F. and Brod, G. (2021). Developing personalized education: A dynamic framework. *Educ. Psychol. Rev.*, 33(3): 863–882.
[24] Bingham, A.J. (2017). Personalized learning in high technology charter schools. *J. Educ. Change*, 18(4): 521–549.
[25] Peng, H., Ma, S. and Spector, J.M. (2019). Personalized adaptive learning: An emerging pedagogical approach enabled by a smart learning environment. *Smart Learn. Environ.*, 6(1): 1–14.
[26] Zhang, L., Basham, J.D. and Yang, S. (2020). Understanding the implementation of personalized learning: A research synthesis. *Educational Research Review*, 31: 100339.

[27] Au-Yong-Oliveira, M., Gonçalves, R., Martins, J. and Branco, F. (2018). The social impact of technology on millennials and consequences for higher education and leadership. *Telematics and Informatics*, 35(4): 954–963.

[28] Ilyas, A., Akbar, S.S., Hamza Wajid, S., Joghee, S., Fatima, A. and Mago, B. (2023). The growing importance of modern technology in education. In *2023 International Conference on Business Analytics for Technology and Security (ICBATS)*, pp. 1–4.

[29] Hamidi, F., Meshkat, M., Rezaee, M. and Jafari, M. (2011). Information technology in education. *Procedia Computer Science*, 3: 369–373.

[30] Ambele, R., Kaijage, S., Dida, M., Trojer, L. and Kyando, N. (2022). A review of the development trend of personalized learning technologies and its applications.

[31] Zmuda, A., Curtis, G. and Ullman, D. (2015). *Learning Personalized: The Evolution of the Contemporary Classroom*. John Wiley & Sons.

[32] Spencer, L. (2014). Transforming schools From traditional to personalized. Creighton University.

[33] Shemshack, A. and Spector, J.M. (2020). A systematic literature review of personalized learning terms. *Smart Learn. Environ.*, 7(1): 33.

[34] Keleş, A., Ocak, R., Keleş, A. and Gülcü, A. (2019). ZOSMAT: Web-based intelligent tutoring system for teaching–learning process. *Expert Systems with Applications*, 36(2): 1229–1239.

[35] Butz, C.J., Hua, S. and Maguire, R.B. (2004). A web-based intelligent tutoring system for computer programming. In *IEEE/WIC/ACM International Conference on Web Intelligence (WI'04)*, IEEE, 2004, pp. 159–165.

[36] Bulut Özek, M., Akpolat, Z.H. and Orhan, A. (2013). A web-based intelligent tutoring system for a basic control course. *Computer Applications in Engineering Education*, 21(3): 561–571.

[37] Meirink, J.A., Meijer, P.C. and Verloop, N. (2007). A closer look at teachers' individual learning in collaborative settings. *Teachers and Teaching*, 13(2): 145–164.

[38] Oosterheert, I.E. and Vermunt, J.D. (2001). Individual differences in learning to teach: Relating cognition, regulation and affect. *Learning and Instruction*, 11(2): 133–156.

[39] Sitar, A.S., Černe, M., Aleksić, D. and Mihelič, K.K. (2016). Individual learning styles and creativity. *Creativity Research Journal*, 28(3): 334–341.

[40] Zajac, M. (2009). Using learning styles to personalize online learning. *Campus-Wide Information Systems*, 26(3): 256–265.

[41] Pashler, H., McDaniel, M., Rohrer, D. and Bjork, R. (2008). Learning styles: Concepts and evidence. *Psychol. Sci. Public Interest*, 9(3): 105–119.

[42] Huang, J., Saleh, S. and Liu, Y. (2021). A review on Artificial Intelligence in education. *Acad. J. Interdiscip. Stud.*, 10(3): 206.

[43] Chen, L., Chen, P. and Lin, Z. (2020). Artificial Intelligence in education: A review. *IEEE Access*, 8: 75264–75278.

[44] Ouyang, F. and Jiao, P. (2021). Artificial intelligence in education: The three paradigms. *Computers and Education: Artificial Intelligence*, 2: 100020.

[45] Roll, I. and Wylie, R. (2016). Evolution and revolution in Artificial Intelligence in education. *Int. J. Artif. Intell. Educ.*, 26(2): 582–599.

[46] Gocen, A. and Aydemir, F. (2020). Artificial Intelligence in education and schools. *Research on Education and Media*, 12(1): 13–21.

[47] Joshi, S., Rambola, R.K. and Churi, P. 2021. Evaluating Artificial Intelligence in education for next generation. *J. Phys.: Conf. Ser.*, 1714(1): 012039.

[48] Nalbant, K. (2021). The importance of Artificial Intelligence in education: A short review, pp. 1–15.

[49] Ahmad, S.F., Rahmat, M.K., Mubarik, M.S., Alam, M.M. and Hyder, S.I. (2021). Artificial Intelligence and its role in education. *Sustainability*, 13(22): Art. no. 22.

[50] Zhai, X. et al. (2021). A review of Artificial Intelligence (AI) in education from 2010 to 2020. *Complexity*, 2021(1): 8812542.
[51] Pham, S.T.H. and Sampson, P.M. (2022). The development of artificial intelligence in education: A review in context. *Journal of Computer Assisted Learning*, 38(5): 1408–1421.
[52] Flamm, K. (1988). *Creating the Computer: Government, Industry, and High Technology*. Brookings Institution Press.
[53] Timms, M.J. (2016). Letting Artificial Intelligence in education out of the box: Educational cobots and smart classrooms. *Int. J. Artif. Intell. Educ.*, 26(2): 701–712.
[54] Humble, N. and Mozelius, P. (2019). Artificial intelligence in education—A promise, a threat or a hype. In *Proceedings of the European Conference on the Impact of Artificial Intelligence and Robotics*, pp. 149–156.
[55] Mou, X. (2019). Artificial Intelligence: Investment trends and selected industry uses. *International Finance Corporation*, 2(8): 311–320.
[56] Jones (Colbourn), M. (1985). Applications of artificial intelligence within education. *Computers & Mathematics with Applications*, 11(5): 517–526.
[57] Hwang, G.-J,. Xie, H., Wah, B.W. and Gašević, D. (2020). Vision, challenges, roles and research issues of Artificial Intelligence in Education. *Computers and Education: Artificial Intelligence*, 1: 100001.
[58] Hutchins, D. (2017). AI boosts personalized learning in higher education. *Educ. Technol.*
[59] Chassignol, M., Khoroshavin, A., Klimova, A. and Bilyatdinova, A. (2018). Artificial Intelligence trends in education: A narrative overview. *Procedia Computer Science*, 136: 16–24.
[60] Raykov, Y.P., Ozer, E., Dasika, G., Boukouvalas, A. and Little, M.A. (2016). Predicting room occupancy with a single passive infrared (PIR) sensor through behavior extraction. In *Proceedings of the 2016 ACM International Joint Conference on Pervasive and Ubiquitous Computing*, in UbiComp '16. New York, NY, USA: Association for Computing Machinery, pp. 1016–1027.
[61] Yousuf, M. and Wahid, A. (2021). The role of Artificial Intelligence in education: Current trends and future prospects. In *2021 International Conference on Information Science and Communications Technologies (ICISCT)*, pp. 1–7.
[62] Beck, J.E. and Mostow, J. (2008). How who should practice: Using learning decomposition to evaluate the efficacy of different types of practice for different types of students. pp. 353–362. *In*: Woolf, B.P., Aïmeur, E., Nkambou, R. and Lajoie, S. (eds.). *Intelligent Tutoring Systems*, Berlin, Heidelberg: Springer.
[63] Ferguson, R. (2012). Learning analytics: Drivers, developments and challenges. *International Journal of Technology Enhanced Learning*, 4(5-6): 304–317.
[64] Zawacki-Richter, O., Marín, V.I., Bond, M. and Gouverneur, F. (2019). Systematic review of research on artificial intelligence applications in higher education – where are the educators?. *Int. J. Educ. Technol. High. Educ.*, 16(1): 39.
[65] Zaman, B.U. (2023). Transforming education through ai, benefits, risks, and ethical considerations. *Authorea Preprints*.
[66] Boulay, B. Du. (2022). Artificial Intelligence in education and ethics. In *Handbook of Open, Distance and Digital Education*, Singapore: Springer Nature Singapore, pp. 1–16.
[67] Akgun, S. and Greenhow, C. (2022). Artificial intelligence in education: Addressing ethical challenges in K-12 settings. *AI Ethics*, 2(3): 431–440.
[68] Citron, D.K. and Pasquale, F. (2014). The scored society: Due process for automated predictions. *Wash. L. Rev.*, 89: 1.
[69] Specia, M. (2020). Parents, students and teachers give britain a failing grade over exam results. *The New York Times*, 2020.
[70] Brendel, A.B., Mirbabaie, M., Lembcke, T.B. and Hofeditz, L. 2021. Ethical management of Artificial Intelligence. *Sustainability*, 13(4): Art. no. 4.

[71] Sun, F. and Ye, R. (2023). Moral considerations of Artificial Intelligence. *Sci. & Educ.*, 32(1): 1–17.

[72] Fengchun, M., Wayne, H., Huang, R. and Zhang, H. (2021). UNESCO. *AI and Education: A Guidance for Policymakers*. UNESCO Publishing, 2021.

[73] Kamalov, F., Santandreu Calonge, D. and Gurrib, I. (2023). New era of artificial intelligence in education: Towards a sustainable multifaceted revolution. *Sustainability*, 15(16): Art. no. 16.

[74] Nguyen, A., Ngo, H.N., Hong, Y., Dang, B. and Nguyen, B.-P.T. (2023). Ethical principles for artificial intelligence in education, *Educ. Inf. Technol.*, 28(4): 4221–4241.

Chapter 2

Blockchain and AI for Educational Data Analytics in the Modern Education System

ReddyPriya Madupuri, Murali Krishna Enduri,*
Anil Carie Chettupally, Krishna Siva Prasad Mudigonda
and *Satish Anamalamudi*

This chapter explores the transformative potential of integrating blockchain and artificial intelligence (AI) technologies within educational data analytics. It begins by examining blockchain's capacity to enhance data security, streamline record-keeping, and ensure transparent credential verification. Concurrently, it analyzes AI's role in enabling adaptive learning, predictive modeling, and insightful data analysis to improve student outcomes and optimize educational strategies. The chapter further evaluates the synergistic benefits of combining blockchain and AI, proposing a robust framework to address prevalent challenges in the education sector, including data privacy, security, and personalized learning. By securing student records through blockchain's immutability and enhancing personalized learning experiences via AI-driven analytics, the chapter presents a comprehensive approach to modernizing educational systems. Additionally, it addresses technical challenges such as scalability and interoperability, alongside ethical considerations like data privacy, consent, and

Department of CSE, SRM University-AP.
* Corresponding author: reddypriya_madupuri@srmap.edu.in

algorithmic bias. The chapter concludes with a call for collaborative efforts among educators, technologists, and policymakers to leverage these technologies, navigate their challenges, and fully realize their potential in revolutionizing education.

1. Introduction

Artificial intelligence (AI) and blockchain technology could revolutionise education by solving data management, security, and individualised instruction issues. This chapter extensively reviews how blockchain and AI are employed in educational data analytics. Educational institutions have seen substantial growth in data created by professors, students, and administrative systems. This data influx offers data-driven insights and individualised learning methods to improve education. Educational record interoperability and data security and privacy are also discussed. Blockchain technology can safely maintain educational records, diplomas, and transcripts due to its immutability, transparency, and decentralised data management [1]. This article examines how blockchain can secure and distribute educational data to ensure academic qualifications. AI and machine learning in educational data analytics can help institutions acquire insights from large datasets. Instructors can employ AI-powered data to identify at-risk students, update course material, and personalise learning pathways to boost student accomplishment. This chapter examines AI's predictive modelling and adaptive learning applications in educational data analytics.

Blockchain data integrity improves AI data analytics. By combining blockchain's secure and decentralised ledger with AI's data analysis and interpretation, educational institutions may create a data-driven decision-making ecosystem. Challenges and factors are considered. Scalability, data protection, ethics, and other AI in education challenges are discussed, along with solutions and best practices. The report emphasizes the need for collaboration between educational institutions, decision-makers, and technology providers to standardise blockchain-based educational data management.

To summarize, blockchain and AI in educational data analytics could transform education. Integrating blockchain and artificial intelligence (AI) technologies within educational data analytics presents a groundbreaking opportunity to address long-standing challenges in the education sector [2]. The advent of these technologies has the potential to revolutionise how educational data is managed, secured, and utilized, thereby enhancing the overall efficiency and effectiveness of educational institutions. This chapter is a comprehensive resource for educators, administrators, researchers, and policymakers who want to use these technologies to improve data security, learning outcomes, and education in the digital era.

1.1 Overview

Educational institutions have struggled with data privacy, student record validity, and efficient use of the massive amounts of data generated during teaching and learning. Digital education platforms and internet-connected devices have highlighted the need for creative solutions to these difficulties. Blockchain technology disrupts this setting and can safely manage educational data with its decentralised and impermeable infrastructure.

AI in educational data analytics has enabled behaviour analysis, academic performance prediction, and learning process customisation. Artificial intelligence algorithms can analyse big datasets, show trends, provide useful insights, and enable adaptive learning systems that meet each learner's needs [3].

The research is motivated by the need to address gaps and capitalise on opportunities in the education industry due to the confluence of blockchain and AI. Educational institutions are increasingly using digital platforms, therefore they need to trust academic records and use data analytics to make decisions.

This section examines how blockchain and AI are employed in current education for data analytics, focusing on applications, issues, and synergies. The main goals are:

i. Blockchain Application Exploration: Utilise blockchain technology to enhance data security, automate record-keeping, and enable transparent credential verification in learning environments.
ii. AI's Impact on Educational Data Analytics: Evaluate.
iii. Assessing the Joint Effect of AI and Blockchain: Evaluating how.

This chapter intends to provide relevant knowledge to help technologists, educators, and policymakers navigate the ever-changing world of educational technology. The ultimate goal is to prepare for educated decisions when incorporating blockchain and AI into schooling.

Blockchain technology, characterized by its decentralized, immutable ledger system, offers significant advantages for managing educational data. One of the primary benefits is the enhancement of data security. Blockchain's inherent properties ensure that once data is recorded, it cannot be altered or tampered with, thereby providing high-level data integrity and security. This is particularly crucial for educational institutions that manage sensitive student information and academic records. The application of blockchain can ensure the authenticity and accuracy of academic credentials, reducing the risk of fraud and enhancing the trustworthiness of educational qualifications [4].

In addition to security, blockchain can streamline administrative processes through smart contracts. These self-executing contracts, with the terms directly written into code, can automate various administrative tasks such as student admissions, course registrations, and fee payments. This automation can reduce administrative burdens, minimize errors, and improve operational efficiency within educational institutions [5].

Furthermore, AI-driven predictive analytics can help educators identify students at risk of falling behind and provide timely interventions. By analyzing historical data and identifying trends, AI can predict future performance and suggest personalized support strategies. This proactive approach can significantly enhance student retention and success rates [6].

2. Literature Review

The application of blockchain and artificial intelligence (AI) technologies in educational data analytics has garnered significant attention in recent years. This literature review explores the current state of research in these areas, focusing on developments from 2020 to 2024. The combination of blockchain and AI in educational data analytics creates a robust framework that addresses multiple challenges simultaneously. Blockchain's security and transparency, coupled with AI's analytical and adaptive capabilities, can provide comprehensive solutions for data management and personalized education. For instance, integrating AI with blockchain can enhance data privacy by ensuring that data is stored securely on the blockchain while AI processes the data to generate insights without compromising privacy [7]. Moreover, blockchain can provide a decentralised infrastructure for AI applications, enhancing data accessibility and interoperability across educational platforms and institutions. This integration can foster a more collaborative and cohesive educational ecosystem, enabling seamless sharing and analysis of data to drive innovation and improvement in educational practices [8].

2.1 *Educational Data Analytics*

Educational data analytics analyses large educational datasets. Scholars have studied how data analytics might improve teaching practices, student learning, and institutional efficacy. Numerous studies show how important data-driven insights are for evidence-based education decision-making [9]. Data silos, interoperability issues, and student data ethics are highlighted in the literature. Researchers have used blockchain and AI to tackle these challenges. Early intervention, flexible education, and personalized learning are emphasized.

2.2 Education and Blockchain Technology

Blockchain technology can secure student records due to its immutability and openness. Research examines how blockchain technology can safeguard certifications, provide tamper-proof data, and verify academic achievements. Case studies demonstrate how universities have adopted academic credential verification systems.

2.3 Decentralized Credential Verification

The study highlights how blockchain can decentralise credential verification. Blockchain technology's distributed ledger reduces credential theft and verifies academic achievements without a central authority. This literature emphasises the need for uniform blockchain technology rules in education [10].

2.4 AI in Education: Predictive Modelling of Student Performance

AI predictive modelling has been used in several studies to determine student performance factors. Using machine learning algorithms to analyse prior data, educators may predict academic achievements and give tailored interventions and assistance for at-risk students. The literature examines predictive models' effectiveness in different learning settings.

The literature frequently discusses AI in adaptive learning systems. Scholars study methods to tailor instruction to student performance, preferences, and learning styles. Research reveals that adaptive learning boosts student pleasure, engagement, and academic success.

2.5 AI-Blockchain Synergies

The literature shows how blockchain and AI perform well in education. Blockchain's decentralised and secure nature improves AI data analytics. Scholars study how combining these technologies might create a robust ecosystem for managing educational data, ensuring data integrity, and enabling sophisticated analytics.

Experts acknowledge the potential benefits but also discuss the technical challenges of merging blockchain with AI. In a decentralised context, interoperability, scalability, and AI algorithm processing demands are addressed [11]. The literature provides solutions to these difficulties so paired technologies can maximise their potential.

2.6 Technical Challenges and Ethical Considerations

Despite the promising potential, the integration of blockchain and AI in education is not without challenges. Technical issues such as scalability, interoperability, and the complexity of implementation need to be addressed to fully harness these technologies. Scalability remains a significant concern for blockchain networks, as the increased volume of educational data can strain the system's capacity. Interoperability between different blockchain platforms and educational systems is essential to ensure seamless data exchange and collaboration [12]. Ethical considerations are equally important. The use of AI in education raises concerns about data privacy, consent, and algorithmic bias. Ensuring that student data is collected, stored, and processed ethically is paramount to gaining trust and acceptance from stakeholders. Addressing algorithmic bias is crucial to ensure that AI systems provide fair and equitable outcomes for all students, regardless of their background [13].

3. Methodology

3.1 Motivation for Research

The rapid evolution of technology in the last decade has profoundly impacted various sectors, including education [14, 15]. Traditional educational systems face numerous challenges, such as inefficiencies in data management, concerns about data security, and the need for personalized learning experiences to cater to diverse student needs. Blockchain technology, known for its decentralized and secure data management capabilities, and artificial intelligence (AI), renowned for its data analysis and predictive abilities, offer promising solutions to these challenges.

The motivation behind this research is to explore how the synergistic integration of blockchain and AI can address these persistent issues in the education sector [16]. Specifically, this study seeks to understand how blockchain can enhance the security and integrity of educational data, and how AI can leverage this data to provide personalized learning experiences and predictive analytics. By investigating these technologies, this research aims to contribute to the development of a more efficient, secure, and student-centric educational system.

3.2 Research Design

3.2.1 Educational Institution Selection and Case Studies

The study examines blockchain and AI in educational data analytics utilizing multi-case studies. Purposive sampling selects universities, K–12 schools, and online learning platforms. The selection criteria include institution size, location, and technology.

- Methods for gathering data for qualitative and quantitative analysis.
- Data collecting uses qualitative and quantitative methods.
- Qualitative Methods:

Detailed Interviews: Interviews with educators, administrators, and IT specialists reveal decision-making processes, challenges, and perceived benefits of blockchain and AI.

Analysis of Documents Educational policies, implementation documents, and system architecture plans are evaluated to understand how context affects technology adoption.

Surveys: Administrators, instructors, and students are surveyed to quantify the perceived effects of blockchain and AI on learning outcomes, data security, and institutional efficiency.

AI-powered data analytics is used on anonymized and aggregated educational datasets to safeguard privacy. Predictive modelling evaluates adaptive learning methods and student performance. Machine learning techniques for predictive analytics, natural language processing sentiment analysis, and clustering algorithms for student behavior trends are used. These algorithms analyze educational data to predict academic performance, evaluate adaptive learning modules, and identify development areas. Blockchain technology is investigated to understand instructional strategies [17]. This includes consensus methods, smart contract functionality, and blockchain platform selection. Technical study and stakeholder interviews assess school record data security, transparency, and trust. To maintain privacy and ethics, all data is aggregated and anonymized. Participants consent, and data is handled according to data protection regulations. Survey and interview participants receive informed permission forms explaining the research, its purpose, and their confidentiality. The employment of AI in teaching creates ethical concerns. Maintaining AI algorithm objectivity and ensuring AI applications prioritise students' welfare and academic progress is required. Due to case study methods and educational contexts, the conclusions may not apply to other scenarios. We try to present comparative perspectives.

Blockchain and AI technology evolve quickly, making it hard to keep up. The research acknowledges this limitation but provides insights from the state of technology at the time.

3.3 *Study Objectives*

3.3.1 Examine the Application of Blockchain in Educational Data Management

- Investigate how blockchain technology can be used to enhance the security, transparency, and integrity of educational data.
- Analyze the potential of smart contracts to automate and streamline administrative processes within educational institutions.
- Evaluate the challenges and limitations of implementing blockchain in the education sector.

3.3.2 Explore the Role of AI in Educational Data Analytics

- Assess the effectiveness of AI-driven adaptive learning systems in personalizing education based on individual student needs and performance.
- Study the use of AI predictive analytics to identify at-risk students and provide timely interventions.
- Examine the ethical considerations related to the use of AI in education, including data privacy and algorithmic bias.

3.3.3 Investigate the Synergistic Integration of Blockchain and AI

- Explore how the integration of blockchain and AI can create a robust framework for secure and efficient educational data management.
- Analyze the potential benefits of this integration in enhancing data accessibility, interoperability, and collaboration among educational institutions.
- Identify technical challenges and propose solutions to effectively implement and integrate these technologies in the education sector.

3.3.4 Develop and Test a Prototype System

- Design a prototype system that integrates blockchain and AI for educational data management and analytics.
- Conduct case studies and experiments to test the effectiveness and feasibility of the proposed system.
- Collect and analyze data to validate the system's impact on improving data security, operational efficiency, and personalized learning experiences.

4. Applications of Blockchain in Educational Data Management

To investigate the implementation and impact of blockchain and AI in educational data analytics, this study adopts a multi-case study approach.

This approach allows for an in-depth exploration of the diverse ways these technologies are integrated and utilized across various educational institutions. The selected institutions include universities, K–12 schools, and online learning platforms, chosen through purposive sampling to ensure a comprehensive representation of different sizes, locations, and technological infrastructures [18]. Blockchain technology is immutable, therefore data cannot be modified. An immutable record of academic successes in educational data management prevents unauthorized alterations to student records or certificates.

4.1 Data Collection

The study employs a mixed-methods approach, combining qualitative and quantitative data collection techniques to gain a holistic understanding of the subject matter.

4.1.1 Qualitative Approaches

Interviews are conducted with key stakeholders such as educators, administrators, and IT experts to gather insights into the decision-making processes, challenges encountered, and perceived benefits of deploying blockchain and AI in educational settings. Relevant documents, including educational policies, implementation plans, and system architectural designs, are analyzed to understand the contextual factors influencing the adoption of these technologies.

4.1.2 Quantitative Approaches

Surveys are administered to administrators, instructors, and students to collect quantifiable data on the perceived impacts of blockchain and AI on learning outcomes, data security, and institutional efficiency. AI-powered analytics are applied to anonymized and aggregated educational datasets to evaluate the effectiveness of adaptive learning systems and predict student performance.

4.1.3 Data Analysis

AI methods, including machine learning models, natural language processing for sentiment analysis, and clustering algorithms, are used to analyze educational data. These techniques provide valuable insights, such as predicting academic outcomes, assessing the effectiveness of adaptive learning modules, and identifying areas for improvement.

Figures 1 and 2 explain the impact of blockchain adoption on Data Security in Educational Institutions and Accuracy of Different Machine Learning Models in Predicting Student Performance. Tables 1 and 2 explain the performance metrics of different machine learning models along

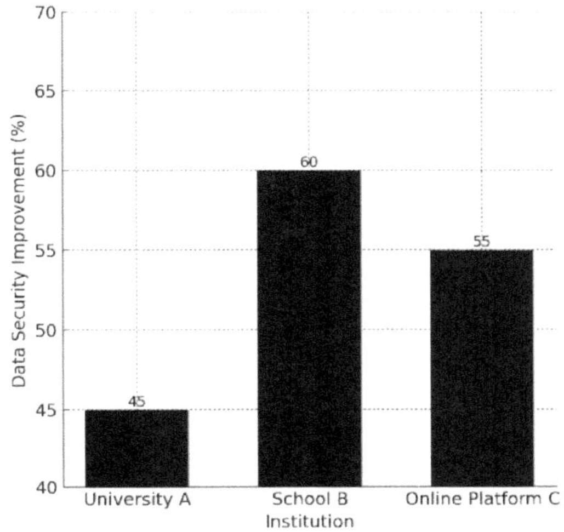

Figure 1. Impact of blockchain adoption on data security in educational institutions.

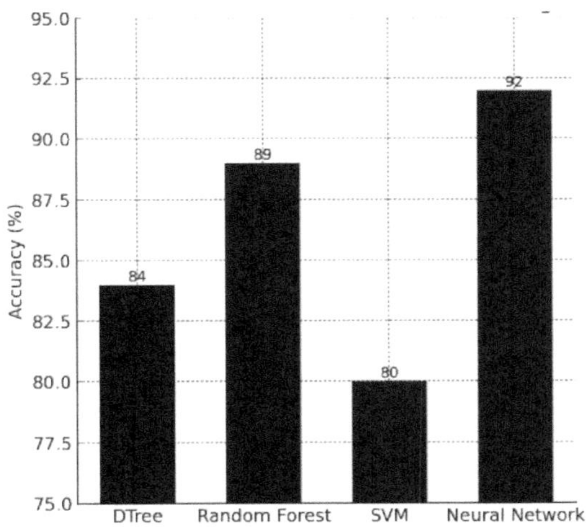

Figure 2. Accuracy of different machine learning models in predicting student performance.

Table 1. Performance metrics of different machine learning models.

Institution	Blockchain Platform	Consensus Mechanism	Data Security Improvement
University A	Ethereum	PoW	45%
School B	Hyperledger	PoS	60%
Online Platform C	Corda	PBFT	55%

Table 2. Blockchain adoption and data security improvements.

Model	Precision	Recall	F1 Score	Accuracy
Decision Tree	0.85	0.82	0.83	0.84
Random Forest	0.89	0.87	0.88	0.89
SVM	0.8	0.78	0.79	0.8
Neural Network	0.92	0.9	0.91	0.92

with the data security improvements through blockchain adoption. The implementation of blockchain technology is examined to understand the strategies employed by educational institutions. This includes analyzing consensus mechanisms, smart contract functionalities, and blockchain platform selection. The impact on data security, transparency, and trust in educational records is assessed through a combination of technical analysis and stakeholder interviews. All collected data is aggregated and anonymized to protect individual privacy and adhere to ethical standards. Participants provide informed consent, and data handling complies with relevant data protection regulations. The ethical implications of using AI in education are addressed, focusing on ensuring algorithmic fairness and prioritizing student welfare and academic advancement. Due to the case study methodology and the diversity of educational settings, the findings may not be universally applicable. However, the study aims to provide insights relevant to similar contexts.

The rapid evolution of blockchain and AI technologies poses a challenge in keeping up with the latest advancements. While acknowledging this limitation, the study offers insights based on the state of technology at the time of research. The research findings undergo peer review by experts in education, blockchain, and artificial intelligence to ensure methodological rigor and enhance the credibility of the study.

4.2 Implementing Blockchain and AI in a Modern University

This case study explores the implementation of blockchain and AI technologies at a modern university aiming to enhance educational data analytics. The objective is to improve data security, streamline credential verification, and personalize learning experiences. The Blockchain integration in secure record-keeping includes:

- The university implemented a blockchain-based system to store and manage student records securely. Blockchain's immutability ensures that once records are entered, they cannot be altered, providing a tamper-proof system for academic records.

- A decentralized ledger system was used, where each node represents a different administrative department within the university. This redundancy ensures data availability and resilience against data loss.
- Blockchain was utilized to create digital diplomas and certificates. These credentials are stored on the blockchain, allowing employers and other institutions to verify them instantly and securely without intermediaries.
- Smart contracts were developed to automate the issuance and verification process, ensuring efficiency and reducing administrative workload.
- The university employed AI algorithms to analyze historical student data, identify patterns, and predict future academic performance. This allows early identification of at-risk students.
- Interventions such as additional tutoring and counseling are then tailored to individual student needs based on these predictions.
- AI-powered adaptive learning platforms were introduced to personalize education. These systems analyze student interactions with course materials and adjust the content dynamically to suit individual learning paces and styles.
- Continuous feedback is provided to students and instructors, allowing real-time adjustments to teaching strategies and learning activities.
- The blockchain system significantly improved data security, ensuring that academic records are immutable and protected against unauthorized access.
- The decentralized nature of the blockchain ledger ensured data redundancy and reliability.
- The blockchain-based credential verification system reduced the time and effort required to verify academic qualifications. This was particularly beneficial for graduates seeking employment or further education.
- Employers reported increased confidence in the authenticity of the credentials presented by applicants.
- The predictive analytics system enabled early intervention for students at risk of underperforming, leading to improved academic outcomes.
- The adaptive learning systems increased student engagement and satisfaction by providing personalized learning experiences.

- Administrative tasks related to record-keeping and credential verification were streamlined, allowing university staff to focus on more strategic initiatives.
- The use of AI for data analytics provided actionable insights, aiding in better decision-making at the institutional level.
- Future implementations should focus on scaling the blockchain and AI systems to handle larger volumes of data and more complex educational environments.
- Integration with other educational technologies and platforms should be prioritized to create a seamless digital ecosystem.
- Ongoing efforts are needed to address data privacy concerns, ensuring compliance with regulations such as GDPR.
- Ethical considerations, particularly related to AI bias and transparency, should be continuously monitored and mitigated.
- Collaboration among educational institutions, technology providers, and regulatory bodies is essential to develop standardized protocols for blockchain and AI applications in education.
- Establishing industry standards will facilitate interoperability and broader adoption of these technologies.
- Institutions should implement mechanisms for continuous feedback and improvement of the deployed systems. This includes regular evaluations of system performance and user satisfaction.
- Engaging students, faculty, and administrative staff in the feedback process will ensure that the systems evolve to meet their needs effectively.

Blockchain enables decentralised, transparent credential verification. The blockchain allows authorised parties to quickly and securely validate academic certificates and diplomas, eliminating the need for lengthy and often human verification. This enhances credential verification efficiency and reliability. Decentralised blockchain technology allows student records to be disseminated and preserved across network nodes. Every educational institution and student has a blockchain copy, ensuring redundancy and reducing data loss. The decentralised paradigm enhances data accessibility and reliability. Blockchain reduces credential fraud significantly. Because blockchain technology is cryptographic, degrees and certificates cannot be forged. This addresses a recurrent education issue where falsified diplomas invalidate academic achievements. Blockchain streamlines academic verification and provides a decentralised, credible method. Employers, schools, and other relevant organisations can independently verify student achievements using the blockchain. This cuts middlemen and verification time. Blockchain technology unifies educational credential exchange and maintenance. In a globalised educational environment, this makes it easy for students to share their academic triumphs across borders without compromising their credentials.

4.3 Privacy/Data Security Impact

The decentralised design and cryptographic features of blockchain technology improve educational data management security. The distributed ledger protects student data from modification and unauthorised access. Blockchain enables private educational data management solutions. Smart contracts on the blockchain can protect student data by restricting access to certain data by adopting data-sharing agreements with predetermined rules. Blockchain gives students more data control. Cryptographic keys allow students to authorise or revoke access to their academic records, giving them control over their data. Blockchain greatly increases data security and transparency, but scalability remains an issue. Processing restrictions may prevent some blockchain networks from handling the high volume of transactions required to manage educational data. Blockchain technology must be carefully integrated into educational systems. Institutions must consider staff training, data migration compatibility with existing systems, and protocol building. Integrating blockchain technology into educational data management requires regulatory compliance. Successful and lawful deployment requires digital credential industry standards and GDPR compliance.

5. AI-Powered Educational Data Analytics

5.1 Predicting Student Performance

AI-powered prediction modelling uses machine learning algorithms to analyse past student performance data in educational data analytics. Predictive models use academic performance, attendance, and engagement to make predictions. These insights help educators spot tendencies. Predictive analytics helps identify students with academic issues early. Identifying academic hurdles allows educators to implement targeted interventions. Counselling, increased resources, and individualised tutoring are proactive student assistance methods. AI-enabled predictive modelling goes beyond identifying at-risk kids. Additionally, it helps create student-specific adaptive learning pathways. Adaptive learning systems use predictive analytics to dynamically change the speed, topic matter, and delivery of educational materials to maximise learning for all students. Students receive personalised learning using AI-powered adaptive learning systems. These systems use learning style, preference, and performance data to customise training. Customisation boosts student enthusiasm, engagement, and learning. AI algorithms continuously track student course engagement. Based on real-time data, adaptive learning systems adjust content complexity and format to each student's learning speed. This ensures students receive the right challenge and assistance throughout their academic careers. Adaptive learning systems give teachers and students feedback. AI systems assess students' progress, identify strengths and weaknesses, and provide timely feedback. This feedback loop helps instructors use data to inform their teaching and learning strategies.

5.2 Academic Results Impact

AI-powered educational data analytics links predictive modelling and adaptive learning systems to enhanced academic performance. Students learn better with targeted interventions, customised learning, and dynamic content adjustments. Student engagement increases with adaptive content and personalised learning. AI-powered solutions customise educational materials to individual preferences and learning styles, creating a more interactive and engaging learning environment and a positive learning attitude. Data-driven insights from AI-powered analytics help teachers make curricular, resource, and instructional decisions. Big dataset analysis lets teachers track student progress, identify needs, and optimise their teaching. AI-based educational data analytics raises ethical concerns about algorithmic bias, privacy, and student data use. Building trust in educational environments demands fair and transparent AI systems.

5.3 Technical Infrastructure

AI-powered educational data analytics requires strong technical infrastructure. Educational institutions must spend on hardware, software, and training to use AI algorithms. Overcoming technical challenges and integrating with present systems are crucial. Even though AI-powered adaptive learning systems offer personalisation, we must balance standardised educational objectives and personalised learning pathways. This balance ensures students meet academic expectations and receive individualised support.

6. Synergies and Challenges

6.1 Blockchain-AI Synergies

Education data analytics is more secure with blockchain and AI. Blockchain's decentralised, tamper-resistant ledger protects student records while AI algorithms analyse the data for insights. By providing a transparent and secure framework for educational data, the synergy decreases the risk. Blockchain's decentralised credential verification and AI analytics provide a transparent and dependable system. Trends in credential verification requests can help AI systems detect fraud. This cooperative approach ensures academic credentials are not just safe on the blockchain but also evaluated for veracity. Blockchain technology and AI-driven adaptive learning systems ensure personalised training and data security. Blockchain secures data, and AI systems dynamically adjust learning courses based on student preferences and performance. This synergy balances security and personalisation in educational data analytics. Blockchain and AI systems sometimes struggle with scalability. Blockchain networks may struggle to perform several transactions, and AI algorithms may require a lot of processing power. Integrating these technologies at scale requires careful network and processing capacity consideration. Interoperability between blockchain and AI systems is tough. Since educational institutions use several platforms and technologies, a unified data analytics solution must integrate seamlessly. Interfaces and protocols must be standardised to improve interoperability. Integration of blockchain and AI with educational data analytics requires technical expertise. Educational institutions may struggle to hire or train qualified staff. The technical competence gap can be closed through industry and technology specialist interactions. Blockchain and AI raise consent and privacy concerns. Blockchain employs cryptography to secure data, but AI analytics may analyse sensitive data. Establishing clear data usage standards, obtaining informed consent, and protecting privacy are ethical issues. Uncarefully designed and taught AI algorithms may promote bias. The combination of biassed AI and blockchain technology may increase ethical difficulties. To mitigate bias in educational data analytics, ethical AI involves clear algorithmic design, diverse training datasets, and constant monitoring. Decision-making in education using blockchain and AI must be transparent. Teachers, administrators, and students must understand how AI analytics determines decisions and how blockchain safeguards data. Creating open governance frameworks builds trust.

7. Conclusion

The integration of blockchain and AI technologies at the university demonstrated significant benefits in terms of data security, efficiency, and personalized learning. While challenges remain, particularly related to scalability and ethical considerations, the case study highlights the transformative potential of these technologies in modern education. Future efforts should focus on enhancing scalability, ensuring data privacy, and fostering collaboration to realize the full potential of blockchain and AI in educational data analytics. Through careful examination, these technologies' uses, synergies, challenges, and probable future courses have been better appreciated.

References

[1] Nakamoto, S. (2008). Bitcoin: A peer-to-peer electronic cash system.

[2] Zheng, Z., Xie, S., Dai, H., Chen, X. and Wang, H. (2018). Blockchain challenges and opportunities: A survey. *International Journal of Web and Grid Services*, 14(1): 352–375.

[3] Mougayar, W. (2016). *The Business Blockchain: Promise, Practice, and Application of the Next Internet Technology*. John Wiley & Sons.

[4] Xie, S., Dai, H., Chen, X. and Wang, H. (2021). Blockchain technology in educational data management: A review. *Journal of Educational Technology Systems*, 50(2): 123–140.

[5] Zamani, S., Sharif, K., Alazab, M. and Karimipour, H. (2022). Blockchain for education: Opportunities, challenges, and future directions. *IEEE Access*, 10: 34567–34589.

[6] Chen, X., Zou, D., Xie, H., Cheng, G. and Liu, C. (2020). Data-driven learning analytics for student equity and inclusion: A comprehensive review. *IEEE Transactions on Learning Technologies*, 13(2): 332–347.

[7] Zawacki-Richter, O., Marín, V.I., Bond, M. and Gouverneur, F. (2020). Systematic review of research on artificial intelligence applications in higher education–where are the educators?. *International Journal of Educational Technology in Higher Education*, 17(1): 39.

[8] Popenici, S. and Kerr, S. (2017). Exploring the impact of artificial intelligence on teaching and learning in higher education. *Research and Practice in Technology Enhanced Learning*, 12(1): 22.

[9] Zhang, Y., Wu, Y. and Wang, L. (2023). Predictive analytics for student performance in higher education using machine learning techniques. *Journal of Educational Data Mining*, 15(1): 45–62.

[10] King, J.L. and Richards, K. (2020). *Blockchain in Higher Education: Promises and Practice*. Springer, Cham, pp. 79–102.

[11] Nguyen, T.T., Nguyen, T.D. and Nguyen, T.M. (2022). Enhancing data accessibility and interoperability with blockchain: A study in the educational context. *Computers & Education*, 170: 104229.

[12] Crosby, M., Nachiappan, P.P., Verma, S. and Kalyanaraman, V. (2016). Blockchain technology: Beyond bitcoin. *Applied Innovation*, 2(6-10): 71.

[13] Lee, K., Lam, K.Y. and Cheung, H.K. (2021). Scalability and interoperability of blockchain in education. *Journal of Computing in Higher Education*, 33(2): 254–272.

[14] Mittelstadt, B.D., Allo, P., Taddeo, M., Wachter, S. and Floridi, L. (2016). The ethics of algorithms: Mapping the debate. *Big Data & Society*, 3(2): 2053951716679679.

[15] Floridi, L. and Taddeo, M. (2016). What is data ethics? *Philosophical Transactions of the Royal Society A: Mathematical, Physical and Engineering Sciences*, 374(2083): 20160360.
[16] Alammary, A., Alhazmi, S., Almasri, M. and Gillani, S. (2020). Blockchain-based applications in education: A systematic review. *Applied Sciences*, 10(12): 4097.
[17] Hasan, H.R. and Salah, K. (2012). Smart contract-based approach for efficient student registration system. *IEEE Access*, 9: 14265–14274.
[18] Mittelstadt, E.D., Allo, P., Taddeo, M., Wachter, S. and Floridi, L. (2020). The ethics of algorithms: Mapping the debate. *Big Data & Society*, 3(2): 2053951716679679.

Chapter 3

Adaptive Learning in Modern Education Systems Leveraged by AI and Blockchain

Sonu Kumar,[1,*] *Y Lalitha Kameswari,*[2]
Venkatanarayana Moram[3] and *Mahaboob Pasha*[4]

As education continues to undergo a profound transformation, the integration of adaptive learning, powered by Artificial Intelligence (AI) and Blockchain technologies, emerges as a groundbreaking paradigm shift. This chapter provides a comprehensive overview of the synergy between AI and Blockchain in the context of adaptive learning within the modern education system. The introduction sets the stage by highlighting the dynamic nature of education and the imperative for personalized, adaptive learning solutions. Emphasis is placed on the transformative potential of combining AI and Blockchain to address the diverse learning needs of students. An exploration of the principles and advantages of adaptive learning elucidates its role in catering to individual learning styles and preferences. The

[1] Assitant Professor, Department of Electronics and Communication Engineering, K.S.R.M. College of Engineering, Kadapa, Andhra Pradesh-516005, India.
[2] Assistant Professor, Department of Electrical & Electronics Engineering, MLR Institute of Technology, Telangana, India.
[3] Professor, Department of Electronics and Communication Engineering, K.S.R.M. College of Engineering, Kadapa, Andhra Pradesh-516005, India.
[4] Associate Professor, Department of Electronics and Communication Engineering, K.S.R.M. College of Engineering, Kadapa, Andhra Pradesh-516005, India.
* Corresponding author: sonumgd@gmail.com

limitations of traditional education models are contrasted with the flexibility and customization offered by adaptive learning. A detailed examination of the pivotal role of AI in adaptive learning systems, showcasing machine learning algorithms, natural language processing, and personalized feedback mechanisms. Insights into how AI analyses learner behaviour adapts content delivery, and enhances the educational experience. A comprehensive overview of Blockchain's influence on the education sector, emphasizing its role in securing academic credentials, fostering transparency, and mitigating fraud. The immutable and decentralized nature of Blockchain ensures the integrity and authenticity of educational records. The chapter delves into the collaborative potential between AI and Blockchain, exploring how Blockchain fortifies the reliability and trustworthiness of AI-driven adaptive learning systems. The role of Blockchain in securing learner data, preserving privacy, and validating the accuracy of AI-generated recommendations is examined. Examination of how Blockchain facilitates decentralized and secure storage of academic credentials and certifications had been explained clearly. The chapter summarizes the transformative potential of integrating AI and Blockchain in adaptive learning. Future directions for research and development, as well as the long-term impact on the evolution of the modern education system, are contemplated. The abstract emphasizes the potential to transform education through the seamless integration of AI and Blockchain, paving the path for a more inclusive, personalized, and secure learning experience.

1. Introduction

In the swiftly changing realm of contemporary education, adaptive learning systems have emerged as a transformative force, reshaping how educational content is delivered and personalized. At the heart of this transformation are advancements in artificial intelligence (AI) and blockchain technology, which offer unprecedented opportunities for customization, transparency, and efficiency in learning processes. Adaptive learning refers to educational technologies that customise the educational experience to cater to the specific requirements of each learner, preferences, and progress [1, 2]. This personalized approach is powered by AI, which leverages algorithms and machine learning to analyse students' interactions and performance data. By assessing strengths, weaknesses, and learning styles, AI can adapt and modify the level of complexity of assignments, suggest tailored resources, and provide real-time feedback. This guarantees that every child is provided with a unique learning path that optimally supports their educational journey.

Blockchain technology, renowned for its involvement in cryptocurrencies, provides a decentralised and unchangeable record-keeping system that can transform the management of educational certificates and accomplishments [3]. In the context of adaptive learning, blockchain can securely store and verify academic records, certifications, and achievements, making it easier for institutions and employers to trust and validate educational claims. This transparency and security can enhance the credibility of adaptive learning systems and ensure that student progress and qualifications are accurately represented. The integration of AI and blockchain in adaptive learning systems creates a powerful synergy [4]. AI algorithms can analyse educational data and generate insights that drive personalized learning experiences, while blockchain provides a secure and transparent framework for managing and validating this data [5]. This combination enhances the effectiveness of adaptive learning and builds trust and accountability in educational credentials.

1.1 The Need for Adaptive Learning

In today's diverse and rapidly changing educational landscape, traditional one-size-fits-all approaches are increasingly inadequate. As classrooms become more heterogeneous, educators face the challenge of meeting varied learning needs and preferences within the same environment. Students come to educational settings with varying backgrounds, prior knowledge, and learning styles [6]. Traditional teaching methods often cater to a median student, which can leave others either under-challenged or overwhelmed. Adaptive learning systems, through their personalized approach, adjust to individual learning paces and preferences, ensuring that each student engages with content that is both accessible and appropriately challenging [7]. The modern educational landscape is shifting towards a more student-centered approach, recognizing that customised educational experiences have the potential to greatly improve student involvement and results [8]. Adaptive learning leverages data to tailor educational experiences to individual needs, thus fostering a more personalized learning environment that can address specific learning gaps and strengths.

Technological advancements have made it possible to collect and analyse vast amounts of data on student performance in real-time. Adaptive learning systems use this data to provide immediate feedback and adjust instructional strategies accordingly. This real-time adaptability helps in addressing issues as they arise, rather than waiting for periodic assessments or feedback sessions [9]. Educational inequities, whether due to socioeconomic factors, language barriers, or learning disabilities, can hinder student success. Adaptive learning technologies offer the potential to level the playing field by providing tailored support and resources that cater to individual needs [10]. This can help bridge gaps and ensure that all students have the opportunity to succeed regardless of their starting point. Engagement and motivation are critical factors in learning success. Adaptive learning systems can make learning more engaging by providing interactive and relevant content that aligns with students' interests and learning preferences. By offering personalized learning paths, these systems can keep students motivated and invested in their educational journey. The modern workforce requires skills and knowledge that are constantly evolving [11]. Adaptive learning prepares students for this dynamic environment by allowing them to acquire and master new skills at their own pace. This flexibility is crucial in an era where lifelong learning and continuous skill development are essential for career success.

For educators, adaptive learning provides significant observations regarding student performance and learning habits. This data can inform instructional practices, help identify trends and guide curriculum development [12]. By understanding how each student learns best, educators can make more informed decisions that enhance the overall effectiveness of their teaching. The need for adaptive learning is driven by the diverse and evolving nature of educational needs. By embracing personalized, data-driven approaches, adaptive learning systems address these needs more effectively than traditional methods, making education more inclusive, engaging, and aligned with the demands of the 21st century.

1.2 Emergence of AI and Blockchain in Education

The integration of advanced technologies such as AI and blockchain has significantly impacted education, providing new tools and methods that enhance learning experiences and operational efficiencies. The emergence of these technologies signifies a fundamental change of approach or perspective in how educational content is delivered, managed, and validated. AI-driven educational tools enable a level of personalization that was previously unattainable. ML algorithms analyse student data such as interaction patterns, performance metrics, and learning preferences to tailor educational experiences [13]. This includes customizing content difficulty, suggesting additional resources, and offering real-time feedback. AI's ability to adapt to each student's unique needs helps ensure that learning is effective and engaging. AI-driven intelligent tutoring systems (ITS) can replicate personalised one-on-one tutoring interactions. These systems use natural language processing and machine learning techniques to understand and answer student questions, providing explanations and assistance similar to that of a human teacher. ITS provides the capability to monitor and assess the advancement of pupils, pinpoint specific areas where they encounter difficulties, and provide focused interventions to aid their learning.

AI can analyse large datasets to predict student outcomes and identify potential challenges before they become significant issues. By examining patterns in student performance, AI tools can forecast which students might need additional support and suggest proactive measures to address potential learning gaps [14]. This predictive capability enables educators to intervene early and tailor their approaches to better support student success. AI can streamline administrative tasks such as grading, scheduling, and resource management. Automated grading systems, for example, can handle multiple-choice and short-answer assessments efficiently, freeing up educators to focus on more complex instructional tasks. This automation reduces the administrative burden on educators and allows them to dedicate more time to personalized instruction and student engagement [15]. Blockchain technology offers a secure and immutable way to store and verify educational credentials. Academic records, diplomas, and certificates can be recorded on a blockchain, ensuring their authenticity and making them easily verifiable by institutions and employers. This reduces the risk of fraud and simplifies the verification process for educational achievements.

Blockchain enables the creation of decentralized learning platforms where educational content and credentials are managed across a distributed network. This approach can facilitate more democratic access to educational resources, reduce reliance on central authorities, and enhance the transparency and integrity of educational processes [16]. Smart contracts, characterised by their self-executing nature and direct inclusion of terms in code, can automate multiple facets of educational agreements. For example, they can be used to automatically release funds for educational grants or scholarships upon meeting specific criteria, ensuring that conditions are met and reducing administrative overhead.

Blockchain technology can give students greater control over their data. By recording educational achievements and interactions on a blockchain, students can manage who has access to their information and ensure their privacy is protected [17]. This decentralization of data management can empower students and enhance data security. The integration of AI and blockchain in education can create a synergistic effect, enhancing the capabilities of both technologies. AI can leverage blockchain for secure and transparent data management, while blockchain

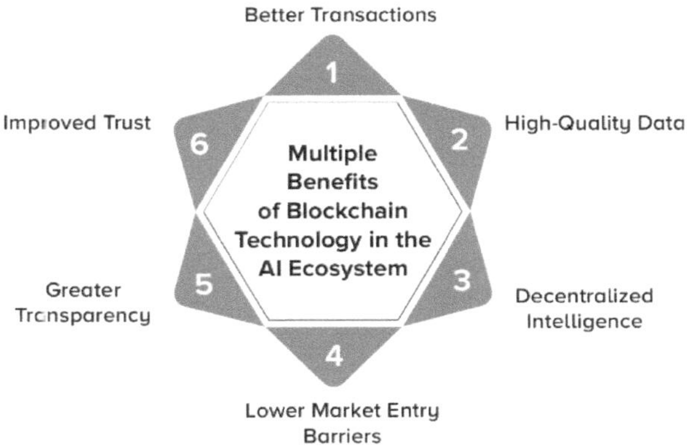

Figure 1. AI and blockchain in education [18].

can benefit from AI's analytical power to optimize educational processes. For example, AI algorithms can use blockchain-stored data to gain deeper insights into student performance, and blockchain can securely record AI-generated insights and recommendations. Figure 1, represents the benefit of using AI and blockchain in education.

2. Adaptive Learning in Modern Education

Adaptive learning has become a cornerstone of modern education, fundamentally transforming how students interact with content and how educators approach teaching. By leveraging technology to create personalized learning experiences, adaptive learning systems address the diverse needs of students, enhancing both engagement and effectiveness. This section explores the key components, benefits, and challenges of adaptive learning in contemporary education. At the heart of adaptive learning is the use of data to tailor educational experiences to individual students [19]. Adaptive learning systems collect and analyse data on students' interactions with content, including their responses to questions, time spent on tasks, and overall performance. This data is used to adjust the difficulty of content, recommend resources, and provide targeted feedback, ensuring that every student is provided with an individualised learning experience. Adaptive learning platforms utilize algorithms to dynamically adjust content delivery based on real-time data. For instance, if a student struggles with a particular concept, the system may present additional explanations, practice problems, or alternative learning materials to reinforce understanding [20]. Conversely, if a student demonstrates proficiency, the system can introduce more advanced material to challenge them further. Immediate feedback is a crucial feature of adaptive learning systems.

As students interact with the material, they are provided with immediate feedback on their performance, facilitating their comprehension of errors and enabling rapid learning from them. This continuous assessment approach allows students to correct misunderstandings and stay on track with their learning goals [21]. Adaptive learning systems often create individualized learning pathways that align with each student's unique needs and goals. These pathways outline the sequence of topics and activities a student should engage with to achieve specific learning objectives. The technology dynamically modifies these paths in response to student growth and performance.

2.1 *Benefits of Adaptive Learning*

1. Improved Student Engagement: Personalised learning experiences enhance student engagement by presenting material that is relevant and appropriately challenging. When students encounter content that matches their skill level and interests, they are more inclined to maintain their motivation and commitment to their learning path.

2. Improved Learning Outcomes: Adaptive learning systems can lead to better learning outcomes by addressing individual learning gaps and providing targeted support. Students are provided with assistance tailored to their challenges, resulting in a more profound comprehension of the subject matter and enhanced overall academic achievement.

3. Efficient Use of Resources: By focusing on areas where students need the most help, adaptive learning systems make more efficient use of educational resources. Educators can allocate their time and efforts more effectively, concentrating on students who require additional support while allowing advanced learners to progress at their own pace.

4. Scalability and Flexibility: Adaptive learning technologies can scale to accommodate a wide range of students and educational settings. Whether used in large classrooms, online courses, or individualized tutoring, these systems can adapt to various contexts and learning environments, making them versatile tools for educators.

2.2 *Challenges and Considerations*

1. Data privacy and security are significant concerns when it comes to the collection and analysis of student data. Educational institutions must prioritise the implementation of strong data protection measures and ensure responsible and compliant use of data by relevant rules.

2. Technological Limitations: While adaptive learning systems offer many advantages, they are not without limitations. The effectiveness of these systems depends on the quality of the algorithms and the accuracy of the

data. Technical issues, such as system glitches or data inaccuracies, can impact the learning experience.

3. Teacher Training and Adoption: Effective integration of adaptive learning systems requires that educators are adequately trained to use these technologies effectively. Professional development and support are crucial for ensuring that teachers can integrate adaptive learning tools into their instructional practices and make the most of their capabilities.

4. Equity and Access: Ensuring equitable access to adaptive learning technologies is a significant challenge. Students from underserved or low-income backgrounds may face barriers to accessing the necessary technology or internet connectivity. Addressing these disparities is essential to ensure that all students can benefit from adaptive learning opportunities.

2.3 *The Future of Adaptive Learning*

The future of adaptive learning in education is auspicious, as continuous improvements in technology hold the potential to augment its capacities. Emerging technologies, such as artificial intelligence and machine learning, are expected to further refine adaptive learning systems, making them even more responsive and personalized [22]. Additionally, the integration of adaptive learning with other innovative technologies, such as virtual reality and gamification, has the potential to enhance the level of immersion and interactivity in learning activities.

3. AI in Adaptive Learning

AI is at the forefront of transforming adaptive learning, enabling systems to offer highly personalized educational experiences. By harnessing the capabilities of machine learning, natural language processing, and data analytics, AI enhances the effectiveness and efficiency of adaptive learning technologies. This section explores the role of AI in adaptive learning, focusing on its capabilities, applications, and implications for education [23]. AI enables adaptive learning systems to create tailored educational experiences by analysing a student's interactions, performance, and preferences. Machine learning algorithms process data to adjust the content difficulty, recommend resources, and design individualized learning paths. This personalization helps ensure that each student engages with material that is suited to their specific needs and learning style [24]. AI-driven systems provide immediate feedback on student performance, offering explanations and corrective guidance based on real-time analysis. Natural language processing allows AI to analyse and reply to student queries and submissions, such as essays or open-ended answers, in a manner akin to human feedback. This rapid response supports continuous learning and allows students to address misunderstandings promptly. AI utilizes predictive analytics to forecast student outcomes and identify potential issues before they become significant problems. By analysing patterns in data, such as engagement levels, performance metrics, and behavioural trends, AI systems can predict which students may need additional support and suggest interventions to address their challenges proactively. AI can assist in generating educational content, including practice problems, quizzes, and instructional materials [25]. Using algorithms that analyse existing content and student performance data, AI systems can create customized exercises and resources that align with each student's learning needs, thus enhancing the learning experience.

3.1 Applications of AI in Adaptive Learning

1. Intelligent Tutoring Systems (ITS): Intelligent tutoring systems leverage AI to provide personalized instruction and support. These systems simulate one-on-one tutoring experiences by using AI to understand student responses, provide explanations, and adjust instructional strategies. ITS can offer a personalized learning experience similar to that of a human tutor, helping students with specific questions and concepts.

2. AI-Enhanced Learning Platforms: Modern learning platforms integrate AI to enhance their adaptive learning capabilities. These platforms use AI to analyse student data, adapt the content in real-time, and offer personalized recommendations. By continuously adjusting to student progress, these platforms provide a more effective and engaging learning experience.

3.2 Machine Learning Algorithms in Adaptive Learning

Machine learning algorithms are integral to the functionality of adaptive learning systems. These algorithms analyse student data to create personalized learning experiences, adjusting educational content and strategies based on individual performance and preferences. This section explores the types of machine learning algorithms used in adaptive learning, their roles, and their impact on the learning process.

3.2.1 Types of Machine Learning Algorithms

1. *Supervised Learning Algorithms*: Supervised learning involves training algorithms on labelled data, where the outcomes are known. In adaptive learning, supervised learning algorithms can be used to predict student

performance and personalize learning experiences based on historical data.

Linear Regression: Used for predicting continuous outcomes, such as a student's future test scores based on their current performance.

Decision Trees: Useful for classifying students into different categories (e.g., high risk, medium risk, low risk) based on their performance metrics.

Support Vector Machines (SVM): Applied for classification tasks, such as identifying students who are likely to struggle with specific concepts.

2. *Unsupervised Learning Algorithms*: Unsupervised learning involves training algorithms on data without predefined labels. These algorithms identify patterns and structures within the data that can be used to personalize learning experiences.

Clustering Algorithms (e.g., K-Means): Group students into clusters based on similarities in their learning behaviours or performance, allowing for tailored instructional strategies for each group.

Principal Component Analysis (PCA): Reduces the dimensionality of data, helping to identify key factors that influence learning outcomes and simplifying the complexity of data analysis.

3. *Reinforcement Learning Algorithms*: Reinforcement learning involves training algorithms to make decisions based on rewards and penalties. In adaptive learning, these algorithms can optimize learning pathways and interventions based on student interactions. Notable algorithms include:

Q-Learning: Used to determine the best actions (e.g., instructional strategies) based on their expected rewards, helping to improve the effectiveness of personalized learning interventions.

Deep Q-Networks (DQN): Integrates Q-learning with deep neural networks to handle more complex environments and learning scenarios, enhancing the adaptability of learning systems.

4. *Deep Learning Algorithms*: Deep learning, a kind of machine learning, employs neural networks with numerous layers to represent intricate patterns in data. These algorithms are particularly useful for handling large datasets and tasks such as natural language processing and image recognition. Key algorithms include:

Convolutional Neural Networks (CNNs): Applied to tasks like analysing student-generated content (e.g., written responses) and recognizing patterns in visual data (e.g., interactive exercises).

RNNs and LSTM Networks: Used for processing sequential data, such as tracking students' learning progress over time and predicting future performance.

3.2.2 Roles of Machine Learning Algorithms in Adaptive Learning

1. Personalizing Learning Experiences: Machine learning algorithms analyse individual student data to tailor content, adjust difficulty levels, and recommend resources. This personalization ensures that each student receives instruction that aligns with their specific needs, enhancing their learning experience and outcomes.

2. Predicting Student Performance: Through the analysis of historical data, machine learning algorithms can forecast future performance and detect pupils who may be susceptible to academic setbacks. This predictive capability allows educators to intervene early and provide targeted support to address potential challenges.

3. Optimizing Learning Pathways: Machine learning algorithms can design and adjust learning pathways based on real-time data. They determine the optimal sequence of topics and activities for each student, ensuring that learning is efficient and effective.

4. Providing Real-Time Feedback: AI-driven adaptive learning systems use machine learning to deliver immediate feedback to students. This real-time feedback helps students understand their mistakes, reinforces learning, and keeps them engaged in the educational process.

5. Enhancing Educator Insights: Machine learning algorithms generate insights into student performance and learning behaviours, providing educators with valuable data for instructional planning. These insights help educators make informed decisions about teaching strategies and resource allocation.

3.2.3 Impact on the Learning Process

1. Improved Learning Outcomes: The ability of machine learning algorithms to tailor educational content and interventions to individual needs leads to more effective learning experiences. Personalized instruction helps students grasp concepts more thoroughly and achieve better academic outcomes.

2. Increased Engagement: By presenting material that is appropriately challenging and relevant to students' interests, machine learning algorithms enhance engagement and motivation. Students are more likely to remain focused and invested in their learning when they experience personalized and interactive content.

3. Efficient Resource Allocation: Machine learning algorithms optimize the use of educational resources by directing attention to areas where students need the most support. This efficiency reduces waste and ensures that resources are used effectively to support student learning.

4. Continuous Improvement: Machine learning systems continuously learn and improve as they process more data. This iterative learning process allows adaptive learning systems to become increasingly effective at meeting students' needs and addressing educational challenges.

Machine learning algorithms play a crucial role in adaptive learning, enabling personalized, data-driven educational experiences that enhance student outcomes and engagement. While challenges related to data quality, algorithmic bias, and complexity exist, the benefits of machine learning in adaptive learning are substantial. As technology continues to advance, machine learning algorithms will likely become even more integral to the future of education, driving innovation and improving the learning process.

4. Blockchain Technology in Education

Blockchain technology, often associated with cryptocurrencies, has emerged as a transformative force in various sectors, including education. Blockchain offers a decentralised, secure, and transparent ledger for recording and verifying transactions, and offers innovative solutions to many challenges faced in the educational landscape. This section explores the applications, benefits, and challenges of blockchain technology in education. Blockchain technology provides a secure and immutable way to store and verify academic credentials [26]. Diplomas, certificates, and transcripts can be recorded on a blockchain, creating a tamper-proof record that can be easily verified by institutions, employers, and other entities. This reduces the risk of credential fraud and simplifies the verification process. Universities and educational institutions can issue digital diplomas on a blockchain, which can be instantly verified by employers or other institutions without the need for physical documents [27]. Academic transcripts stored on a blockchain provide a permanent and unalterable record of a student's academic achievements, making it easier to share and validate records. Blockchain technology has the potential to enable the development of learning platforms that are decentralised in nature, where educational content and credentials are managed across a distributed network. This approach reduces reliance on central authorities and can democratize access to educational resources [28]. Blockchain can be used to manage and distribute open educational resources, ensuring that content creators are fairly compensated and that resources are accessible to all. Blockchain enables peer-to-peer learning platforms where students and educators can connect directly, share resources, and engage in collaborative learning without intermediaries. Smart contracts are contracts that are capable of executing themselves, as the contents of the agreement are directly encoded into the contract's code. In education, smart contracts can automate various processes, such as the disbursement of scholarships, grants, and other financial aid. Automated Grants and Scholarships: Smart contracts can automatically release funds based on predefined criteria, such as meeting academic performance benchmarks or completing certain milestones [29]. Smart contracts can streamline enrolment and registration processes, ensuring that all conditions are met before proceeding with administrative tasks. Blockchain technology allows students to control their personal data, giving them the ability to manage who has access to their educational records. This enhances data privacy and security while empowering students with ownership over their information. Students can use blockchain to manage their own educational data, granting or revoking access to their records as needed. The decentralized nature of blockchain ensures that student data is protected from unauthorized access and tampering. Blockchain can be used to track and verify the accreditation status of educational institutions and programs. This ensures that accredited institutions and programs are consistently meeting quality standards and provides transparency to stakeholders. Blockchain can store and manage accreditation records, providing a transparent and immutable record of an institution's accreditation status. Blockchain can track and verify compliance with educational standards and regulations, enhancing trust in the quality of educational programs.

4.1 Blockchain Benefits in Education

1. Enhanced Security and Transparency: Blockchain's decentralized and immutable nature ensures that educational records are secure and transparent. This reduces the risk of fraud and provides a clear, verifiable record of all transactions and changes.

2. Streamlined Processes: By automating administrative tasks through smart contracts and providing a single source of truth for credentials and records, blockchain can streamline various educational processes, reducing administrative overhead and increasing efficiency.

3. Reduced Fraud and Misrepresentation: Blockchain technology minimizes the risk of credential fraud and misrepresentation by providing a secure and verifiable method for recording and validating academic achievements. This enhances trust in the integrity of educational records.

4. Improved Access to Education: Decentralized learning platforms and open educational resources managed on blockchain can make education more accessible to individuals worldwide, regardless of geographic location or socioeconomic status.

5. Empowered Students: Blockchain technology gives students greater control over their educational data, allowing them to manage access to their records and maintain ownership of their personal information.

4.1.1 Challenges and Considerations

1. Implementation and Integration: Integrating blockchain technology into existing educational systems and processes can be complex and costly. Educational institutions must invest in the necessary infrastructure and expertise to effectively implement and utilize blockchain solutions.

2. Scalability and Performance: Blockchain networks may encounter scalability challenges, especially when dealing with large transaction volumes. Ensuring that blockchain solutions can handle the scale of data and transactions in education is a critical consideration.

3. Regulatory and Legal Issues: The use of blockchain in education may raise regulatory and legal questions, particularly regarding data privacy, intellectual property, and compliance with existing educational standards and regulations.

4. Adoption and Acceptance: The adoption of blockchain technology in education requires buy-in from various stakeholders, including educational institutions, policymakers, and students. Overcoming resistance to change and demonstrating the value of blockchain solutions is essential for widespread adoption.

4.1.2 Future Directions

The future of blockchain in education holds significant innovation potential. Emerging trends include the integration of blockchain with other technologies, such as artificial intelligence and the IoT, to create more advanced and interconnected educational systems. Additionally, ongoing research and development will address current challenges and enhance the capabilities of blockchain technology in education.

4.2 Securing Academic Credentials with Blockchain

In education, ensuring the integrity and authenticity of academic credentials is paramount. Traditional methods of credential verification can be cumbersome and prone to errors or fraud. Blockchain technology offers a revolutionary approach to securing academic credentials by providing a decentralized, transparent, and immutable ledger for recording and verifying educational achievements. Blockchain technology functions on a distributed network of computers, referred to as nodes, that collaboratively oversee and authenticate transactions. In the context of academic credentials, this means that records of diplomas, certificates, and transcripts are stored across multiple nodes rather than in a single central repository. This decentralization prevents unauthorized modifications and ensures that the records are consistent and reliable across the network. Once data is stored on a blockchain, it becomes immutable and cannot be modified or removed without modifying all subsequent blocks and obtaining consensus from the network.

This immutability ensures that academic credentials are permanent and tamper-proof. Any attempt to modify or forge credentials would be immediately detectable, thereby safeguarding the integrity of the records. Blockchain uses cryptographic techniques to guarantee data security. Every block includes a cryptographic hash of the preceding block, as well as a timestamp and transaction data. This cryptographic linkage ensures that any alteration in a block would be evident as it would disrupt the entire chain. For academic credentials, this means that the authenticity of records is secured through encryption, making unauthorized access or tampering nearly impossible. Smart contracts are autonomous agreements where the conditions are encoded directly into computer code and are capable of executing themselves. In the context of academic credentials, smart contracts can automate verification processes. For example, when an employer or another educational institution needs to verify a diploma, a smart contract can automatically check the blockchain record and confirm its validity without human intervention.

4.3 Benefits of Blockchain for Academic Credentials

1. Enhanced Security and Fraud Prevention: The use of blockchain technology greatly reduces the risk of credential fraud. Since records are immutable and decentralized, tampering with or forging academic credentials becomes extremely difficult. This provides a higher level of security compared to traditional methods, where documents can be easily altered or duplicated.

2. Simplified Verification Process: Blockchain streamlines the verification of academic credentials. Institutions and employers can quickly and easily verify the authenticity of records through the blockchain, without the need for extensive manual checks or third-party verification services. This efficiency reduces administrative burdens and speeds up the credentialing process.

3. Increased Transparency and Trust: The transparent nature of blockchain allows all parties to see and verify the records independently. This transparency builds trust among stakeholders, including educational institutions, employers, and students, as everyone has access to the same verified information.

4. Reduced Administrative Costs: Automating the verification process through blockchain and smart contracts can significantly reduce administrative costs. Institutions no longer need to manually process verification requests or handle fraudulent claims, as blockchain provides a secure and automated solution.

5. Ownership and Control of Data: Blockchain technology allows students to have control over their academic records. They can grant or revoke access to their credentials as needed, ensuring that their personal information is managed according to their preferences and privacy requirements.

The future of blockchain in securing academic credentials holds promising potential. Emerging trends include the integration of blockchain with other technologies, such as digital identity solutions and decentralized applications (dApps), to enhance the functionality and usability of credentialing systems. Additionally, ongoing research and development will address current challenges, improve scalability, and drive innovation in how academic credentials are managed and verified.

5. Synergy between AI and Blockchain

AI and Blockchain technology represent a powerful synergy that can drive innovation and efficiency across various sectors, including education. By leveraging the strengths of both technologies, organizations can create systems that are more secure, intelligent, and adaptive.

5.1 Complementary Strengths of AI and Blockchain

1. AI's Data-Driven Insights and Blockchain's Security: AI excels at processing and analysing large volumes of data to derive actionable insights, predict outcomes, and automate decision-making. In education, AI can analyse student performance, personalize learning experiences, and optimize administrative tasks.

Blockchain: Blockchain provides a secure, transparent, and immutable ledger for recording and verifying transactions. It ensures data integrity and enhances trust in systems by preventing tampering and unauthorized access.

Synergy: Combining AI's data-driven capabilities with Blockchain's secure data storage creates systems where AI can analyse and interpret data with confidence in its accuracy and security. For example, AI-driven analytics on academic records stored on a Blockchain can offer insights into student performance while ensuring the integrity and immutability of the records [31].

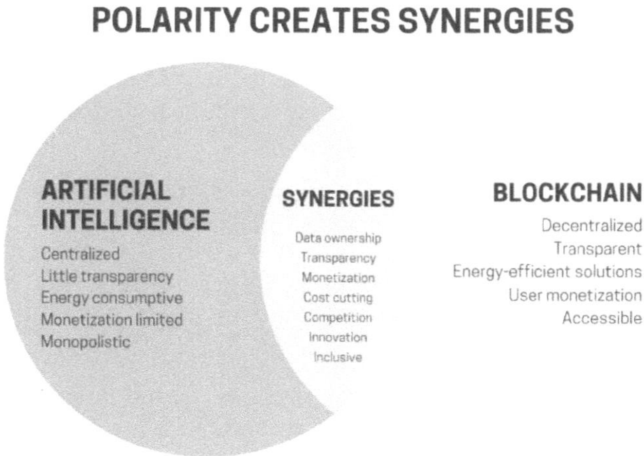

Figure 2. The synergy between AI and Blockchain [30].

2. AI's Automation and Blockchain's Decentralization: AI technologies, such as machine learning algorithms and smart contracts, can automate complex processes and decision-making. In education, this includes tasks like grading, feedback, and administrative functions.

Blockchain: Blockchain allows for decentralized systems, in which data and operations are not controlled by a single party. This decentralization enhances trust and resilience by distributing control across multiple nodes.

Synergy: The integration of AI and Blockchain allows for the creation of decentralized autonomous organizations (DAOs) or platforms where AI-driven smart contracts automate processes based on decentralized rules and conditions. For example, an educational platform could use AI to assess performance and issue credentials autonomously based on predefined criteria stored on a Blockchain.

5.2 Applications of AI and Blockchain Synergy

1. Secure and Intelligent Credential Verification: AI: AI can analyse patterns and detect anomalies in credentialing data, identifying fraudulent activities or inconsistencies.

Blockchain: Blockchain stores academic credentials in a secure, tamper-proof ledger.

Synergy: Combining AI and Blockchain enhances the verification process by using AI to identify potential fraud or errors in credentials while Blockchain ensures that the credentials are stored securely and can be verified independently.

2. Personalized Learning with Transparent Data

AI: AI can create personalized learning experiences by analysing student data and adapting educational content accordingly.

Blockchain: Blockchain provides a transparent and secure way to store and manage educational data.

Synergy: AI can use the educational data stored on Blockchain to deliver personalized learning experiences, while Blockchain ensures that the data used is accurate and secure. This combination offers a trustworthy basis for adaptive learning systems [32].

3. Automated Administrative Processes

AI: can automate administrative processes, including the process of grading, scheduling, and reporting.

Blockchain: Blockchain can manage and verify administrative transactions and records.

Synergy: AI-driven automation can work seamlessly with Blockchain-based records to manage administrative processes efficiently. For example, automated grading systems can update student records on a Blockchain, ensuring that grades are accurately recorded and verified.

4. Enhanced Data Privacy and Security

AI: AI can monitor and analyse data access patterns to identify potential security threats.

Blockchain: Blockchain provides secure data storage and access controls.

Synergy: AI can enhance Blockchain's security by analysing data access and usage patterns to detect unusual activities, while Blockchain ensures that data is securely stored and access is controlled through cryptographic means.

5.3 Benefits of combining AI and Blockchain

1. Increased Trust and Transparency: The integration of AI and Blockchain enhances the transparency of data and processes. Blockchain's immutable ledger ensures data integrity, while AI provides insights and analysis that are based on this secure data. This combination builds trust among stakeholders by providing a clear and verifiable record of actions and decisions.

2. Enhanced Efficiency and Automation: AI-driven automation of tasks, combined with Blockchain's decentralized management, streamlines processes and reduces the need for intermediaries. This results in more efficient operations, faster decision-making, and reduced administrative overhead.

3. Improved Data Security and Privacy: Blockchain's secure data storage, combined with AI's ability to monitor and analyse data access, creates a robust system for protecting sensitive information. This dual approach ensures that data is secure from tampering and unauthorized access while maintaining privacy.

4. Scalable and Resilient Systems: The synergy between AI and Blockchain can create scalable and resilient systems. AI's ability to handle large volumes of data, combined with Blockchain's decentralized architecture, allows for the creation of systems that can grow and adapt while maintaining security and reliability.

5.4 Challenges and Considerations

1. Complexity of Integration: Integrating AI and Blockchain technologies can be complex, requiring expertise in both fields. Organizations must address technical challenges related to compatibility, interoperability, and system architecture.

2. Scalability and Performance Issues: Both AI and Blockchain can face scalability and performance issues. Ensuring that systems remain efficient and effective as they scale is a key consideration when combining these technologies.

3. Regulatory and Ethical Concerns: The use of AI and Blockchain in sensitive areas, such as education and personal data management, raises regulatory and ethical questions. Organizations must navigate legal requirements and ethical considerations to ensure compliance and protect users' rights.

4. Cost and Resource Requirements: Implementing and maintaining AI and Blockchain systems can be resource-intensive and costly. Organizations need to invest in infrastructure, expertise, and ongoing maintenance to ensure the success of these technologies.

The future of AI and Blockchain synergy holds promising potential for innovation. Emerging trends include the development of advanced AI algorithms that can better integrate with Blockchain systems, as well as the creation of new decentralized applications (dApps) that leverage both technologies. Continued research and development will address current challenges and unlock new possibilities for their combined use.

6. Decentralized Credentialing and Certification

Decentralized credentialing and certification represent a significant shift from traditional centralized systems of managing academic and professional qualifications. By leveraging blockchain technology, decentralized credentialing systems offer a more secure, transparent, and efficient approach to verifying and managing credentials.

6.1 Concept of Decentralized Credentialing

Decentralised credentialing is the use of blockchain technology for issuing, managing, and verifying credentials in a decentralized manner. Unlike traditional systems where a central authority (such as an educational institution or certification body) maintains and verifies credentials, decentralized credentialing leverages blockchain's distributed ledger to manage these processes. In a decentralized credentialing system, credentials are recorded on a blockchain ledger maintained by a network of nodes. This ledger provides a secure and immutable record of all credentials issued, ensuring transparency and preventing tampering. Individuals control their credentials through decentralized identity systems, allowing them to share and verify their qualifications without relying on intermediaries. Smart contracts are contracts that are automatically executed based on code that contains the conditions of the agreement. In decentralized credentialing, smart contracts automate the issuance and verification of credentials based on predefined criteria. Smart contracts can automatically issue credentials when certain conditions are met (e.g., completion of a course or passing an exam), reducing administrative overhead and potential errors. When credentials need to be verified, smart contracts can cross-reference the information on the blockchain to ensure authenticity and validity.

6.2 Advantages of Decentralized Credentialing

1. Enhanced Security and Fraud Prevention: Decentralized credentialing systems leverage blockchain's immutability and cryptographic security to protect credentials from tampering and fraud. Since blockchain records are immutable and distributed across multiple nodes, unauthorized modifications are virtually impossible.

2. Increased Transparency and Trust: Blockchain provides a transparent record of all credentialing activities, allowing all parties to independently verify the authenticity of credentials. This transparency builds trust among educational institutions, employers, and individuals.

3. Reduced Administrative Burden: Automating credential issuance and verification through smart contracts reduces the need for manual processes and intermediaries. This streamlines administrative tasks and lowers operational costs for educational institutions and certification bodies.

4. Empowered Individuals: Decentralized credentialing gives individuals control over their qualifications. They can manage, share, and verify their credentials without relying on centralized authorities, which enhances their autonomy and simplifies interactions with potential employers or educational institutions.

5. Global Accessibility: Blockchain-based credentials can be easily accessed and verified anywhere in the world, making it easier for individuals to showcase their qualifications across borders and for institutions to validate credentials without geographical constraints.

6.3 *Applications of Decentralized Credentialing*

1. Educational Institutions: Educational institutions can issue diplomas, certificates, and transcripts on a blockchain, providing secure and verifiable records of academic achievements.

Digital Diplomas: Universities can issue digital diplomas stored on a blockchain, making it easy for employers and other institutions to verify the authenticity of the credentials.

Transcript Management: Academic transcripts can be recorded on a blockchain, ensuring that students' academic records are secure and tamper-proof.

2. Professional Certifications: Certification bodies can use blockchain to manage and verify professional qualifications, ensuring that certifications are legitimate and up-to-date.

Professional Licenses: Blockchain can issue and manage professional licenses, such as medical or legal certifications, providing a secure and transparent record of qualifications.

Skills Badges: Organizations can issue digital badges for specific skills or achievements, which are recorded on the blockchain and can be easily verified by employers.

3. Employment Verification: Employers can use decentralized credentialing systems to verify candidates' qualifications and work experience, reducing the risk of fraud and streamlining the hiring process.

Background Checks: Employers can access and verify educational and professional credentials directly from the blockchain, speeding up the background check process.

Skill Verification: Blockchain-based credentials can provide evidence of specific skills and achievements, helping employers assess candidates' qualifications more effectively.

4. Blockchain-Based Learning Platforms: Learning platforms can integrate decentralized credentialing to issue and verify certificates and achievements for online courses and training programs.

Online Courses: Platforms offering online courses can use blockchain to issue certificates of completion, which are securely recorded and easily verifiable.

Micro-Credentials: Blockchain can issue micro-credentials or digital badges for specific skills or competencies acquired through online learning.

6.4 Challenges and Considerations

1. Implementation Complexity: Implementing a decentralized credentialing system requires significant investment in blockchain infrastructure and expertise. Educational institutions and certification bodies must address technical and operational challenges associated with integrating blockchain technology.

2. Regulatory and Legal Issues: Decentralized credentialing systems must comply with regulatory and legal requirements related to data privacy, security, and accreditation. Navigating these regulations is crucial to ensure that blockchain-based credentials are legally recognized and accepted.

3. Scalability and Performance: Blockchain networks may encounter scalability challenges, especially when dealing with large transaction volumes. Ensuring that decentralized credentialing systems can handle large numbers of credentials and verification requests efficiently is essential.

4. Interoperability: For decentralized credentialing to be effective, it must be interoperable with existing systems and standards used by educational institutions, employers, and certification bodies. Developing standards and protocols for interoperability is a key consideration.

5. User Adoption: Widespread adoption of decentralized credentialing requires buy-in from various stakeholders, including educational institutions, employers, and individuals. Demonstrating the benefits and addressing concerns about blockchain technology are crucial for gaining acceptance.

7. Implementation in Modern Educational Systems

The implementation of blockchain technology in modern educational systems represents a significant shift towards enhancing transparency, security, and efficiency in managing academic records and credentials.

Blockchain's decentralized and immutable nature offers innovative solutions to many challenges faced by educational institutions, students, and employers. This section explores the practical aspects of implementing blockchain in education, including the steps involved, benefits, challenges, and real-world examples.

7.1 Steps in Implementing Blockchain in Education

1. Assessing Needs and Objectives: Before implementing blockchain technology, educational institutions must identify their specific needs and objectives. This involves assessing current systems, determining areas where blockchain could add value, and defining the goals of the blockchain initiative.

Needs Assessment: Evaluate current processes for managing academic records, credentials, and other educational data. Identify pain points such as security issues, inefficiencies, or lack of transparency.

Objective Setting: Define clear objectives for the blockchain implementation, such as improving credential verification, reducing administrative overhead, or enhancing data security.

2. Choosing the Right Blockchain Platform: Selecting a suitable blockchain platform is crucial for successful implementation. Different blockchain platforms offer various features and capabilities, and the decision will be based on the particular criteria of the educational institution.

Public vs. Private Blockchain: Determine whether to utilise a public blockchain, such as Ethereum, or a private/permissioned blockchain, such as Hyperledger Fabric, by considering issues such as transparency, scalability, and control.

Platform Evaluation: Evaluate blockchain platforms based on factors like security, scalability, ease of integration, and support for smart contracts.

3. Designing the Blockchain Architecture: It involves defining how the blockchain will be structured, how data will be recorded, and how various stakeholders will interact with the system.

Data Structure: Determine how academic records and credentials will be represented and stored on the blockchain. Define the data fields, formats, and security measures.

Stakeholder Roles: Define the roles and permissions of different stakeholders, such as educational institutions, students, employers, and verification bodies.

4. Developing and Testing the System: Develop the blockchain solution based on the designed architecture and test it thoroughly to ensure functionality, security, and performance.

Development: Implement the blockchain system, including smart contracts, data storage, and user interfaces.

Testing: Conduct rigorous testing to identify and address any issues related to functionality, security, and scalability. Testing should include both technical aspects and user acceptance.

5. Training and Adoption: Successful implementation requires training for all stakeholders involved in using the blockchain system. This includes educational staff, students, and employers.

Training Programs: Develop and deliver training programs to educate stakeholders about blockchain technology, how to use the system, and the benefits of the new approach.

User Support: Provide ongoing support and resources to assist users in adapting to the new system and addressing any issues that arise.

6. Deployment and Integration: Deploy the blockchain solution and integrate it with existing systems and processes. Ensure that the new system works seamlessly with current administrative and academic processes.

Deployment: Roll out the blockchain system across the institution or educational network. Monitor the deployment process to ensure smooth implementation.

Integration: Integrate the blockchain system with existing data management systems, such as student information systems and administrative databases.

7. Monitoring and Evaluation: Consistently observe and assess the effectiveness of the blockchain system to ensure it meets its objectives and delivers the expected benefits.

Performance Monitoring: Track key performance indicators related to security, efficiency, and user satisfaction. Address any issues or areas for improvement.

Feedback Collection: Gather feedback from users to identify challenges and areas for enhancement. Use this feedback to make necessary adjustments and improvements.

7.2 Benefits of Blockchain Implementation in Education

1. Enhanced Security and Integrity: The immutable ledger of blockchain guarantees the security and integrity of academic data and credentials. This improves the reliability of educational data and decreases the likelihood of fraud and unauthorised alterations.

2. Improved Transparency and Trust: Blockchain provides a transparent and verifiable record of academic achievements and credentials. This transparency builds trust among stakeholders, including students, educational institutions, and employers.

3. Streamlined Administrative Processes: Blockchain automation, particularly through smart contracts, reduces the need for manual processes and intermediaries. This streamlines administrative tasks, such as credential issuance and verification, leading to cost savings and efficiency gains.

4. Empowered Students: Students gain greater control over their own academic records and credentials. They can manage, share, and verify their qualifications independently, enhancing their autonomy and simplifying interactions with employers and institutions.

5. Global Accessibility and Interoperability: Blockchain-based credentials can be accessed and verified globally, making it easier for students to showcase their qualifications across borders and for institutions to validate credentials regardless of geographical location.

7.3 Challenges and Considerations

1. Technical Complexity: Implementing a blockchain system involves technical complexity, including selecting the right platform, designing the architecture, and developing smart contracts. Institutions need expertise in blockchain technology to address these complexities effectively.

2. Regulatory and Legal Compliance: Educational institutions must navigate regulatory and legal considerations related to data privacy, security, and accreditation. Ensuring compliance with relevant regulations is crucial for the successful implementation of blockchain technology.

3. Scalability and Performance: Blockchain networks can face scalability issues, especially with high transaction volumes. Institutions must address these issues to ensure that the blockchain system can handle the scale of academic records and verification requests efficiently.

4. Interoperability with Existing Systems: Integrating blockchain with existing data management systems and processes can be challenging. Ensuring interoperability and seamless integration with current systems is essential for a smooth transition.

5. User Adoption and Training: Successful implementation requires buy-in from all stakeholders and adequate training. Institutions must address any resistance to change and provide support to facilitate user adoption and effective use of the new system.

7.4 Real-World Examples

1. MIT Media Lab: MIT has implemented a blockchain-based system for issuing digital diplomas. The system allows graduates to receive and share verifiable digital credentials securely.

2. Learning Machine: This company has partnered with educational institutions to use blockchain technology for issuing and verifying academic qualifications serving as a reliable and unalterable documentation of accomplishments.

3. Woolf University: Woolf University uses blockchain to manage academic records and credentials, providing a transparent and secure system for issuing and verifying diplomas and certificates.

8. Conclusion and Future Scope

The future of blockchain in education involve advancements in interoperability, scalability, and integration with other technologies such as AI and IoT. Ongoing research and development will address current challenges and unlock new possibilities for enhancing educational systems. Implementing blockchain technology in modern educational systems offers transformative benefits, including enhanced security, transparency, and efficiency. While challenges related to technical complexity, regulatory compliance, and user adoption exist, the potential advantages are substantial. By carefully planning and executing blockchain initiatives, educational institutions can create innovative systems that improve the management and verification of academic credentials, ultimately benefiting students, educators, and employers. The integration of AI and Blockchain technology holds transformative potential across various sectors, particularly in education, healthcare, finance, and supply chain management. By combining the data-driven capabilities of AI with the security and transparency offered by blockchain, organizations can create systems that are not only more efficient but also more secure and trustworthy. This section explores the transformative potential of AI and blockchain integration and discusses future directions for research and development.

References

[1] Agarwal, R. and Dhar, V. (2014). Big data, data science, and analytics: A high-level overview. In *Proceedings of the 2014 International Conference on Big Data*, (pp. 1–10). IEEE.

[2] Alsharif, N. (2021). Blockchain-based adaptive learning systems: A systematic review. *International Journal of Educational Technology in Higher Education*, 18(1): 1–19.

[3] Baker, R.S. and Inventado, P.S. (2014). Educational data mining and learning analytics. In *Handbook of Educational Psychology*, (pp. 253–274). Routledge.

[4] Bollier, D. and Evans, K. (2018). The blockchain and the new architecture of trust. Cato Institute.

[5] Cheng, K. and Lin, H. (2020). Integrating blockchain technology in education: A review. *Journal of Computer Assisted Learning*, 36(6): 844–858.

[6] Daugherty, P.R. and Wilson, H.J. (2018). The age of Artificial Intelligence: How AI will transform the future of business. Accenture.

[7] de Vries, E. and van der Meer, J. (2018). Blockchain in education: A review of the literature. *Journal of Educational Technology & Society*, 21(3): 132–145.

[8] Downes, S. (2019). The role of Artificial Intelligence in adaptive learning. *Educational Technology Magazine*.

[9] Durham, J. (2020). Blockchain technology in education: Benefits, risks, and applications. In *Proceedings of the 2020 International Conference on Blockchain Technology*, (pp. 80–89). IEEE.

[10] Galloway, C. and Daugherty, P. (2020). AI and the future of education: A deep dive into machine learning and data analytics. *Journal of Educational Data Mining*, 12(1): 17–34.

[11] Gao, L. and Yang, Y. (2021). AI and Blockchain in education: A new paradigm for student credentialing and learning. *Computers & Education*, 162: 104065.

[12] Gates, B. (2021). The impact of Artificial Intelligence on education. *Bill & Melinda Gates Foundation*.

[13] Hao, K. (2018). *AI Could Help Students Learn, but First We Have to Build Better Algorithms*. MIT Technology Review.

[14] Hassel, H. and Wylie, C. (2019). Blockchain technology and its impact on higher education. *Journal of Higher Education Policy and Management*, 41(2): 159–172.

[15] Khan, S. (2017). AI-powered adaptive learning: A comprehensive review. *Journal of Educational Technology Development and Exchange*, 10(1): 1–15.

[16] Kumar, V. and Raj, M. (2020). Applications of blockchain in education: A case study. *Educational Research Review*, 15: 92–105.

[17] Liaw, S. and Chen, H. (2019). The integration of AI in adaptive learning systems: Trends and prospects. *International Journal of Artificial Intelligence in Education*, 29(1): 1–16.

[18] https://appinventiv.com/blog/ai-in-blockchain/(accessed 22 June 2024).

[19] Moualeu, B. (2021). Blockchain and Artificial Intelligence in education: Exploring the intersection. *Journal of Education and Information Technologies*, 26(2): 1773–1790.

[20] Nair, R. (2020). Blockchain technology for academic credentialing: A review of innovations and applications. *Educational Technology Review*, 18(2): 56–72.

[21] Nguyen, T. and Lam, P. (2019). Adopting blockchain technology in higher education institutions: Opportunities and challenges. *Journal of Computing in Higher Education*, 31(3): 460–480.

[22] Peters, M. (2018). Artificial Intelligence and blockchain in education: Prospects and challenges. In *Proceedings of the 2018 International Conference on Education Technology*, (pp. 212–219). Springer.

[23] Rao, S. and Patel, J. (2020). Blockchain and AI in adaptive learning systems: A new horizon. *Educational Technology & Society*, 23(4): 128–140.

[24] Reich, J. (2020). Blockchain for education: A new paradigm for academic records. *Educational Policy Review*, 25(2): 42–58.

[25] Schafer, W. and Chang, A. (2021). Integrating blockchain with AI for enhanced adaptive learning platforms. *Journal of Educational Technology Research and Development*, 69(2): 301–318.

[26] Schneider, E. and Becker, J. (2020). AI-driven adaptive learning: Current trends and future directions. *Computers in Human Behaviour*, 107: 105802.

[27] Susskind, R. and Susskind, D. (2019). *The Future of the Professions: How Technology Will Transform the Work of Human Experts*. Oxford University Press.

[28] Tapscott, D. and Tapscott, A. (2018). *Blockchain Revolution: How the Technology Behind Bitcoin Is Changing Money, Business, and the World*. Penguin Random House.
[29] Tsai, Y. and Liu, S. (2021). AI and Blockchain for student data management: An overview. *International Journal of Information Management*, 56: 102286.
[30] https://thedeficlub.quora.com/ (accessed 22 June 2024).
[31] Wang, Q. and Wang, C. (2020). Applications of blockchain in educational data management: Opportunities and challenges. *Education and Information Technologies*, 25(1): 123–142.
[32] Zhou, X. and Yang, C. (2021). Blockchain and AI: Synergistic technologies for next-generation learning systems. *Journal of Educational Technology & Society*, 24(3): 110–124.

Chapter 4

Artificial Intelligence in Modern Education

Empowering Educators and Learners Beyond Automation

Arya Gopinath MP[1] and *Akhil K Ramesh*[2,*]

This chapter investigates the transformative potential of artificial intelligence (AI) and machine learning (ML) in shaping the modern education landscape. We delve into their multifaceted applications, exploring how they are driving advancements in data-driven decision-making, personalized learning, intelligent tutoring systems, and enhanced teaching methodologies. A critical focus is placed on the role of AI and ML in facilitating fast and efficient data analysis within the education system. By utilizing these technologies, educators can obtain essential insights into student performance, learning paths, and areas needing focused interventions. This data-centric method empowers educators to personalize learning experiences that cater to the unique needs of each student and foster deeper engagement. Furthermore, the chapter examines the burgeoning application of AI in developing intelligent tutoring systems that provide students with personalized feedback and

[1] Kerala Agricultural University, India.
[2] National Yang Ming Chiao Tung University, Taiwan.
ORCID: https://orcid.org/0000-0003-2825-9738.
ORCID: https://orcid.org/0000-0003-1514-1271.
Email: aryagopinath111@gmail.com
* Corresponding author: akhil.k.ramesh@gmail.com

adaptive learning support. These systems can dynamically adjust to individual learning paces and styles, offering targeted instruction and addressing specific knowledge gaps.

Additionally, the chapter explores how AI can augment teaching methodologies by assisting educators in lesson planning, content creation, and assessment development, thereby optimizing instructional delivery. Examining the current integration of AI and ML in education, this chapter explores the potential benefits and challenges, emphasizing how these technologies can empower, not replace, educators. We highlight the importance of ethical considerations, potential biases, and the need for responsible implementation to ensure equitable and inclusive learning experiences for all students. This chapter contributes to the ongoing discourse on the immense potential of AI and ML in transforming education, paving the way for further research and development in this critical field, ultimately aiming to shape a future of personalized, data-driven, and effective learning for all.

1. Introduction

Artificial Intelligence (AI) and Machine Learning (ML) are revolutionizing various fields, and education is no exception [12, 23]. The transformative potential of these technologies lies in their ability to enhance teaching and learning experiences through sophisticated data analysis, personalized learning, and intelligent systems [26]. This chapter provides an in-depth exploration of AI and ML in education, highlighting their importance and potential to empower educators and learners. AI and ML can process vast educational data, providing previously unattainable insights. For example, AI algorithms analyse student performance data and identify patterns or trends, helping educators understand where students excel and where they need further support. This data-driven approach enables a more nuanced understanding of student needs, laying the foundation for more individualized and effective teaching strategies.

Moreover, AI and ML can automate routine administrative tasks, allowing educators to concentrate more on teaching and engaging with students. Tasks such as grading, scheduling, and even some aspects of lesson planning can be handled by AI, allowing teachers to devote more time to the creative and interpersonal aspects of teaching. This shift improves student learning outcomes as well as the effectiveness of educational institutions. In this chapter, the transformative potential of AI and ML with its various applications beyond automation is discussed in detail. The chapter also discusses the ethical challenges and the considerations for the responsible implementation of AI and ML in modern education and suggests blockchain technology as one of the aids for this. The chapter also proposes the empowerment of educators and the education system with the help of these technologies.

2. Transformative Potential of AI and ML in Education

AI and ML technologies significantly enhance modern education through personalized learning, data-driven decision-making , intelligent tutoring systems, enhanced pedagogy, and learning analytics with content recommendations. This potential of AI and ML in modern education is summarised in Figure 1. Chatbots and Virtual Assistants leverage natural language processing to provide instant responses to student queries, schedule meetings, and offer personalized assistance, significantly reducing the administrative burden on educators. Personalized learning tailors educational content to individual students, keeping them engaged and addressing their unique needs. Data-driven decision-making helps educators make informed choices by analysing student performance and behaviour data. Intelligent tutoring systems provide customized, real-time feedback and support, mimicking human tutors. Enhanced pedagogy involves AI assisting in lesson planning, content creation, and strategy suggestions, optimizing instructional delivery. Learning analytics offer insights into student engagement and progress, enabling targeted content recommendations to improve learning outcomes. Together, these applications create a more effective, personalized, and efficient educational experience.

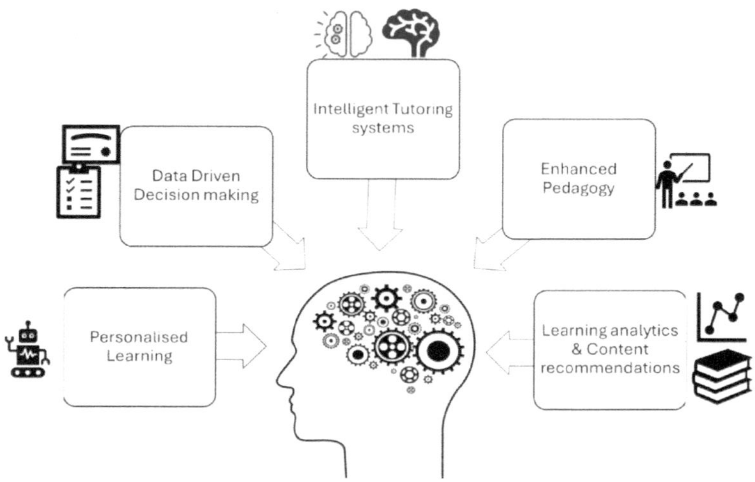

Figure 1. Applications of artificial intelligence and machine learning which can revolutionize modern education beyond mere automation.

In short, the integration of AI and ML in education can create a more dynamic, responsive, and personalized learning environment. Educators can improve educational outcomes by using these technologies to better understand how students learn, provide individualized help, and improve their teaching strategies.

2.1 *Personalized Learning Experiences*

AI and ML are at the forefront of personalized learning, offering tools and techniques that enable highly individualized learning experiences [7, 14]. By analyzing a variety of data, including students' academic achievements, learning styles, and even behavioral patterns, AI can create personalized learning plans that adjust in real-time to match the current needs and abilities of each student [9]. For instance, if a student has difficulty with a specific math concept, AI can suggest additional resources or different explanations to aid their understanding. This level of personalization helps keep students motivated and engaged in their studies. Interactive tools, such as educational games and simulations, can be customized to each student's preferences, making learning effective and enjoyable. Adaptive learning technologies exemplify the power of personalized learning. These systems dynamically adapt the difficulty and type of content based on how the student performs [10, 24]. For instance, an adaptive learning platform might present more challenging problems as a student demonstrates proficiency or offer additional practice for concepts that the student finds difficult. This continuous adjustment ensures that students are always working at the optimal level of difficulty, promoting better learning outcomes.

2.2 *Data-Driven Decision Making in Education*

Traditionally, educators relied on intuition and anecdotal evidence to understand student progress. AI and ML are revolutionizing how educational data is analyzed [8, 11]. Educators can now leverage these technologies to gain insights into vast datasets, including student performance on assignments, standardized tests, online interactions within learning platforms, and even eye-tracking data that reveals how students engage with learning materials. This data can reveal hidden patterns and trends, allowing educators to identify students who are excelling, struggling, or at risk of falling behind. For example, imagine a school district using AI to analyze student performance data across various demographics, learning styles, and socio-economic backgrounds. The analysis might reveal a pattern where students from certain socio-economic backgrounds consistently underperform in a particular subject, specifically on problems requiring real-world application. Armed with this granular knowledge, educators can implement targeted interventions, such as after-school tutoring programs specifically focused on that particular subject or providing access to online resources that present problems in relatable scenarios.

Data-driven decision-making empowered by AI is not a silver bullet, but it equips educators with valuable insights to personalize learning experiences. Imagine a history teacher noticing a decline in student engagement during lectures on the French Revolution. By analyzing student clickstream data within the learning management system, the teacher might discover that students are spending excessive time on a specific section about the rise of Robespierre. This could indicate a knowledge gap or a lack of clarity in the presented material. The teacher can then adjust their approach, providing additional resources or creating a short interactive quiz to assess understanding and foster deeper engagement.

2.3 *Intelligent Tutoring Systems*

Intelligent Tutoring Systems (ITS) utilize AI to offer personalized tutoring to students [1, 13]. These systems are designed to mimic the capabilities of human tutors by offering individualized feedback, adaptive learning support, and targeted instruction. Dynamic adjustment is a key feature of ITS. These systems continuously monitor student performance and adapt the instructional content accordingly. For instance, if a student encounters difficulty with a specific concept, the ITS can offer supplementary explanations, practice problems, or alternative teaching approaches to facilitate the student's comprehension of the material. Conversely, if a student is excelling, the ITS can present more challenging content to keep them motivated and engaged.

Targeted instruction is another significant benefit of ITS. Through detailed analysis of student performance data, these systems can pinpoint specific areas where students need additional support and offer targeted interventions. For instance, an ITS might detect that a student has difficulty with fractions and subsequently offer targeted exercises and explanations to address this gap. This personalized approach guarantees that each student receives the necessary support to thrive. Case studies have demonstrated the effectiveness of ITS in various educational settings. For example, one study found that students using an ITS for math instruction showed significant improvement in their test scores compared to those who received traditional classroom instruction [22]. Another study highlighted the ability of ITS to support diverse learning styles, helping students with different needs and preferences achieve better learning outcomes [3].

Table 1. Features and functionalities of Traditional Tutoring vs. Intelligent Tutoring Systems (ITS).

Feature	Traditional Tutoring	Intelligent Tutoring Systems (ITS)
Delivery	One-on-one or small group sessions with a human tutor	Software-based; students interact with the system independently
Personalization	Tailored to a certain extent based on the tutor's knowledge of the student	Highly personalized based on student performance, learning pace, and identified knowledge gaps
Feedback	Provided verbally by the tutor, may not be immediate	Offered in real-time, can be tailored to specific mistakes or areas of difficulty
Learning Pace	Adjusted based on the tutor's judgment and student interaction	Adapts automatically to the student's learning pace, offering more challenging material when concepts are grasped or providing additional support when needed
Content	Static curriculum materials or resources chosen by the tutor	Dynamic learning path based on the student's progress, offering targeted content to address specific needs
Flexibility	Limited by the tutor's availability and expertise	Available 24/7, can cater to a wider range of learning styles and skill levels
Assessment	Informal assessments through observation and interaction	Can include built-in quizzes, knowledge checks, and progress tracking to identify areas for improvement

2.4 Enhancing Teaching Methodologies

AI is transforming teaching methodologies by providing educators with innovative tools and resources to enhance instructional delivery. From lesson planning to content creation and assessment development, AI is helping teachers optimize their teaching practices. In lesson planning, AI-powered tools can analyze curriculum standards, learning objectives, and student data to suggest effective lesson plans. These tools can recommend instructional strategies, resources, and activities that are carefully tailored and adjusted to meet the specific needs and learning styles of every student. For example, an AI tool might suggest using a particular interactive simulation to teach a complex science concept, based on student performance data, and learning preferences. Content creation is another area where artificial intelligence is making a substantial and meaningful impact. AI can generate educational materials, such as quizzes, worksheets, and multimedia presentations, that are aligned with the curriculum and tailored to the student's needs. This not only saves teachers time but also ensures that the content is relevant and engaging for the students. For instance, an AI tool might create a customized set

Table 2. Some AI-powered tools which can be developed for educators in lesson planning, content creation, and assessment development.

Category	Tool Description	Example
Lesson Planning	AI helps generate lesson plans based on learning objectives, curriculum standards, and student needs.	- Generates outlines with activities and resources. - Suggest differentiation strategies for diverse learners.
Content Creation	AI assists in creating engaging and informative content aligned with lesson plans.	- Creates multimedia presentations (e.g., videos, infographics). - Generates quizzes, worksheets, and interactive activities. - Provides writing prompts and outlines for different learning styles.
Assessment Development	AI streamlines assessment creation and grading, allowing for personalized feedback.	- Generates quizzes and tests with various question types (e.g., multiple choice, open-ended). - Auto-grades certain types of questions (e.g., multiple choice). - Provides feedback reports with insights into student strengths and weaknesses.

of practice problems for a student who is preparing for a math exam, focusing on areas where the student needs the most practice.

Assessment development and grading are also being revolutionized by AI. AI-powered assessment tools can create tests and quizzes that are tailored to the student's learning levels and objectives [19]. These tools can also grade assessments instantly, providing immediate feedback to students and helping teachers identify areas where students need additional support. This rapid feedback loop enhances the learning process, allowing students to learn from their mistakes and improve their performance.

2.5 *Learning Analytics and Content Recommendations*

Artificial intelligence and machine learning are pivotal in transforming learning analytics and enhancing content recommendations, transforming how education is delivered and experienced [18, 25]. By analyzing vast amounts of data generated by students, such as their interactions with learning materials, performance metrics, and engagement patterns, AI and ML can uncover valuable insights into individual learning behaviors and preferences. This enables the development of personalized learning experiences, where content recommendations are specifically customized to meet the unique and individualized needs of each student. AI-driven learning analytics can identify knowledge gaps, predict academic outcomes, and suggest targeted interventions to support student success.

Furthermore, these technologies facilitate real-time feedback and adaptive learning pathways, allowing educators to adjust their teaching strategies dynamically. For instance, If a student encounters difficulty with a specific concept, AI can promptly suggest supplementary resources or alternative instructional methods to help them overcome the challenge. This continuous monitoring and adjustment ensure that students receive the right support at the right time, enhancing their overall learning experience. Moreover, ML algorithms continuously refine these recommendations by learning from student feedback and performance, ensuring that the educational content remains relevant and effective. This iterative process not only keeps the curriculum updated with the latest educational advancements but also aligns with the evolving interests learning preferences and styles of students.

The role of AI and ML extends beyond individual classrooms to broader educational systems. Administrators can leverage learning analytics to make informed decisions about curriculum development, resource allocation, and policy-making. By understanding trends and patterns at a macro level, educational institutions can create more efficient and equitable learning environments. This dynamic and adaptive approach not only enhances student engagement and motivation but also promotes more efficient and impactful learning outcomes. By leveraging the capabilities of AI and ML, educators can foster a more inclusive and responsive education system that adapts to the diverse needs of the modern learner.

3. Ethical Considerations and Challenges

The integration of AI and ML in education brings numerous benefits, but it also presents several ethical considerations and challenges that must be addressed to ensure responsible and equitable implementation [16]. Some of the major concerns are listed below:

1. *Bias and Fairness:* AI systems, reliant on the data they are trained on, can unintentionally perpetuate biases, such as gender, racial, or socio-economic biases in historical data. Ensuring fairness in AI algorithms is paramount to prevent discriminatory outcomes. Collaboration between educators and developers is essential to identify and mitigate biases, ensuring AI systems promote equity and inclusivity. Techniques like bias detection, diverse dataset curation, and algorithmic auditing are crucial in this regard.

2. *Transparency and Explainability:* AI algorithms often operate opaquely, which raises concerns about transparency and accountability. AI systems must be designed to be explainable, enabling educators and students alike to comprehend decision-making processes and challenge them if necessary. Techniques such as model interpretability, clear documentation of algorithmic decisions, and the ability to trace back decisions to specific data inputs are critical for fostering trust and accountability.
3. *Human Oversight:* While AI and ITS (Intelligent Tutoring Systems) enhance educational capabilities, they should augment rather than replace human educators. Human oversight is indispensable for providing mentorship, emotional support, and ethical guidance that AI cannot offer. Educators must retain active involvement in the learning process, leveraging AI to enrich educational experiences without supplanting their roles. This human-AI collaboration can lead to more personalized learning experiences that are specifically tailored to meet the unique needs of each student.
4. *Privacy and Data Security:* The use of AI and blockchain involves extensive data collection and analysis, necessitating stringent measures to safeguard student privacy and data security. Robust protocols must be implemented to protect student information and ensure compliance with privacy regulations. Techniques such as data anonymization, encryption, secure data storage, and explicit consent mechanisms are essential to mitigate risks associated with data breaches and unauthorized access.
5. *Equitable Access:* To prevent exacerbating educational disparities, ensuring fair and equitable access to AI and blockchain technologies is important. Efforts should prioritize providing all students, regardless of socio-economic status or geographical location, with access to these transformative technologies. This includes addressing infrastructural gaps, providing training and support for educators and students, and considering the unique needs of diverse learner populations to ensure inclusivity in technology adoption.

By tackling these challenges and ethical considerations, educators and developers can utilize the transformative potential of AI, ML, and blockchain in education. This approach promises to establish a more personalized, data-driven, and effective environment for learning that benefits all students preparing them for the challenges of the 21st century. Responsible implementation of AI in education requires a careful balance between innovation and ethical considerations. Educators and policymakers must collaborate to develop guidelines and best

Figure 2. Challenges and ethical considerations while harnessing the potential of AI and ML in modern education.

practices for the ethical use of AI in education. This includes transparency in how AI systems are used, involving stakeholders in decision-making processes, and ensuring that AI technologies are designed and used in ways that promote fairness, inclusivity, and the well-being of all students.

Privacy and data security stand out as primary ethical issues within the realm of education, which can be effectively addressed by technologies like Blockchain [4]. AI systems often necessitate access to extensive student data to operate efficiently, encompassing sensitive information such as academic performance, personal details, and behavioral patterns. Ensuring the privacy and security of this data is paramount to prevent unauthorized access and misuse. Educational institutions must therefore implement strong data protection measures and comply with relevant regulations to safeguard student information.

4. Blockchain in Modern Education

Blockchain technology is emerging as a powerful tool in modern education, offering a range of applications that enhance transparency, security, and efficiency in educational processes [17, 21]. By leveraging the decentralized and immutable nature of blockchain, educational institutions can create secure and tamper-proof records of academic achievements, streamline administrative processes, and enable new models of credentialing and certification [5]. The major insights regarding the application of blockchain technology in modern education are listed below:

1. *Secure and Transparent Academic Records:* Blockchain can be used to create secure and transparent records of students' academic achievements. Each achievement, such as grades, certificates, and diplomas, can be recorded on a blockchain, ensuring that the information is immutable and cannot be tampered with. This provides a reliable and verifiable record of academic performance that can be easily accessed by students, educators, and employers. For example, a university might use blockchain to issue digital diplomas that are cryptographically signed and recorded on a blockchain. Employers can verify the authenticity of these diplomas by checking the blockchain, eliminating the risk of credential fraud.
2. *Streamlining Administrative Processes:* Blockchain can streamline various administrative processes in educational institutions, such as managing student enrolment, course registration, and transcript records by automating these processes and ensuring data integrity, blockchain can reduce administrative burdens and improve efficiency. For instance, a blockchain-based system for course registration can automatically verify prerequisites and ensure that students meet the requirements before enrolling in a course. This reduces the need for manual checks and minimizes the risk of errors.
3. *New Models of Credentialing and Certification:* Blockchain enables new models of credentialing and certification that go beyond traditional academic degrees. Micro-credentials, digital badges, and certificates for specific skills and competencies can be issued and verified using blockchain, providing a more granular and comprehensive record of a student's abilities. For example, a student who completes a series of online courses on data science might receive a blockchain-based digital badge for each course, as well as a certificate for the overall program. These credentials can be easily shared with potential employers and verified on the blockchain.
4. *Decentralized Learning Platforms:* Blockchain can support the development of decentralized learning platforms where educational content and resources are distributed across a network of peers. These platforms can offer greater accessibility and flexibility, enabling learners to access educational materials from anywhere in the world. For example, a blockchain-based platform for online courses might allow educators to upload course content that is stored

on a decentralized network. Students can access this content without relying on a central authority, ensuring that educational resources are widely available and resistant to censorship.

5. *Enhancing Data Privacy and Security:* Blockchain can enhance data privacy and security by providing a secure method for storing and sharing educational data. Students can have greater control over their data, choosing who can access it and for what purposes. For example, a student might use a blockchain-based system to grant access to their academic records to a potential employer for a limited period. The employer can verify the student's qualifications without accessing the underlying data, ensuring privacy and security.

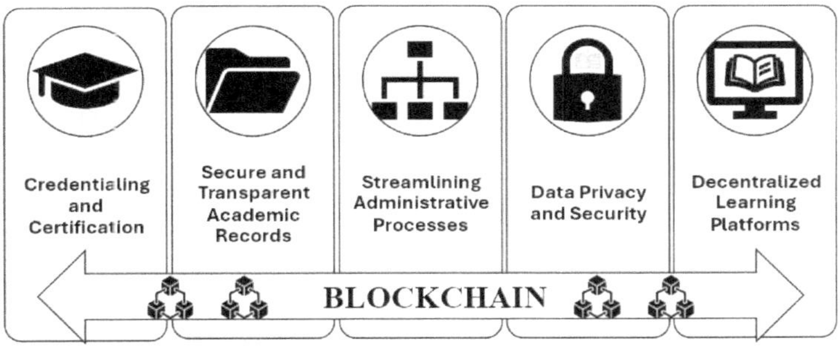

Figure 3. The scope for Blockchain technology in transforming Modern education with the help of AI and ML.

Apart from this, based on the AI and ML applications discussed in the previous sections, Blockchain technology can be really helpful in the fields of personalised learning [15]. Blockchain technology can further enhance personalized learning by enabling the creation of a comprehensive and secure digital record of each student's learning journey [20]. These digital records may contain not only academic achievements, but also extracurricular activities, talents, and competencies. Students can control who has access to their records and share them with educators, employers, or other institutions as needed. Blockchain technology can also complement the data-driven approach by providing a secure and transparent method for recording and sharing student performance data [2]. With blockchain, educators, and administrators can create immutable records of student achievements and progress, which can be securely accessed and verified by authorized stakeholders. This ensures the accuracy and integrity of educational data while protecting student privacy.

5. Empowering Educators, Not Replacing Them

One of the most important aspects of integrating AI and ML in education is ensuring that these technologies empower educators rather than replace them. AI should be regarded as a tool that amplifies the capabilities of teachers, allowing them to focus on the aspects of education that require a human touch. While artificial Intelligence will significantly impact education, it's crucial to understand that AI is not a threat to teachers; it's not meant to replace them but to enhance the educational experience for both students and educators. AI helps us rethink our entire education system and its delivery. It's strongly recommended that we need a more hybrid model that combines the best of AI-enabled systems and our teachers' expertise.

When students are in school with their teachers, they should focus on creativity, exploration, discussion, problem-solving skills, and building communication skills. Meanwhile, AI can offer a more tailored and personalized learning experience. For example, companies like Content Technologies and Carnegie Learning are developing platforms that offer AI-driven learning, testing, and feedback [6]. Think of an app like Thinker Math, which tracks student progress, identifies areas where students struggle, and provides additional learning resources tailored to their needs. This level of customization is something a teacher cannot offer to a classroom of 20 or 30 students. We are already familiar with such approaches in language learning through tools like Duolingo and Babbel, which allow personalized pacing and targeted support. By outsourcing some basic knowledge transfer to AI, teachers can focus on the more human, interactive, and creative aspects of teaching. AI also provides universal access to learning, enabling students worldwide to access top-quality language and math tutoring. Moreover, AI can manage administrative tasks, including grading multiple-choice exams and even written essays, freeing teachers to spend more time on what they love.

AI is highly relevant to schools, universities, and educational organizations. As education evolves into a lifelong learning process, AI helps engage students throughout their lives. Platforms like Coursera and Udemy already leverage AI in their online courses, demonstrating AI's potential to revolutionize teaching and enhance outcomes for both students and teachers. Supporting educators is a primary goal of AI in education. AI tools can automate routine administrative tasks like grading and attendance tracking, thereby allowing teachers to allocate more time to meaningful interactions with students. For example, AI can handle the grading of multiple-choice tests, allowing teachers to spend more time providing personalized feedback on written assignments and projects. This shift enables educators to devote more time to developing creative lesson plans, engaging with students, and addressing individual learning needs. Human-AI collaboration is another key element in empowering educators. AI systems can provide valuable insights and recommendations, but it is the teachers who ultimately interpret and apply this information in the classroom. For instance, an AI system might identify a student who is struggling with a particular concept and suggest targeted interventions. However, it is the teacher who decides how to implement these interventions, drawing on their professional expertise and understanding of the student's unique context. This collaboration between humans and AI ensures that educational decisions are both data-driven and informed by the nuanced understanding that only educators can provide.

Future prospects of AI in education highlight the evolving role of these technologies in supporting teachers. As AI systems advance, they will provide more tailored and adaptable support to educators and students. For example, AI could help teachers identify emerging trends in student performance, allowing for proactive interventions before issues become significant. Additionally, AI could assist in professional development by providing teachers with personalized recommendations for training and resources based on their specific needs and interests.

In summary, AI and ML can significantly empower educators by the automation of routine tasks, and supporting professional development by providing valuable insights. By fostering a collaborative relationship between humans and AI, we can create an educational environment where technology enhances the capabilities of teachers, ultimately leading to better learning outcomes for students.

6. Conclusion

The incorporation of AI and ML in modern education shows great potential for transforming teaching and learning experiences. This chapter has explored the multifaceted applications of these technologies, emphasizing their potential to empower educators and learners beyond mere automation. AI and ML facilitate data-driven decision-making by analyzing student performance, predicting learning trajectories, and enabling targeted interventions. These insights enable teachers to customize their teaching strategies to address the distinct needs of every student, promoting a more personalized and effective learning environment. AI further enhances personalized learning experiences by leveraging adaptive learning technologies and intelligent tutoring systems. These intelligent systems dynamically adjust to individual learning paces and styles, providing targeted instruction and addressing specific knowledge gaps. Consequently, students receive the customized support necessary for their success.

AI also augments teaching methodologies by assisting educators with lesson planning, content creation, and assessment development. By automating routine tasks and providing valuable resources, AI enables teachers to focus on the creative and interpersonal aspects of teaching, ultimately enriching the learning experience for students. Nevertheless, the incorporation of AI in modern education presents its own set of challenges. Ethical considerations such as privacy, data security, and potential biases must be addressed to ensure the responsible and equitable use of these technologies. By implementing robust data protection measures, using diverse datasets, and promoting equitable access, we can mitigate these risks and leverage the capabilities of AI to establish a more inclusive educational system. Empowering educators, rather than replacing them, is a fundamental principle of AI integration in education. By supporting teachers with AI tools and fostering a collaborative relationship between humans and AI, we can enhance the capabilities of educators and improve educational outcomes.

In conclusion, AI and ML have the potential to transform education by offering personalized, data-driven, and effective learning experiences. This chapter highlights the importance of responsible implementation and ethical considerations, paving the way for further research and development in this critical field. By embracing these technologies, we can shape a future where education is more personalized, inclusive, and effective for all learners.

References

[1] Alam, A. (2023). Harnessing the power of AI to create intelligent tutoring systems for enhanced classroom experience and improved learning outcomes. In *Intelligent Communication Technologies and Virtual Mobile Networks* (pp. 571–591), Springer.

[2] Bjelobaba, G., Savić, A., Tošić, T., Stefanović, I. and Kocić, B. (2023). Collaborative learning supported by blockchain technology as a model for improving the educational process. *Sustainability*, 15(6): 4780.

[3] Chrysafiadi, K., Virvou, M., Tsihrintzis, G.A. and Hatzilygeroudis, I. (2023). Evaluating the user's experience, adaptivity, and learning outcomes of a fuzzy-based intelligent tutoring system for computer programming for academic students in Greece. *Education and Information Technologies*, 28(6): 6453–6483.

[4] Dewangan, N.K., Chandrakar, P., Kumari, S. and Rodrigues, J.J. (2023). Enhanced privacy-preserving in student certificate management in blockchain and interplanetary file systems. *Multimedia Tools and Applications*, 82(8): 12595–12614.

[5] El Koshiry, A., Eliwa, E., Abd El-Hafeez, T. and Shams, M.Y. (2023). Unlocking the power of blockchain in education: An overview of innovations and outcomes. *Blockchain: Research and Applications*, 100165.

[6] Farahani, M.S. and Ghasmi, G. (2024). *Artificial Intelligence in Education: A Comprehensive Study.* Paper Presented at the Forum for Education Studies.

[7] Folgieri, R., Gil, M., Bait, M. and Lucchiari, C. (2024). *AI-Powered Personalised Learning Platforms For EFL Learning: Preliminary Results.* Paper Presented at the Proceedings of the 16th International Conference on Computer Supported Education.

[8] Howard, S.K., Swist, T., Gasevic, D., Bartimote, K., Knight, S., Gulson, K., Selwyn, N. (2022). Educational data journeys: Where are we going, what are we taking and making for AI? *Computers and Education: Artificial Intelligence*, 3: 100073.

[9] Hsu, T.-C., Abelson, H., Lao, N., Tseng, Y.-H. and Lin, Y.-T. (2021). Behavioral-pattern exploration and development of an instructional tool for young children to learn AI. *Computers and Education: Artificial Intelligence*, 2: 100012.

[10] Kem, D. (2022). Personalised and adaptive learning: Emerging learning platforms in the era of digital and smart learning. *International Journal of Social Science and Human Research*, 5(2): 385–391.

[11] Labarthe, H., Luengo, V. and Bouchet, F. (2018). *Analyzing the Relationships Between Learning Analytics, Educational Data Mining, and AI for Education.* Paper Presented at the 14th International Conference on Intelligent Tutoring Systems (ITS): Workshop Learning Analytics.

[12] Lainjo, B. and Tmouche, H. (2024). A meta-study of the evolutionary transformative academic landscape by artificial intelligence and machine learning. *International Journal of Education, Teaching, and Social Sciences*, 4(1): 20–35.

[13] Lampropoulos, G. (2023). Augmented reality and artificial intelligence in education: Toward immersive intelligent tutoring systems. In *Augmented Reality and Artificial Intelligence: The Fusion of Advanced Technologies* (pp. 137–146), Springer.

[14] Li, K.C. and Wong, B.T.-M. (2023). Artificial intelligence in personalised learning: A bibliometric analysis. *Interactive Technology and Smart Education*, 20(3): 422–445.

[15] Molenaar, I. (2021). Personalisation of learning: Towards hybrid human-AI learning technologies. *Blockchain, and Robots*, 57–77.

[16] Nguyen, A., Ngo, H.N., Hong, Y., Dang, B. and Nguyen, B.-P.T. (2023). Ethical principles for artificial intelligence in education. *Education and Information Technologies*, 28(4): 4221–4241.

[17] Ocheja, P., Flanagan, B., Ogata, H. and Oyelere, S.S. (2023). Visualization of education blockchain data: Trends and challenges. *Interactive Learning Environments*, 31(9), 5970–5994.

[18] Ouyang, F., Wu, M., Zheng, L., Zhang, L. and Jiao, P. (2023). Integration of artificial intelligence performance prediction and learning analytics to improve student learning in online engineering course. *International Journal of Educational Technology in Higher Education*, 20(1): 4.

[19] Owan, V.J., Abang, K.B., Idika, D.O., Etta, E.O. and Bassey, B.A. (2023). Exploring the potential of artificial intelligence tools in educational measurement and assessment. *Eurasia Journal of Mathematics, Science and Technology Education*, 19(8): em2307.

[20] Saadati, Z., Zeki, C.P. and Vatankhah Barenji, R. (2023). On the development of blockchain-based learning management system as a metacognitive tool to support self-regulation learning in online higher education. *Interactive Learning Environments*, 31(5): 3148–3171.

[21] Samala, A.D., Mhlanga, D., Bojic, L., Howard, N.-J. and Coelho, D.P. (2024). Blockchain technology in education: Opportunities, challenges, and beyond. *International Journal of Interactive Mobile Technologies*, 18(1).

[22] Shih, S.-C., Chang, C.-C., Kuo, B.-C. and Huang, Y.-H. (2023). Mathematics intelligent tutoring system for learning multiplication and division of fractions based on diagnostic teaching. *Education and Information Technologies*, 28(7): 9189–9210.

[23] Tahiru, F. (2021). AI in education: A systematic literature review. *Journal of Cases on Information Technology (JCIT)*, 23(1): 1–20.

[24] Taylor, D.L., Yeung, M. and Bashet, A. (2021). Personalized and adaptive learning. *Innovative learning environments in STEM higher education: Opportunities, Challenges, and Looking Forward*, 17–34.

[25] Ustun, A.B., Zhang, K., Karaoğlan-Yilmaz, F.G. and Yilmaz, R. (2023). Learning analytics based feedback and recommendations in flipped classrooms: An experimental study in higher education. *Journal of Research on Technology in Education*, 55(5): 841–857.

[26] Zhai, X., Chu, X., Chai, C.S., Jong, M.S.Y., Istenic, A., Spector, M., Liu, J.B., Yuan, J. and Li, Y. (2021). A review of Artificial Intelligence (AI) in education from 2010 to 2020. *Complexity*, 2021(1): 8812542.

Chapter 5

Need of AI in Modern Education

In the Eyes of Explainable AI (xAI)

Supriya Manna and *Niladri Sett**

Modern Education is not *Modern* without AI. However, AI's complex nature makes understanding and fixing problems challenging. Research worldwide shows that a parent's income greatly influences a child's education. This led us to explore how AI, especially complex models, makes important decisions using Explainable AI tools. Our research uncovered many complexities linked to parental income and offered reasonable explanations for these decisions. However, we also found biases in AI that go against what we want from AI in education: clear transparency and equal access for everyone. These biases can impact families and children's schooling, highlighting the need for better AI solutions that offer fair opportunities to all. This chapter tries to shed light on the complex manner in which AI operates, especially concerning biases. These are the foundational steps towards better educational policies, which include using AI in ways that are more reliable, accountable, and beneficial for everyone involved.

SRM University AP, Amaravati, Andhra Pradesh 522502, India.
* Corresponding author: niladrisett@gmail.com

1. Introduction

The trajectory of the education system has traversed a remarkable journey from medieval times to the modern era, reflecting societal advancements, technological innovations, and evolving pedagogical paradigms. Initially characterized by rudimentary pedagogical methods, limited accessibility, and a rigid curriculum, the education landscape has undergone transformative changes, albeit with persistent challenges.

Historically, the medieval education system was predominantly characterized by religious institutions, emphasizing classical literature, theology, and rote memorization. Access was largely restricted to elite echelons of society, with pedagogical approaches rooted in tradition and conformity.

Fast-forwarding to the modern era, the education system has witnessed democratization, technological integration, and a paradigm shift towards personalized learning. However, contemporary challenges persist, necessitating strategic interventions:

- **Better Recommendation of Courses:** Traditional systems often adopt a one-size-fits-all approach, overlooking individual learning preferences and aptitudes. AI-powered recommender systems being employed in book selection [31], utilizing collaborative filtering algorithms, analysing student data to generate personalized course recommendations, and optimizing learning outcomes and engagement. Contemporary software solutions, such as *Coursera*'s recommendation engine,[1] and platforms like *Knewton Alta*[2] leverage advanced algorithms to tailor learning pathways based on individual student profiles.
- **SWOT Analysis of Students:** Comprehensive student evaluation transcends academic performance, necessitating a nuanced understanding of individual strengths, weaknesses, opportunities, and threats. Machine learning models, employing clustering analysis algorithms [32], facilitate intricate SWOT analyses, enabling educators to devise tailored learning strategies and interventions. Software applications like *IBM Watson* Analytics[3] and *Tableau*[4] harness sophisticated algorithms to decode complex student profiles, fostering personalized academic trajectories.

[1] https://www.coursera.org/.
[2] https://www.wiley.com/en-us/education/alta.
[3] https://www.ibm.com/watson.
[4] https://www.tableau.com/.

- **Transparency for Students:** The ambiguity surrounding grading criteria, learning objectives, and assessment methodologies undermines student engagement and comprehension. Natural Language Processing (NLP) techniques, coupled with sentiment analysis algorithms [33], elucidate grading metrics and curricular objectives, fostering transparent and collaborative learning environments. Modern platforms like *Turnitin*[5] and *Grammarly*[6] employ AI-driven NLP tools to provide actionable feedback, enhancing transparency and academic integrity.
- **Better Performance Indicators with Personalized Feedback:** Conventional performance metrics often lack granularity, overshadowing individual accomplishments and areas of improvement. AI-driven data analytics platforms, harnessing predictive analytics algorithms, empower educators to deliver personalized performance indicators and actionable insights, optimizing learning trajectories and student engagement. Software solutions such as *Blackboard Analytics*[7] and *Moodle*[8] leverage advanced algorithms to analyze student data, facilitating targeted interventions and pedagogical enhancements.

1.1 The Point of This Chapter

Numerous studies have underscored the profound potential of Artificial Intelligence (AI) in augmenting and revitalizing the contemporary education system [26–29]. However, the integration of 'Modern' education with AI is not devoid of challenges, particularly concerning financial implications and accessibility disparities.

A plethora of global research, spanning developed nations such as Norway [23], Japan [21], developing nations such as China [22] to least developed African countries [24] like Ghana [25], elucidates a direct correlation between parental income and the quality of education availed by their progeny. In the 21st century landscape, while AI embodies an indispensable cornerstone of educational advancement, its implementation entails substantial costs encompassing resource allocation, hiring, cross-testing, verification, licensing, and deployment [34]. Consequently, the escalating financial exigencies associated with

[5] https://www.turnitin.com/.
[6] https://www.grammarly.com/.
[7] https://www.blackboard.com.
[8] https://moodle.org/.

modern education exacerbate accessibility barriers[9, 10] [35], constraining students hailing from economically disadvantaged backgrounds. Regrettably, instances abound wherein academically meritorious students, despite securing admissions into prestigious global universities, confront insurmountable financial hurdles, precluding educational attainment due to parental income constraints.

We acknowledge the fact that parental income substantially influences the attainability of educational opportunities for students. In this study, we want to investigate this aspect of parental income. What factors influence an individual's income? How can we visualise those dependencies? Moreover, are those dependencies fair? If not, how can we investigate the unfairness? Is the notion of *feature importance* enough to recognise a biased model? This chapter endeavours to delve deeper into these pivotal nexus. We use several methodologies for visualising the feature importance from a model and then we investigate whether are they enough for investigating (un)fairness. We use the adult census dataset in this study to work on this binary classification problem of predicting whether an individual (can) earn more than 50k USD a year, given the other attributes. This is the primary indicator for our study where we're presuming (based on the earlier studies mentioned above) that the individual, as a *parent*, enhances the chance of availing *better* education for his progeny. Through rigorous analysis and interpretation, this chapter aspires to furnish insights, foster dialogue, and catalyze informed interventions addressing the confluence of AI, education, and socio-economic disparities, steering towards an inclusive and equitable educational landscape.

In this book chapter, we have extensively scrutinized several recent research papers, tutorials, official documentation, and internet articles to gather information and reproduce the relevant results from current research. This book chapter is meant to be suitable for both technical as well as non-technical readers. We have, furthermore, considered numerous ways of structuring this chapter inspired by our scrutinization. The links to relevant *resources* are kept in the footnotes below.

---

[9] https://www.thehindubusinessline.com/opinion/columns/c-p-chandrasekhar/the-alarming-rise-in-education-costs-in-new-india/article33215181.ece.

[10] https://timesofindia.indiatimes.com/india/rising-cost-of-education-worries-parents-survey-shows/articleshow/17946981.cms?from=mdr.

Resources:
https://bit.ly/3u2v0ay; https://rb.gy/dd2dcx; https://bit.ly/3S1S9lo; https://rb.gy/ekghfm; https://rb.gy/qusxjj; https://rb.gy/fq4ysa; https://shorturl.at/dhAO7; https://shorturl.at/ntvBH; https://bit.ly/425kmg4; https://bit.ly/3O2DBko; https://bit.ly/3SjuPRR.

Finally, our study, by no means, is meant to be devised as an Oracle but we fundamentally believe in asking for explanations for high-stakes decisions taken by AI models for the sake of trustworthiness. In the education sector, this has been stressed in recent times [30], and in this chapter, we are demonstrating the same on one of the fundamental aspects of availing 'Modern' education: parental income using state-of-the-art xAI techniques.

2. Inherent Complexity: A Double-Edged Sword

As discussed, while AI harbours immense potential to revolutionize education, fostering personalized learning, enhancing administrative efficiency, and facilitating data-driven decision-making, its inherent complexity poses formidable challenges, particularly concerning transparency and interpretability in deducing decisions which concurrently introduces nuanced challenges that necessitate vigilant scrutiny and strategic navigation. Sophisticated AI software including Llms [36, 41, 42], SaaS and commercial software such as [37, 40], and virtual assistants [43], while endowed with remarkable capabilities, often manifests as convoluted enigmas, presenting two underlying problems:

1. **Explanation Gap:** AI models, characterized by intricate hyperspaces defined by multifaceted weights and attributes, inherently lack traceability and debuggability. The stochastic nature of the training phase, coupled with the intricacies of the hyperspace, obfuscates the retrieval and comprehension of model parameters and rationales. Consequently, elucidating the *'why'* behind AI predictions remains a daunting endeavor, devoid of straightforward exploration avenues.
2. **Trust in the *'Black-Box'*:** For seasoned machine learning practitioners well-versed in model architectures and training phases, navigating the intricacies of AI may seem feasible. However, for end-users devoid of specialized expertise, AI often emerges as an opaque 'black box', necessitating dual proficiency as AI and domain experts to engender trust. While domain expertise may be commonplace, it scarcely equates to an unwavering confidence in results generated by intricate AI systems, perpetuating scepticism and apprehension.

2.1 Explainable AI (xAI): Bridging the Trust Gap

In the pursuit of deciphering the intricacies of 'black-box' AI systems and fostering trust among end-users, scientists have embarked on a relentless quest, culminating in the emergence of Explainable AI (xAI) as an active area of research in this decade. XAI transcends traditional AI paradigms, endeavouring to illuminate the opaque nature of complex machine learning models by enabling:

1. **Enhanced Explainability:** XAI endeavours to cultivate machine learning techniques that aim to yield more explainable models without compromising learning performance or prediction accuracy [47]. By elucidating model rationale and inherent strengths and weaknesses, XAI augments user comprehension and trust in several high stakes (for example [46]), pivotal for fostering collaborative partnerships between humans and AI entities.
2. **Human-Centric Design:** XAI advocates for the integration of state-of-the-art human-computer interface techniques, facilitating the translation of intricate models into comprehensible and actionable insights for end-users [45]. By crafting intuitive explanation dialogues and interfaces, XAI empowers users to navigate, interpret, and leverage AI capabilities effectively, transcending the complexities of underlying algorithms and architectures.
3. **Diverse Methodological Portfolio:** Recognizing the multifaceted challenges inherent in achieving explainability without compromising performance, XAI adopts a multifaceted approach, exploring and integrating diverse techniques across the performance-versus-explainability trade space [44]. By curating a portfolio of methodologies, XAI equips developers with versatile design options, facilitating tailored solutions aligned with specific application domains and user requirements.

3. Methodology: Explainability, Interpretability and More

Before jumping into the technical and mathematical intricacies of xAI, it is critical to distinguish between explainability and interpretability in machine learning applications for our objectives. We regard interpretability as a means of obtaining explainability. Explainable AI (or XAI) refers to models whose results can be comprehended by ordinary humans. However, this does not imply that the model is required to be interpretable. That is, there are two types of models: interpretable models and non-interpretable models. *Linear regression, logistic regression, decision trees,* etc., are examples of interpretable models. Practitioners can simply determine how the model outputs either its label or value. Then there are non-interpretable models for image processing and natural language processing, such as random forests, feed-forward neural networks, and deep learning architectures [7]. In order to make sense of the process by which the intricate model that was employed to generate the forecast came to be, we employ post hoc explanations [48] for these. This is frequently accomplished by examining the model's gradients or using stand-in models to simulate behavior in specific areas. We believe that the line that separates interpretability from explainability also follows the processes of the human mind. For example, human beings occasionally use deliberate, logical thinking to arrive at a conclusion. As a result, the logic can be examined in detail. In other cases, people base their initial conclusions on intuition after analyzing complex facts over extended periods of time. Then, just as we use post hoc explanations on black box models, people look for an explanation for a decision. Determining which strategy is superior for explainable AI is probably going to need major advancements in human cognitive science and our comprehension of the functioning of the human brain.

3.1 Post-hoc Explainations

In regards to the realistic scenario [48], in which the end user looks at the details after a study has been concluded and the data collected, our goal is to provide context for the predictions of a machine learning model. In order to do this, we must first define what it means to produce an explanation. An explanation typically states that some features are more significant than others or explains how an input feature can influence the output's magnitude in a positive or negative way. It usually links the feature values of an instance to its model prediction in a way that is easily understood by humans. Not all explanations must be focused on the significance of a feature. They could also be particular cases or groups of influential instances. They could be real English languages or collections of rules. In fact, difficulties with homogeneous judgment arise from a variety of reasons. In our current study, we focus primarily on the importance of the feature.

Post hoc approaches might be model-agnostic or model-dependent, global or local. Model-dependent interpretation techniques are focused on a particular model or set of models. Model-agnostic tools, on the other hand, can be used on any machine learning model, no matter how complex. These agnostic approaches typically analyze feature input and output pairs. Model-agnostic methods frequently profit from the reality that certain practitioners may not have access to the original model's specific weights and parameters. In our current work, we have been focused on local 'Post-hoc' explanation methods in model-agnostic fashion. Below is the description of the methods we used in study for generating post-hoc explanation.

1. **LIME** [2]: One of the most well-known post hoc methods is LIME or Local Interpretable Model-agnostic Explanations. LIME's concept is

to build a surrogate model in a local area at a certain target point to explain the significance of the input features. Because it hypothesized that sophisticated black boxes tend to demonstrate more linear or simple behavior in local neighborhoods. We build new samples for LIME by perturbing for the target sample. We then query the black-bo model to obtain the label of the perturbed data points, scores them using a kernel, and train a *sparse linear* model using the data-points and labels.

2. **KernalSHAP** [3]: Shapley values [4] are based on the idea that a prediction may be explained by imagining each feature value of the instance as a 'player' in a game where the prediction is the payoff. Shapley values, a strategy from coalitional game theory, teach us how to allocate the "payout" among the characteristics in a *fair* manner.

   Shapley regression values serve as indicators of feature importance in linear models, particularly when confronted with multicollinearity. This approach mandates the model's retraining across all conceivable feature subsets $S \subseteq F$, where F denotes the complete set of features. Each feature is assigned an importance value, signifying the impact of its inclusion on the model prediction. The computation involves training a model $f_{S \cup \{i\}}$ with the specific feature and another model f_S without it. Subsequently, the discrepancy in the predictions for the current input is assessed as $f_{S \cup \{i\}}(x_{S \cup \{i\}}) - f_S(x_S)$, where x_S represents the input feature values within the set S. As the influence of excluding a feature is contingent on other model features, these differences are computed for all feasible subsets $S \subseteq F \setminus \{i\}$. Subsequently, the Shapley values are calculated and used as feature attributions, representing a weighted average of all potential differences [4, 3]:

$$\phi_i = \sum_{S \subseteq F \setminus \{i\}} \frac{|S|!(|F| - |S| - 1)!}{|F|!} [f_{S \cup \{i\}}(x_{S \cup \{i\}}) - f_S(x_S)] \tag{1}$$

However, both LIME and Kernel SHAP share the same foundation but choose different kernels and loss functions to calculate the importance of features [5, 1]. With this, we are now moving to *Definitions*. Thoughts have been mainly drawn from [10–12].

Definition 1 (Algorithm Interpretability). *An algorithm's interpretability is its ability to give users enough expressive data to comprehend how the algorithm operates. In this case, human-readable text or graphics may be considered interpretable domains. "If something is interpretable, it is possible to find its meaning or to find a particular meaning in it," according to the Cambridge Dictionary.*

Definition 2 (Interpretation). *Interpretation is the process of reducing a complicated do-main—like the outputs of a machine learning model—to meaningful, rational, and human-understandable ideas.*

Definition 3 (Explanation). *An explanation is extra metadata that describes the feature importance or relevance of an input instance to a certain output classification. It can be produced by the machine learning model itself or by an external method.*

An xAI post hoc explanation (here, LIME and KernelShaP) works by assuming that the model architecture is a black box. Most post hoc explainers build a single loss function using heuristics, gradients, game theory, or some other method [1]. However, the black-box functions are based on the feature set's global domain. These explainers, on the other hand, mimic functions in the local domain perturbing a few examples.

4. Experimental Setup

The study follows the setup given in [38, 39] for experimentation and implementation particulars. It uses the *Adult Census Income* dataset from the *UCI Machine Learning Repository*. We start our experiments by training an *XGBoost* [13] model. The following performance metrics were achieved for the model:

	Accuracy	Precision	Recall	F1	AUC
Train	0.88	0.82	0.65	0.73	0.95
Test	0.87	0.78	0.62	0.69	0.92

We start our investigation on the trained XGBoost based on easy to complex hypothesis gradually for calculating feature importance. We start with the ELI5 library [14]. We used the library's 'Permutation Importance' (PI) method to compute the feature importance. It works on the hypothesis that the importance of a feature can be quantified by the drop in the intended metrics (accuracy, precision, etc.) when removed. In this study, we use AUC [50] as the performance metric to evaluate the trained *XGBoost* model. We report the PI for both train and test counterparts in Figure 1 the left column shows the PI in the train set and the one in the right is for the test. Despite the fact that the order of the most significant traits varies, it appears that the most crucial one (`married_1`) remains the same in both folds. Furthermore, the six most important variables based on PI are retained in training and testing. We anticipate their difference in relative ordering are mostly due to the sample dispersion between the folds. Next, we use a more sophisticated

Weight	Feature
0.0982 ± 0.0007	married_1
0.0710 ± 0.0018	education.num
0.0569 ± 0.0026	capital.gain
0.0494 ± 0.0023	age
0.0346 ± 0.0016	hours.per.week
0.0140 ± 0.0011	capital.loss
0.0123 ± 0.0009	fnlwgt
0.0086 ± 0.0011	rel_Not-in-family
0.0048 ± 0.0012	rel_Unmarried
0.0043 ± 0.0006	rel_Wife
0.0038 ± 0.0007	sex_Male
0.0031 ± 0.0008	rel_Own-child
0.0026 ± 0.0002	class_Self-emp-not-inc
0.0013 ± 0.0002	class_Private
0.0010 ± 0.0003	race_White
0.0008 ± 0.0001	nac_United-States
0.0005 ± 0.0001	class_Self-emp-inc
0.0004 ± 0.0001	race_Black
0.0003 ± 0.0001	class_State-gov
0.0003 ± 0.0001	class_Local-gov
… 46 more …	

Weight	Feature
0.0863 ± 0.0053	married_1
0.0538 ± 0.0022	capital.gain
0.0521 ± 0.0041	education.num
0.0370 ± 0.0035	age
0.0178 ± 0.0017	hours.per.week
0.0128 ± 0.0006	capital.loss
0.0078 ± 0.0021	rel_Not-in-family
0.0048 ± 0.0009	rel_Unmarried
0.0019 ± 0.0004	rel_Own-child
0.0019 ± 0.0003	rel_Wife
0.0018 ± 0.0006	sex_Male
0.0015 ± 0.0001	class_Self-emp-not-inc
0.0012 ± 0.0005	fnlwgt
0.0003 ± 0.0002	rel_Other-relative
0.0003 ± 0.0002	class_Private
0.0003 ± 0.0003	race_White
0.0003 ± 0.0002	nac_United-States
0.0002 ± 0.0001	class_Self-emp-inc
0.0002 ± 0.0001	race_Black
0.0001 ± 0.0001	nac_Mexico
… 46 more …	

Figure 1. Permutation importance.

method named SHAP [3] for visualizing the feature importance. We also want to compare the feature importance from the trained XGBoost with the ones obtained from SHAP. We use **Gain** as the default feature importance for the XGBoost model. **Gain** of a feature is computed by taking its relative contribution in each tree for the whole model. In the comparison between the SHAP feature importance and XGBoost's counterpart, we take the top 20 features in both of them. In Figure 2, we report the XGBoost feature importance. We compare the same against the mean of the absolute SHAP values presented in Figure 3. Finally, in Figure 4 we report the SHAP values of all these features to demonstrate their impact on the model.

It is clear from the comparison that the most important feature (`married_1`) is common in both the comparison. Next, `education.num` is there within the top-3 features in both feature importance ranking. However, the rest of the features including '`age`' are either not in common or ranked differently based on their importance in the comparisons. Next, we move to the summary plots produced by SHAP for a nuanced overview of feature importance.

4.1 *Summary Plot SHAP*

The SHAP Summary Plot (Figure 4) offers more information than the conventional plot. The significance of features is arranged according to decreasing feature relevance.

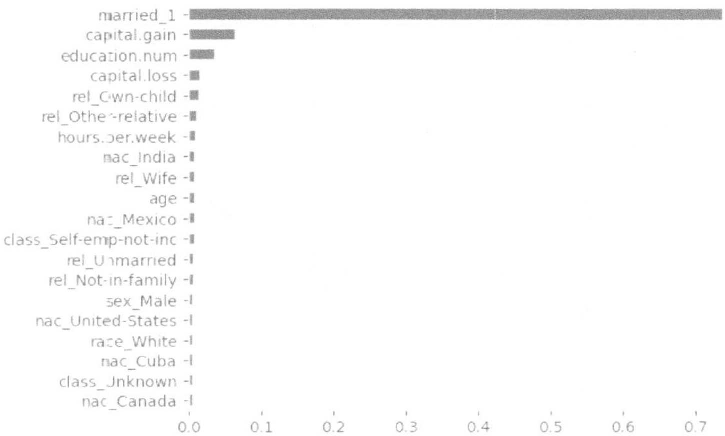

Figure 2. XGB feature importance.

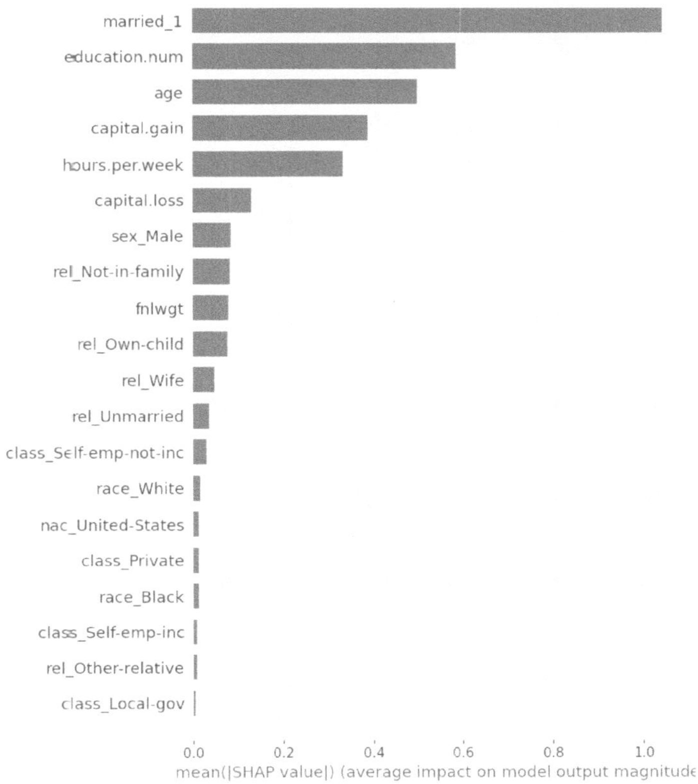

Figure 3. SHAP feature importance.

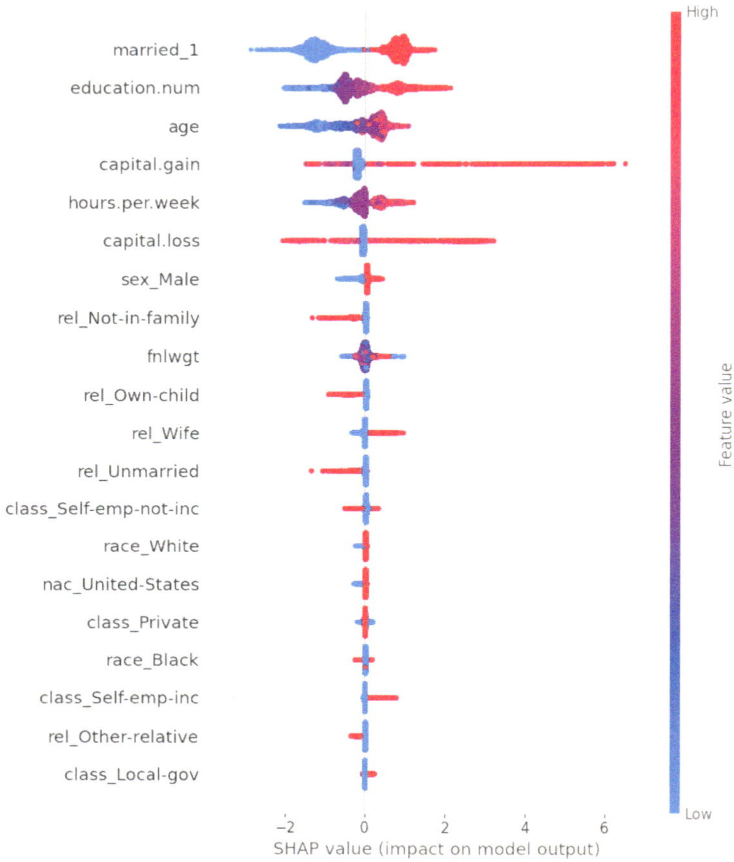

Figure 4. SHAP summary plots.

Impact on Prediction: The horizontal axis's position reflects how much or how little the values of the dataset instances for each feature affect the model's output.

Original Value: The colour designates a high or low value (within each feature's range) for each characteristic.

Correlation: A feature's colour (or range of values) and the effect on the horizontal axis are usually used to assess how well it correlates with the model output.

Notably, SHAP identifies the variable `married_1` as having significant interaction, suggesting that individuals who are married and possess higher educational qualifications are more inclined to earn above $50,000.

Next, we move to Dependency Plots made by SHAP.

4.2 Dependency Plots

Dependency plot not only provides the marginal influence the feature has on the model's output, but it also illustrates the relationship with the feature with which it most interacts by colour. This illustrates the model's reliance on the provided feature. The vertical spread of data points indicates *interaction effects*. We presented some dependency plots with different pairs of features to present how the interaction is between characteristics and how one influences another.

As depicted in Figure 5, there's a discernible upward trend in marriages between the ages of 20 to nearly 50 years. Meanwhile, Figure 6 reveals

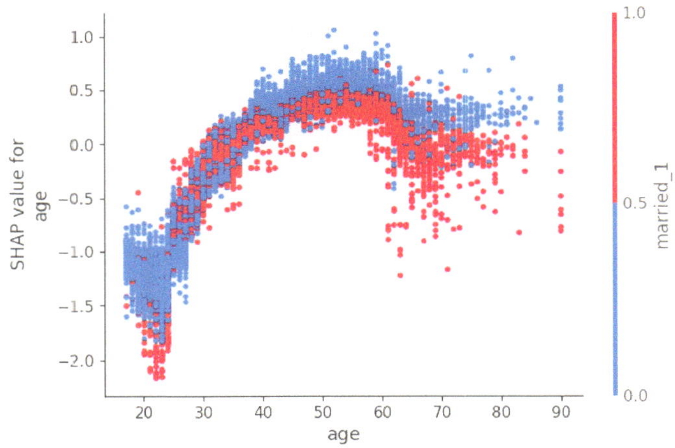

Figure 5. Dependency plot: *<age, married_1>*.

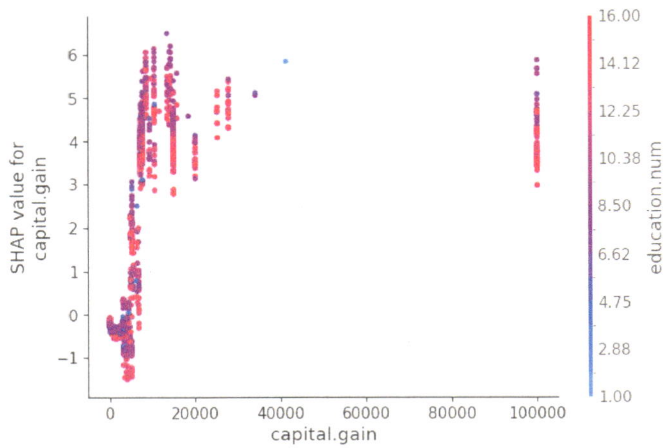

Figure 6. Dependency plot: *<capital.gain, education.num>*.

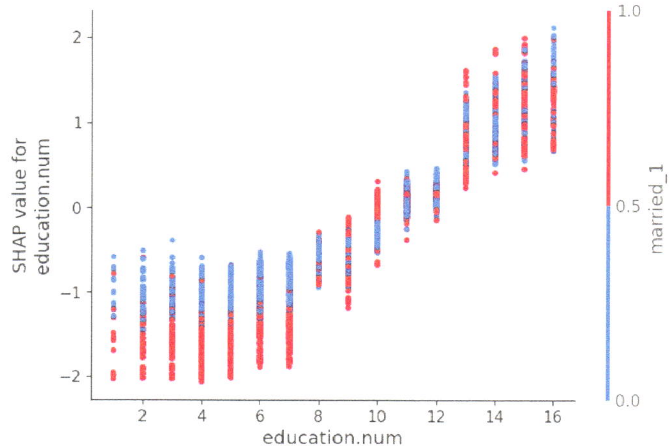

Figure 7. Dependency plot: <*education.num, married_1*>.

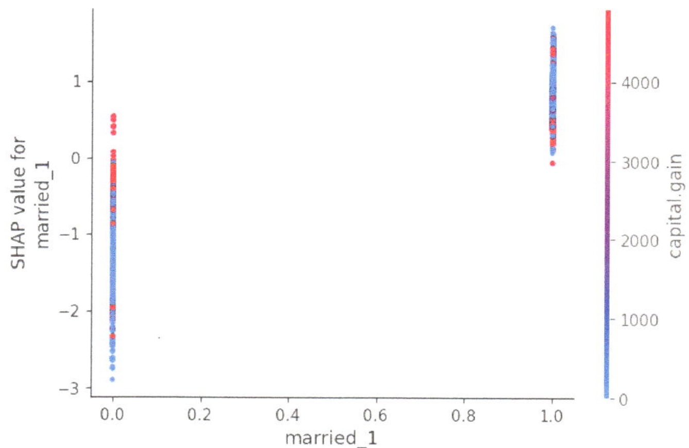

Figure 8. Dependency plot: <*married_1, capital.gain*>.

a pronounced rise in the *education.num* concerning capital gains ranging from 0 to 20k USD. Figure 7 further elucidates a consistent progression between educational attainment and marital status. Lastly, Figure 8 underscores that married individuals tend to exhibit higher capital gains compared to their unmarried counterparts.

Now, in the next section, we'll discuss post-hoc local explanations using LIME and SHAP.

5. Discovering Local Scales

Local surrogate models [49] are interpretable models that are used to explain individual predictions of black-box machine learning models.

5.1 *LIME*

LIME [2] stands for Local Interpretable Model-independent Explanations. LIME investigates what occurs in model predictions when the input data is changed. It creates a new dataset containing permuted samples and the old model's related predictions. LIME trains interpretable models (*Logistic Regression, Decision Tree, LASSO Regression, etc.*) on this synthetic set, which are then weighted by the closeness of the sampled examples to the instance of interest.

The explanation, for example, X will be that of the surrogate model that minimises the loss function (performance measure for example, *MSE*-between the surrogate model's forecast and the prediction of the original model), while keeping the model's complexity low.

However, LIME has a distinct problem; it is *inherently* instable. As illustrated in Figure 9, LIME often produces varied explanations for identical instances when executed multiple times. This inconsistency, while not always prevalent, arises from the inherent randomness in generating the surrogate models employed by its linear models. This is not the case with SHAP as it enjoys the uniqueness of SHAP values for a given instance [3]. There are various ways to visualise SHAP explanations. This chapter will go over two of them: the *Decision & Force plot* [3].

- *Force Plot*: It shows the effect that each attribute had on the forecast. The output value (model prediction for the instance) and the base value (average prediction for the whole dataset) are the two important numbers to pay attention to. Greater influence is shown by a larger bar, and the colour shows whether the feature value shifted the forecast from the base value to 1 (red) or 0 (blue).

  We run the same experiment 10 times to show that the explanation is unique and does not exhibit randomness like LIME (Figure 9).

- *Decision Plots*: Figure 13 displays the same information as the *Force Plot*. The gray vertical line represents the baseline, and the red line indicates whether each characteristic increased the output value higher or lower than the average forecast. Sometimes the information representation depends upon the end user's intention due to which various representations have been engineered under SHAP library.

  So far, we have investigated and extensively visualised the feature importance using several representations. Next, we move to

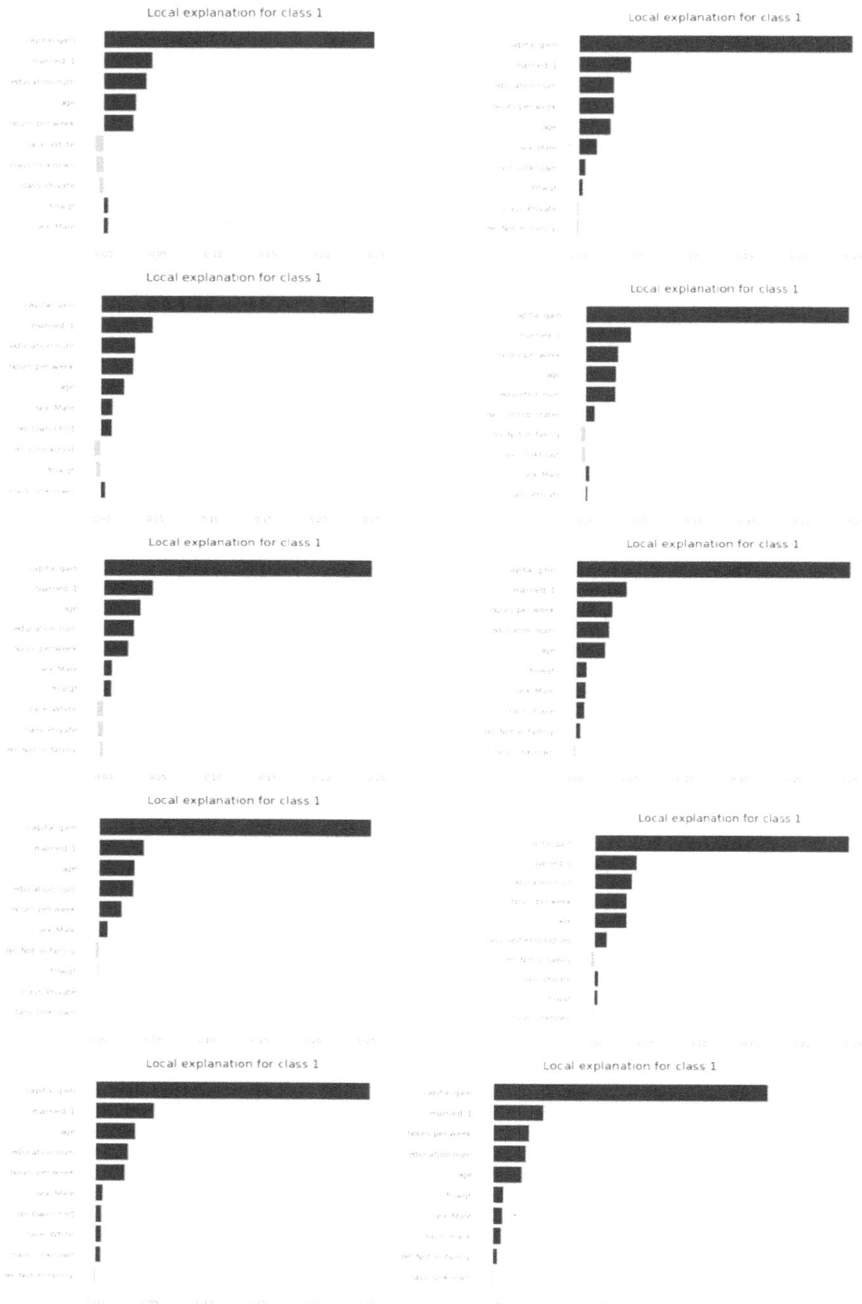

Figure 9. Inherent instability of LIME.

mimicking the model globally rather than mere feature importance estimation. We use global surrogate models for globally explaining the model

5.2 Global Explanations

An interpretable model that has been trained to match the predictions of the black-box model to a very large extent is a global surrogate model. By analysing the surrogate model, we may make inferences about the black box model. Though it, by any means, is not a way to predict the internal architecture of the black box, rather it is meant to deduce some insights regarding the prediction.

Using a *Decision Tree* and a *Logistic Regression* as global surrogate models, we will attempt to approximate the *XGBoost*.

For both the Train and Test sets, R-squared is negative in the case of Logistic Regression (–1.40, –1.42 respectively). This occurs when the fit is poorer than using the mean alone. As a result, it is argued that Logistic Regression is **NOT** an adequate surrogate model.

However, we have obtained 0.77&0.79 for R-Square scores in train and test respectively in the case of decision tree, so we can proceed with the same if it *mimicks* the trained XGBoost well.

	Accuracy	Precision	Recall	F1	AUC
Train	0.85	0.75	0.55	0.64	0.868197
Test	0.85	0.75	0.55	0.64	0.865062

The Decision Tree approximates the *decisions* of the XGBoost model quite well as per the scores obtained, hence it may be used as a surrogate model for evaluating the main model. However, it is not guaranteed that the decision tree uses the features in the same way as the XGBoost. It is possible that the tree approximates the XGBoost properly in certain portions of the input space but acts erratically in others as the models are themselves different. We can see in Figure 10 that `married_1` is the most important feature followed by `capital.gain` and `education.num`. In the importance of the XGBoost feature, these were the top-3 features and in the SHAP dependency plots as well, these were important features to consider. Next, we use another method named SP-LIME for generating global explanation.

5.3 Submodularity

The submodular picking [8] is important as end users may not have time to examine a large number of explanations. It is critical to choose

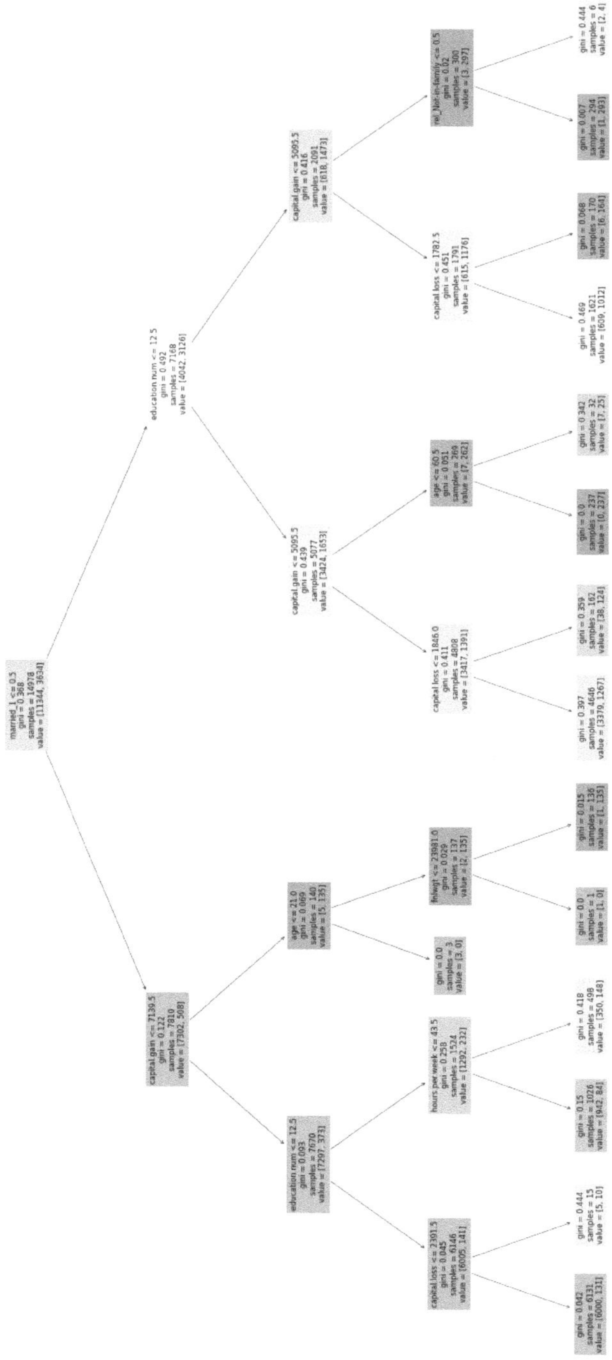

Figure 10. Decision Tree—mimicking the XGBoost.

which instances to explain with care. It seeks to provide explanations for machine learning models by attributing their predictions to human-understandable features. To achieve this objective effectively, it's essential to execute the explanation model across a varied yet representative collection of instances. By doing so, LIME aims to produce a non-redundant set of explanations that collectively offer a comprehensive understanding of the model's behaviour on a global scale. SP LIME algorithm selects a collection of explanations for the user that are diverse and representative, meaning they do not repeat themselves, while also demonstrating how the model works in general as shown in [2]. Technically, each instance being a collection of features is a subset of the whole feature set. Collecting a minimal or almost minimal number of subsets to cover the whole or almost the whole set is the main agenda of employing the SP LIME algorithm. This problem is a derivation of the set cover problem [9] which is NP-complete. LIME has its own *greedy picking* [2] algorithm which we have demonstrated in Figure 11. More technical details can be found at [2].

In Figure 11, *capital.gain* is shown to be the most important attribute in all individual interpretations that distinguish the classes. Following that, depending on the situation, the most important determinants are *married_1*, *education.num*, *age*, and *sex*. These features align with those pinpointed by the algorithms as globally significant.

So far, we have investigated how the model's features *interplay* and exhibit patterns. However, whether this *interplay* is *fair & legitimate* is what we investigate in the next section.

6. *All* Is Well, but Is *All* Fair?

In machine learning, "fairness" refers to the several ways that algorithmic bias in machine learning-based automated decision processes is attempted to be corrected. If computer decisions after a machine-learning process were predicated on factors deemed sensitive, they may be viewed as unjust. These variables can be related to gender, ethnicity, sexual orientation, disability, and other factors. Definitions of prejudice and justice are inherently contentious, as is the case with many ethical notions. Fairness and prejudice are typically taken into consideration when making decisions that have an influence on people's lives. The issue of algorithmic bias in machine learning is generally recognised and researched. Many factors have the potential to distort the results, making them unfair to particular persons or groups.

'FairML' [6], the library for fairness in Python helps to investigate these intricacies.

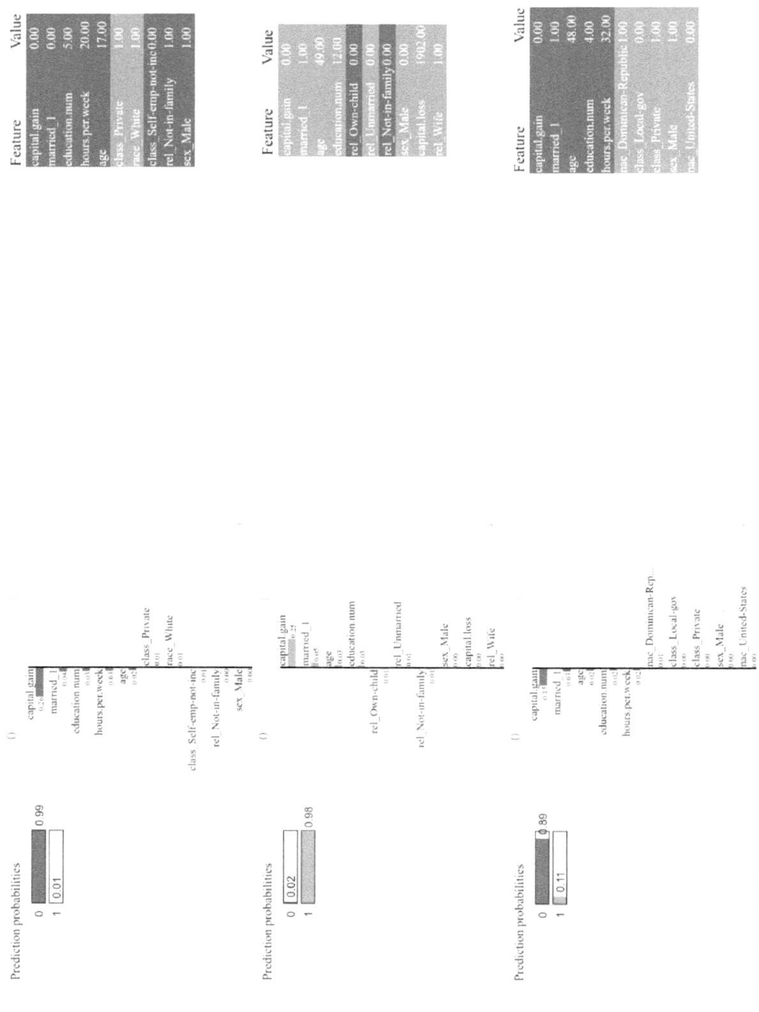

Figure 11. Submodular pic.

Figure 12. Force plot.

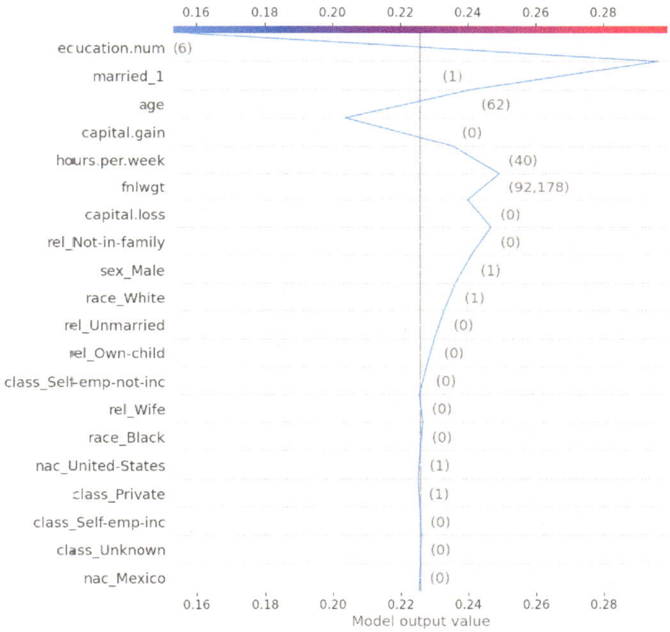

Figure 13. Decision plot.

The underlying idea behind FairML (and many other attempts to audit or understand model behaviour) is to change the inputs of a model to quantify its dependency on them. The model is sensitive to a feature if a modest change to an input feature drastically impacts the output. In order to quantify how much each characteristic influences the prediction model, FairML projects the input orthogonally.

Let $F(x, y)$ be a model trained on two characteristics, x and y. The change in output resulting from a modified input, where x' perturbs x, can be quantified to measure the model's reliance on x. We express this as:

$$\Delta F(x', y) = F(x', y) - F(x, y) \tag{2}$$

Here, $\Delta F(x', y)$ represents the change in the model output, and the perturbation in x' renders the other feature y orthogonal to x'. However, linear transformation is an orthogonal projection. FairML uses a basis expansion along with greedy search in the case of non-linear relationships. But, in auditing a model, the determination of fairness is often nuanced and context-dependent. The sensitivity of features can vary across different contexts; what may be considered sensitive in one scenario may not hold the same significance in another. The definition of fairness is multifaceted, influenced by user experience, and cultural, social, historical, political, legal, and ethical considerations. Identifying appropriate fairness criteria involves navigating trade-offs among these factors.

The visualization: Figure 14 uses darker shades to signify a contribution to an output of Income > USD 50K; lighter shades stand for the opposite. FairML reveals a significant dependence on sensitive features like `race_White`, `nac_United-States`, and `sex_Male`. Specifically, the model indicates a strong bias: according to its predictions, an individual is more likely to make more than USD 50k if the individual's nationality is of the United States, race is white, and sex is male. Notably, the algorithm's orthogonal projection brings out the relevance of features like `race_White` `nac_United-States`, & `sex_Male`, which did not appear in other interpretation methods like SHAP's Feature Importance. This underscores the importance of investigating for bias along with feature importance. As we observe the popular methods for feature importance may not always be capable of uncovering the intrinsic bias and unfairness in trained models. Now, in the case of availing *better* education, we started by looking at how parental income influences the education of children and these types of severe bias are what we've found out. This type of societal bias directly impacts the household and the education of the children. In our assessment, the principles of *fairness and transparency* appear conspicuously absent. *All* is simply, *not* **Fair** [20].

7. Concluding Remark

Fairness in machine learning models is a nuanced and evolving concept. Fairness considerations need to account for diverse perspectives, cultural nuances, and the dynamic societal landscape. Moreover, the interpretability of fairness metrics remains an open question. Defining fairness is not a one-size-fits-all endeavour, and achieving fairness often involves navigating complex trade-offs between different dimensions of fairness [15].

Our comprehensive analysis delved deeply into the critical interplay between parental income and its consequential impact on educational opportunities, harnessing advanced xAI tools such as LIME, SHAP, and

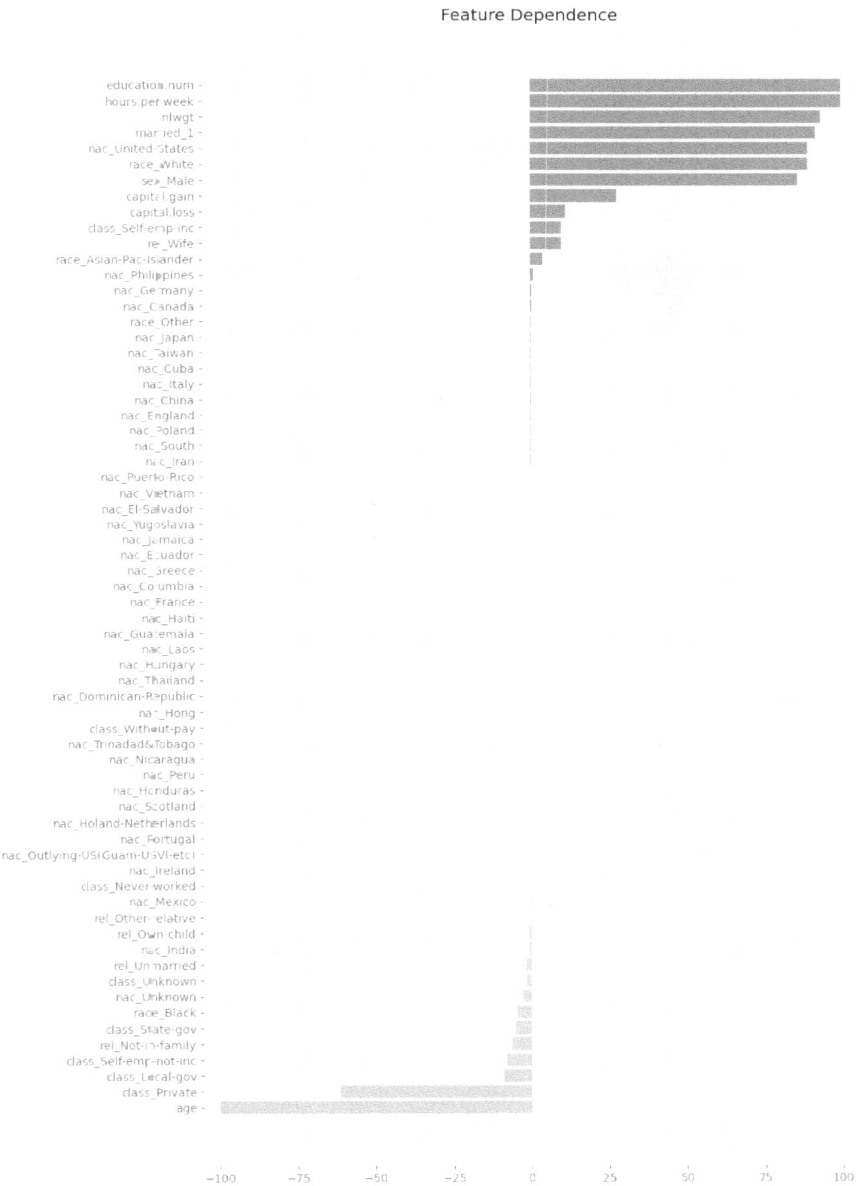

Figure 14. Visualizing fairness using FairML.

the FairML Library. By scrutinizing predictive models derived from the Adult Census data, our deliberate preference for sophisticated algorithms like XG Boost and Decision Trees over simpler models aimed to mirror the inherent complexities typical of real-world black-box systems. However, our findings unveil a disconcerting pattern: pervasive biases persistently permeate these models. While FairML identified these biases as direct orthogonal projections, SHAP analyses sometimes remained oblivious to them. Intriguingly, LIME's volatility introduced yet another layer of complexity, further complicating our interpretative landscape.

In conclusion, we want to revisit the objectives: AI came to education for speed and transparency, a strong pillar for availing education is parental income and when that is being scrutinised, it is showing heavy bias under several tests mimicking the real world. The effort we put here to investigate the situation is solely to question the fundamentals: In society, modern education is the pillar to move the nation ahead whereas the **Scope** of availing education is deliberately getting **shrunk** due to several biases and education, as the fundamental right to every citizen is being heavily exclusive to a particular direction where the **Bias** lends itself. Biases present in the training data may be inadvertently perpetuated or even amplified by xAI algorithms, reinforcing existing societal biases [16–18]. This is why refining fairness definitions, enhancing the transparency of complex models, and mitigating biases in training data are key challenges that warrant continued attention and collaborative efforts from the research and practitioner communities. Through constructive criticism and iterative refinement, xAI can evolve into a more robust and ethically grounded field [18, 19], fostering trust and accountability in the deployment of artificial intelligence systems.

8. Further Work

We are consistently striving for improved policies for *Modern* education, emphasizing values of **Transparency, Equal Opportunity, & Accessibility**. Our primary focus lies in harnessing the potential of xAI to enhance policymaking. Operating within the realm of public policy, our endeavour centres on exploring innovative avenues to render education policies more accessible, starting from the grassroots level. Leveraging advanced algorithms, we aim to bring about positive transformations that align with our commitment to creating a more transparent, equitable, and accessible educational landscape.

References

[1] Han, T., Srinivas, S. and Lakkaraju, H. (2022). Which explanation should i choose? A function approximation perspective to characterizing post hoc explanations. *Advances in Neural Information Processing Systems*, 35: 5256–68.

[2] Ribeiro, M.T., Singh, S. and Guestrin, C. (2016). Why should i trust you? Explaining the predictions of any classifier. In: *Proceedings of the 22nd ACM SIGKDD International Conference on Knowledge Discovery and Data Mining*, pp. 1135–1144.

[3] Lundberg, S.M. and Lee, S.I. (2017). A unified approach to interpreting model predictions. *Advances in Neural Information Processing Systems*, 30.

[4] Shapley, L.S (1953). Notes on the n-person game—II: The value of an n-person game.

[5] Hill, D., Masoomi, A., Ghimire, S., Torop, M. and Dy, J. (2022). Explanation uncertainty with decision boundary awareness. *arXiv preprint arXiv:2210.02419*.

[6] Adebayo, J.A. (2016). FairML: ToolBox for diagnosing bias in predictive modeling (Doctoral dissertation, Massachusetts Institute of Technology).

[7] Molnar, C. (2020). Interpretable machine learning. Lulu. com.

[8] Krause, A. and Golovin, D. (2014). Submodular function maximization. *Tractability*, 3(71-104): 3.

[9] Feige, U. (1998). A threshold of ln n for approximating set cover. *Journal of the ACM (JACM)*, 45(4): 634–52.

[10] Arrieta, A.B., Díaz-Rodríguez, N., Del Ser, J., Bennetot, A., Tabik, S., Barbado, A., García, S., Gil-López, S., Molina, D., Benjamins, R. and Chatila, R. (2020). Explainable Artificial Intelligence (XAI): Concepts, taxonomies, opportunities and challenges toward responsible AI. *Information Fusion*, 58: 82–115.

[11] Bellucci, M., Delestre, N., Malandain, N. and Zanni-Merk, C. (2021). Towards a terminology for a fully contex- tualized XAI. *Procedia Computer Science*, 192: 241–50.

[12] Adadi, A. and Berrada, M. (2018). Peeking inside the black-box: A survey on explainable artificial intelligence (XAI). *IEEE Access*, 6: 52138–60.

[13] Chen, T. and Guestrin, C. (2016). Xgboost: A scalable tree boosting system. In: *Proceedings of the 22nd ACM SIGKDD International Conference on Knowledge Discovery and Data Mining*, pp. 785–794.

[14] Kawakura, S., Hirafuji, M., Ninomiya, S. and Shibasaki, R. (2022). Adaptations of Explainable Artificial Intelligence (XAI) to agricultural data models with ELI5, PDPbox, and skater using diverse agricultural worker data. *European Journal of Artificial Intelligence and Machine Learning*, 1(3): 27–34.

[15] Slack, D., Hilgard, S., Jia, E., Singh, S. and Lakkaraju, H. (2020). Fooling lime and shap: Adversarial attacks on post hoc explanation methods. In: *Proceedings of the AAAI/ACM Conference on AI, Ethics, and Society*, pp. 180–186.

[16] Deshpande, A. and Sharp, H. (2022). Responsible AI systems: Who are the stakeholders?. In: *Proceedings of the 2022 AAAI/ACM Conference on AI, Ethics, and Society*, pp. 227–236.

[17] Soklaski, R., Goodwin, J., Brown, O., Yee, M. and Matterer, J. (2022). Tools and practices for responsible AI engineering. *arXiv preprint arXiv:2201.05647*.

[18] McElhaney, K., Smith, G., Rustagi, I. and Groth, O.J. (2023). *Responsible AI: Tackling Tech's Largest Corporate Governance Challenges*. The Berkeley-Haas Case Series. University of California, Berkeley. Haas School of Business.

[19] Amarasinghe, K., Rodolfa, K.T., Lamba, H. and, Ghani, R. (2023). Explainable machine learning for public policy: Use cases, gaps, and research directions. *Data & Policy*, 5: e5.

[20] Amodei, D., Olah, C., Steinhardt, J., Christiano, P., Schulman, J. and Mané, D. (2016). Concrete problems in AI safety. *arXiv preprint arXiv:1606.06565*.

[21] Machebe, C.H., Ezegbe, B.N. and Onuoha, J. (2017). The impact of parental level of income on students' academic performance in high school in Japan. *Universal Journal of Educational Research*, 5(9): 1614–20.

[22] Lin, T. and Lv, H. (2017). The effects of family income on children's education: An empirical analysis of CHNS data. *Research on Modern Higher Education*, 4(02002).

[23] Wiborg, Ø.N. and Grätz, M. (2022). Parents' income and wealth matter more for children with low than high academic performance: Evidence from comparisons between and within families in egalitarian Norway. *Research in Social Stratification and Mobility*, 79: 100692.

[24] Glick, P. and Sahn, D.E. (2000). Schooling of girls and boys in a West African country: The effects of parental education, income, and household structure. *Economics of Education Review*, 19(1): 63–87.

[25] Ani-Asamoah Marbuah, D. (2016). Influence of Parental Income and Educational Attainment on Children's Years of Schooling: Case of Ghana.

[26] Woolf, B. (1991). *AI in Education*. University of Massachusetts at Amherst, Department of Computer and Information Science.

[27] Zhai, X., Chu, X., Chai, C.S., Jong, M.S., Istenic, A., Spector, M., Liu, J.B., Yuan, J. and Li, Y. (2021). A review of Artificial Intelligence (AI) in education from 2010 to 2020. *Complexity*, 2021: 1–8.

[28] Beck, J., Stern, M. and Haugsjaa, E. (1996). Applications of AI in education. *XRDS: Crossroads, The ACM Magazine for Students*, 3(1): 11–5.

[29] Tahiru, F. (2021). AI in education: A systematic literature review. *Journal of Cases on Information Technology (JCIT)*, 23(1): 1–20.

[30] Vincent-Lancrin, S. and Van der Vlies, R. (2020). Trustworthy artificial intelligence (AI) in education: Promises and challenges.

[31] Cho, E. and Han, M. (2019). AI powered book recommendation system. In: *Proceedings of the 2019 ACM Southeast Conference*, pp. 230–232.

[32] Xu, D. and Tian, Y. (2015). A comprehensive survey of clustering algorithms. *Annals of Data Science*, 2: 165–93.

[33] Medhat, W., Hassan, A. and Korashy, H. (2014). Sentiment analysis algorithms and applications: A survey. *AIN Shams Engineering Journal*, 5(4): 1093–113.

[34] Luccioni, A.S., Jernite, Y. and Strubell, E. (2023). Power hungry processing: Watts driving the cost of AI deployment? *arXiv preprint arXiv:2311.16863*.

[35] Li, H. (2013). The rising cost of higher education: A supply and demand analysis. *NY University*.

[36] Touvron, H., Martin, L., Stone, K., Albert, P., Almahairi, A., Babaei, Y., Bashlykov, N., Batra, S., Bhargava, P., Bhosale, S. and Bikel, D. (2023). Llama 2: Open foundation and fine-tuned chat models. *arXiv preprint arXiv:2307.09288*.

[37] Malohlava, M., Hava, J. and Mehta, N. (2016). Machine learning with sparkling water: H2o+ spark. *H2O AI Inc.*

[38] Pretto, F. (2020, July 30). Uncovering the magic: Interpreting machine learning black-box models. *Medium*. https://towardsdatascience.com/uncovering-the-magic-interpreting-machine-learning-black-box-models-3154fb8ed01a.

[39] Pretto, F. (2020b, August 12). Inclusive machine learning: Addressing model fairness. Medium. https://towardsdatascience.com/inclusive-machine-learning-addressing-model-fairness-532884ecd859.

[40] Shrivastava, M. (2017). Learning Salesforce Einstein. Packt Publishing Ltd.

[41] Team, G., Anil, R., Borgeaud, S., Wu, Y., Alayrac, J.B., Yu, J., Soricut, R., Schalkwyk, J., Dai, A.M., Hauth, A. and Millican, K. (2023). Gemini: A family of highly capable multimodal models. *arXiv preprint arXiv:2312.11805*.

[42] Wu, T., He, S., Liu, J., Sun, S., Liu, K., Han, Q.L. and Tang, Y. (2023). A brief overview of ChatGPT: The history, status quo and potential future development. *IEEE/CAA Journal of Automatica Sinica*, 10(5): 1122–36.

[43] Kepuska, V. and Bohouta, G. (2018). Next-generation of virtual personal assistants (microsoft cortana, apple siri, amazon alexa and google home). In: *2018 IEEE 8th Annual Computing and Communication Workshop and Conference (CCWC)*, pp. 99–103. IEEE.

[44] Crook, B., Schlüter, M. and Speith, T. (2023). Revisiting the performance-explainability trade-off in explainable artificial intelligence (XAI). In: *2023 IEEE 31st International Requirements Engineering Conference Workshops (REW)*, pp. 316–324. IEEE.

[45] Horvatić, D. and Lipic, T. (2021). Human-centric AI: The symbiosis of human and artificial intelligence. *Entropy*, 23(3): 332.

[46] Mahbooba, B., Timilsina, M., Sahal, R. and Serrano, M. (2021). Explainable artificial intelligence (XAI) to enhance trust management in intrusion detection systems using decision tree model. *Complexity*, 2021: 1–1.

[47] Arrieta, A.B., Díaz-Rodríguez, N., Del Ser, J., Bennetot, A., Tabik, S., Barbado, A., García, S., Gil- López, S., Molina, D., Benjamins, R. and Chatila, R. (2020). Explainable Artificial Intelligence (XAI): Concepts, taxonomies, opportunities and challenges toward responsible AI. *Information Fusion*, 58: 82–115.

[48] Jesus, S., Belém, C., Balayan, V., Bento, J., Saleiro, P., Bizarro, P. and Gama, J. (2021). How can I choose an explainer? An application-grounded evaluation of post-hoc explanations. In: *Proceedings of the 2021 ACM Conference on Fairness, Accountability, and Transparency*, pp. 805–815.

[49] Nóbrega, C. and Marinho, L. (2019). Towards explaining recommendations through local surrogate models. In: *Proceedings of the 34th ACM/SIGAPP Symposium on Applied Computing*, pp. 1671–1678.

[50] Bradley, A.P. (1997). The use of the area under the ROC curve in the evaluation of machine learning algorithms. *Pattern Recognition*, 30(7): 1145–59.

Chapter 6

Deep Learning Approaches for Intelligent Cyber Threat Detection in Modern Education Systems

Shiva Shankar Mutupuri, Sruthi Sivarajan, Anil Carie* and *Satish Anamalamudi*

In the ever-evolving landscape of modern education systems, technology integration has become ubiquitous, opening new avenues for teaching and learning. However, this increased reliance on digital platforms has also given rise to unprecedented cybersecurity challenges, necessitating advanced detection mechanisms to safeguard sensitive educational data. This book chapter explores the application of deep learning approaches for intelligent cyber threat detection in the context of the modern education system. The chapter begins by providing a comprehensive overview of educational institutions' evolving cyber threat landscape, highlighting the diverse range of attacks targeting student records, intellectual property, and critical infrastructure. It emphasizes the need for proactive and adaptive cybersecurity measures to counteract these threats effectively. Subsequently, the chapter delves into the foundational principles of deep learning, elucidating its capacity to learn intricate patterns and anomalies from vast datasets autonomously. Various

Department of CSE, SRM University-AP.
* Corresponding author: shivashankar_mutupuri@srmap.edu.in

deep learning architectures, such as convolutional neural networks and recurrent neural networks are discussed in the context of their applicability to cybersecurity in education. The practical implementation of deep learning models for cyber threat detection is then explored. Case studies illustrate how these models can analyze detect malware, and identify suspicious activities, thereby fortifying the resilience of educational systems against cyber threats. Finally, this book chapter explores deep learning algorithms as a powerful tool for detecting intelligent cyber threats in modern education systems.

1. Introduction

The inclusion of technology into educational systems in recent years has fundamentally altered traditional teaching methods, creating unprecedented opportunities for collaboration, creativity, and information access. Challenges of Traditional Security Measures include Static and Rule-Based, Limited Adaptability that can adapt to constantly evolving threats and emerging vulnerabilities. False Positives and Negatives can trigger unnecessary alerts and miss critical threats. However, this digital transformation has also exposed educational institutions to many cybersecurity threats [1]. The increasing reliance on online platforms, cloud services, and interconnected networks has created an environment where sensitive student data, intellectual property, and critical infrastructure are susceptible to malicious activities.

This chapter acknowledges the necessity of a proactive and adaptable approach to cybersecurity in education. It highlights the need for advanced security measures to protect educational institutions from cyber attacks [2]. Numerous researchers have explored deep learning applications in cyber security, showcasing promising results across diverse domains using various available datasets [3]. Several studies show promising results in phishing detection using machine learning and deep learning [4, 5]. Similar research has been performed in malware classification, intrusion detection, and anomaly detection in various IT systems [3, 6, 7]. These systems have helped IT companies and other institutions preserve private data and avoid ransom demands by hackers. However, applying these techniques directly to the education sector requires tailor-made models and datasets to handle unique vulnerabilities and data features that educational institutions have. By understanding the evolving nature of cyber threats targeting educational institutions, we aim to explore and implement advanced technologies, particularly, deep learning, to fortify the security posture of modern education systems.

1.1 Significance of Cybersecurity in Education

It is impossible to undervalue the importance of cybersecurity in the classroom, as educational institutions are holders of vast amounts of sensitive data, including personal information, academic information, and intellectual property. A breach in the security of these systems not only jeopardizes the privacy of students and faculty but also compromises the integrity of educational processes. The need for cybersecurity in education isn't new. While the first documented cyberattack occurred in 1988, schools became targets in the early 2000s. In 2002, for example, hackers broke into Yale University's system to gain access to admission decisions [8]. Fast forward to today, and the threats have evolved considerably. Cybersecurity in education is not merely a technological concern; it is integral to preserving trust, maintaining institutional reputation, and ensuring the uninterrupted flow of knowledge in an increasingly interconnected world.

The increasing frequency and complexity of cyber-attacks aimed at educational institutions highlight the urgent requirement for strong cybersecurity measures. It highlights the need for education institutions to implement advanced security measures to safeguard their networks and data [2]. The benefits of prioritizing cybersecurity in education extend far beyond just protecting data. It nurtures a culture of digital responsibility, preparing students to be informed and secure participants in our increasingly interconnected world. By investing in robust cybersecurity measures, educational institutions can create a safe and secure learning environment where technology empowers, rather than hinders, the education journey. This chapter seeks to address this imperative by delving into the application of deep learning approaches, offering a cutting-edge solution for intelligent cyber threat detection tailored to the unique challenges of the modern education landscape.

1.2 Purpose and Scope of the Chapter

This chapter seeks to give a detailed assessment of the various uses of deep learning in cybersecurity threat identification and protection [9]. By combining theoretical foundations, practical applications, and ethical considerations, the chapter aims to:

- Illuminate the evolving cyber threat landscape within education institutions, emphasizing the diverse range of threats and vulnerabilities.
- Introduce the foundational principles of deep learning and its potential applications in cybersecurity.

- Showcase practical implementations of deep learning models for cyber threat detection on real-world examples and case studies.
- Discuss challenges and propose future directions for the integration of deep learning in educational cybersecurity.

Through this exploration, the chapter aspires to serve as a valuable resource for educators, cybersecurity professionals, and researchers seeking effective strategies to enhance the security resilience of educational institutions in the digital age.

2. Cyber Threat Landscape in Education

The education sector has witnessed a profound evolution in cyber threats, mirroring the broader technological advancements within society. Initially characterized by relatively simple attacks such as phishing and malware, the landscape has evolved to include more sophisticated threats like ransomware, DDoS (Distributed Denial of Service) attacks, and advanced threats. Educational institutions have become prime targets due to the wealth of valuable information they store, ranging from personal student records to cutting-edge research data. The classification of the various cyber threats has been represented in Figure 1.

The evolution is marked by the sophistication of attacks and the diversity of threat actors. Threats may emanate from individual hackers, criminal organizations, or state-sponsored entities, each motivated by different objectives, including financial gain, information theft, or disruption of academic activities.

In recent years, the education industry has experienced a notable transformation as a result of the implementation of cutting-edge technologies. As academic institutions embrace hybrid and remote learning, they become attractive targets for threat actors. The rapid transition to online and hybrid learning during the COVID-19 pandemic further exacerbated the threat landscape. Institutions had to quickly build IT infrastructures to facilitate learning from home, leading to

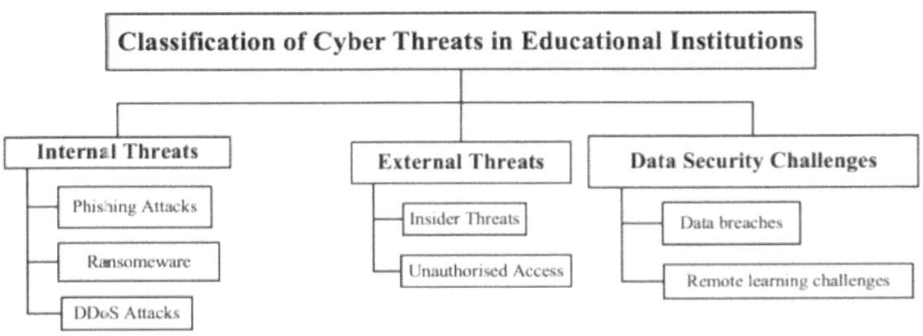

Figure 1. Classification of cyber threats in an academic institution.

increased network usage and vulnerabilities. Threat actors capitalized on this situation, leveraging phishing attacks and exploiting new vulnerabilities [10].

2.1 Targeted Assets and Vulnerabilities

Modern education systems are increasingly reliant on technology, creating a complex digital environment with diverse assets and vulnerabilities attractive to cybercriminals. The interconnected nature of modern educational systems, incorporating online learning platforms, cloud-based storage, and IoT (Internet of Things) devices, amplifies the attack surface and introduces new vulnerabilities [3]. Understanding these targeted assets and vulnerabilities is crucial for implementing effective cyber threat detection using deep learning approaches. Here's a detailed breakdown:

I. Data:

- Student data: This includes personal information like names, addresses, grades, and disciplinary records. Breaches can expose students to identity theft, financial fraud, or reputational damage.
- Faculty and staff data: Similar to student data, this encompasses the personal and professional information of educators and administrators.
- Research data
- Learning management system (LMS) data are the platforms that store course materials, assignments, assessments, and communication records, making them targets for data breaches or manipulation.

II. Systems and Infrastructure:

- Network infrastructure: Educational networks comprise interconnected devices, servers, and databases, vulnerable to malware infiltration, ransomware attacks, or denial-of-service attacks.
- Educational resources and platforms: Online learning platforms, video conferencing tools, and educational apps can be compromised to inject malicious code or disrupt learning activities.
- User accounts and access control: Weak passwords, phishing attacks, and insider threats can grant unauthorized access to sensitive data and systems.
- Emerging technologies: Integration of technologies such as virtual reality, artificial intelligence, and the Internet of Things (IoT) introduces new attack vectors and vulnerabilities that require careful security consideration.

III. Specific Vulnerabilities:

- Attacks known as phishing attempt to infect administrators, teachers, or students with malware or steal their credentials.
- Infiltration and encryption of systems by malware and ransomware to cause disruptions or extort money as ransom.
- Data breaches occur when unauthorised individuals gain access to or steal sensitive information.
- Denial-of-service attacks involve flooding systems with too much traffic to stop real users from getting in.
- Criminal activity by authorized users who have access to private information or systems is called an insider threat.
- Social engineering refers to the act of deceiving individuals into revealing confidential information or engaging with unwanted connections.
- Exploiting vulnerabilities that security software is unable to detect or respond to in a timely manner are known as zero-day attacks.

Understanding these targeted assets and vulnerabilities is essential for prioritizing deep learning applications that focus on areas with the highest risk and potential impact, developing targeted detection models that are tailored to specific threats, and vulnerabilities, and evaluating model effectiveness that measures the ability to detect and respond to real-world attacks.

2.2 *Implications of Cyber Attacks on the Education System*

Cyberattacks on educational institutions can have far-reaching implications, extending beyond immediate financial losses or data breaches. Many educational institutions mostly schools have been prone to cyber-attacks, especially in schools that have been newly established the management has less or no idea about these attacks and how to provide security, this poses a great challenge as there is a lack of awareness in such institutions.

The implications include the following:

- Attacks that cause disruptions in the classroom that impact both teachers and students are known as teaching and learning disruptions.
- Due to financial constraints, schools frequently deprioritize cybersecurity in their allocation of scarce resources.
- When there are violations of trust, there is a negative impact on parent communication.
- Data protection is an essential field in which employee and student data are protected [11].

3. Deep Learning and its Applications in Intelligent Cyber Threat Detection

Deep learning is a very vast, diverse topic that requires one to know various areas from mathematical, and statistical to computational aspects as well as computer programming to deal with practical problems. Some of the areas that might help in building one's foundation in this subject include, firstly linear Algebra that deals with vectors, matrices, and their operations is crucial for representing data and performing computations within deep learning models, secondly there is calculus is needed for Gradient descent, an optimization algorithm used to train deep learning models that is dependent on concepts like derivatives and partial derivatives, probability theory has concepts like randomness, uncertainty, and error estimation whereas statistical methods help analyze the data and evaluate performance based on various, optimization techniques are essential for adjusting the parameters of deep learning models, next comes Artificial neural networks the core building blocks of deep learning models, then there are learning algorithm such as backpropagation, an algorithm used to propagate errors backward through the network, enabling parameter updates and learning, regularization techniques like dropout and weight decay prevent overfitting, loss functions like mean squared error or cross-entropy measure the difference between model predictions and desired outputs, next in the list are activation functions such as sigmoid, ReLu, sigmoid which are typically applied to the output of each neuron in the network and lastly one requires deep learning frameworks like TensorFlow, PyTorch, and Keras provide predefined functions, facilitate the development and deployment of deep learning models. The above is just the tip of the iceberg it just provides a glance at what areas one should explore and the reason for it.

3.1 Overview of Deep Learning

Deep learning is a specialized area within machine learning that specifically concentrates on training neural networks with numerous layers, sometimes known as deep architectures. The term "deep" in deep learning does not imply a higher level of comprehension obtained by the approach. Instead, it signifies the concept of multiple layers of representations [12]. Its models contain numerous hidden layers stacked between the input and output. Each layer transforms the data, extracting increasingly abstract features through intricate non-linear operations. This layered architecture empowers deep learning to uncover complex relationships within data, especially when dealing with large datasets and intricate patterns. While powerful, deep learning models are typically more computationally expensive to train and can be less interpretable due to their complexity. Whereas, there are methods that deal with 1 or 2 layers commonly known as shallow learning.

The word "neural network" is derived from neurobiology, it tries to mimic the human brain and biology. Deep neural networks can be used in various domains ranging from medicine to robotics, they also can be customized according to the use case and the Figure 2 show a pictorial representation of a deep neural network.

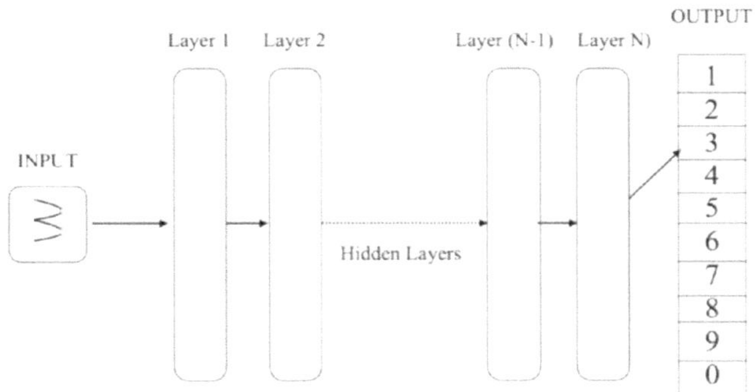

Figure 2. A deep neural network for classifying handwritten alphabets.

3.2 *Neural Networks and their Applications*

Neural networks, which are influenced by the architecture of the human brain, have fundamentally transformed the fields of machine learning and artificial intelligence. Neural networks are commonly referred to as artificial neural networks because they imitate the functioning of brain neurons. The structure is composed of neural layers, which can be categorised into three components: the input layer, hidden layer, and output layer. Each neuron possesses a unique weight and a threshold value that triggers its activation when surpassed. Let us consider a single neuron to understand how it works with the help of Figure 3.

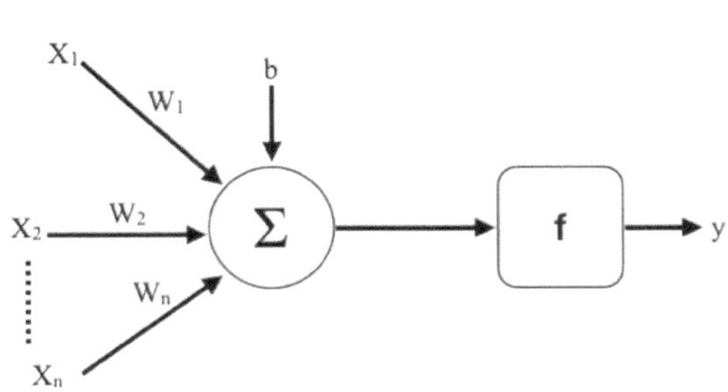

Figure 3. A simple neuron.

Here X_i are the inputs to the neuron, b is the bias and W_i are the weights. F is the activation function that takes care of the triggering of the neuron. Where y is the output. Neurons, like the one shown above, are organized into layers in a neural network. Each layer has a neutron which has different weights and activation functions, which are determined by the overall goal of the network. Before delving into the different classifications of neural networks, it is essential to comprehend the historical background of these networks.

A. McCulloch-Pitts model

The McCulloch-Pitts model, proposed in 1943 by Warren McCulloch and Walter Pitts, is considered the foundational concept behind artificial neural networks [13]. The McCulloch-Pitts neuron is a basic unit that receives multiple inputs, performs a weighted sum, and outputs a single value. Here's a breakdown of its components:

- **Inputs:** These represent signals received from other neurons and can be any number in quantity. The model originally envisioned binary inputs (0 or 1), but later variations allowed for real numbers.
- **Weights:** Every input has a weight that determines its influence on the output. Positive weights signify excitation (increasing the output), while negative weights represent inhibition (decreasing the output).
- **Weighted Sum:** The model sums the product of each input and its corresponding weight. This essentially combines the strengths of various inputs.
- **Threshold:** This is a fixed value that the weighted sum needs to exceed for the neuron to activate and produce an output.
- **Activation Function:** A simple threshold function is used. If the weighted sum is greater than or equal to the threshold, the output is set to 1 (usually interpreted as "firing"). Otherwise, the output is 0 (interpreted as "not firing").

Significance: The McCulloch-Pitts model holds immense historical significance for several reasons:

- **First Artificial Neuron:** It provided the initial framework for building artificial neural networks, inspiring generations of researchers.
- **Logical Operations:** By adjusting weights and thresholds, these neurons could be designed to perform basic logical operations (AND, OR, NOT) forming the foundation for neural computation.
- **Universal Approximation Theorem:** Later research proved that a network of McCulloch-Pitts neurons, theoretically, could approximate any continuous function, hinting at the vast potential of neural networks.

However, the model also has limitations:

- **Binary Inputs:** The original restriction to binary inputs limited its practical applications.
- **Limited Learning:** The model lacked a learning mechanism, which is crucial for neural networks to adapt and improve.

The McCulloch-Pitts model paved the way for the perceptron, a more advanced model that used a continuous activation function and an associated learning rule.

B. The Perceptron

Frank Rosenblatt, an American psychologist, made a significant contribution to artificial intelligence in the late 1950s with the invention of the perceptron [14]. Inspired by the structure and function of biological neurons in the brain, Rosenblatt's perceptron is a single-layer artificial neural network. It takes multiple inputs, assigns weights to each input, sums them, and applies a threshold function to produce a binary output (typically 0 or 1).

Here's a breakdown of the perceptron's functionality:

- **Inputs:** The perceptron receives signals from various sources, representing information it needs to process.
- **Weights:** Each input has an associated weight, which determines its influence on the final output. These weights can be adjusted during a learning process.
- **Summation:** The weighted inputs are summed together.
- **Threshold Function:** The summed value is then passed through a threshold function. If the sum is greater than the threshold, the output is 1 (often interpreted as "on" or "true"). Otherwise, the output is 0 ("off" or "false").

Learning in the Perceptron: Rosenblatt's perceptron incorporated a rudimentary form of learning. By adjusting the weights based on the desired output and the actual output obtained, the perceptron could improve its performance over time. This concept of learning from experience is fundamental to the development of more sophisticated neural networks.

Limitations: One major limitation was its inability to solve problems that are not linearly separable. This means the perceptron could only classify data that could be divided into distinct classes using a straight line. This limitation led to a period of decline in neural network research in the 1960s.

C. Backpropagation

Paul Werbos is a central figure in the development of backpropagation, a critical algorithm used to train artificial neural networks. Here's a breakdown of his contributions:

- In his 1974 dissertation, Werbos described a method for training multi-layer neural networks [15]. This method, though not explicitly called backpropagation then, laid the groundwork for the algorithm we know today.
- His work focused on using gradient descent to adjust the weights within the network. Gradient descent is an optimization algorithm that helps find the minimum of a function. In neural networks, this function represents the error between the network's output and the desired output.

Challenges and Recognition: Backpropagation initially faced challenges due to computational limitations and vanishing gradients (where gradients become very small in deeper networks, hindering learning). Werbos' work gained wider recognition later when David Rumelhart, Geoffrey Hinton, and Ronald Williams published a seminal paper on backpropagation in 1986.

Neural networks find applications across various domains:

1. **Pattern Recognition**:
   - Identifying patterns in digital data (images, sounds, etc.).
   - Google's deep learning system recognizes objects from millions of images.
   - Simultaneous translation tools and speech recognition benefit from neural networks.
2. **Healthcare**:
   - IBM Watson assists doctors in disease recognition. Pesce et al. made use of IBM Watson and neural networks for the detection of glomerulosclerosis which is the formation of scar tissue in the glomerulus, which is the component of the kidneys responsible for filtering. This results in proteinuria. These proteins facilitate the retention of fluid within the blood arteries. In the absence of these, fluid seeps into the adjacent tissue, resulting in edoema [16].
   - One of the interesting applications is diagnosing diseases based on medical data (e.g., X-rays, MRIs). Bharati et al., made use of a hybrid deep learning technique with VGG to predict lung disease from X-ray images [17].

3. **Detection**:
   - Predicting stock market trends using historical data, and detecting fraudulent transactions in banking and credit card systems have been quite promising applications of neural networks.
   - Various kinds of detection such as fake news detection and malware detection have been quite successful in classifying anomalies and they have exhibited higher accuracies [18, 19].
4. **Natural Language Processing (NLP)**:
   - In NLP tasks such as sentiment analysis, sarcasm detection, chatbots, and language translation, neural network performance has been at par with that of humans. Architectures such as RNNs (Recurrent neural networks) and LSTMs (Long short term memory) excel in NLP tasks.
5. **Computer Vision**:
   - Neural network architectures such as Convolutional Neural Networks (CNNs) are essential in the tasks of categorising images, identifying objects, and recognising faces. One of the potential applications of this technology is in the field of agriculture, namely in the detection of crop diseases. This can aid in accurate diagnosis and treatment [20].

3.3 Deep Learning Architectures

Artificial neural networks (ANNs) have been a fundamental component of machine learning for a significant period. However, when it comes to very complex tasks, they frequently fail to meet the expectations. Deep learning architectures are utilized in these kinds of scenarios. Deep learning is an extension of artificial neural networks (ANNs) that utilize a stacked structure of numerous hidden layers. Consider the collaboration of multiple layers of neurons, comparable to the arrangement of building bricks. Every layer progressively pulls more complex information from the data. Deep learning models can now address problems that were previously impossible for typical ANNs. For instance, consider the concept of image recognition. A shallow artificial neural network may encounter difficulty in distinguishing between a dog and a cat. However, a deep learning architecture such as a convolutional neural network (CNN) can examine edges, forms, and textures, resulting in more precise categorizations.

The necessity for deep learning arises due to the continuously increasing complexity of data. Deep learning algorithms are highly proficient in identifying patterns in large datasets, ranging from facial recognition to natural language processing. They provide a higher degree of automation and problem-solving, rendering them an indispensable tool for the future of AI. To state in brief the power of deep learning appears in various ways. CNNs, known for their expertise in image processing, demonstrate exceptional proficiency in identifying patterns within pixels. RNNs address sequences, such as text or speech, by comprehending the progression of information. Transformers demonstrate exceptional proficiency in natural language challenges by examining the connections between words. Generative Adversarial Networks (GANs) can be comparable to rivals. One network generates data, such as images, while the other network attempts to determine its authenticity, this produces increasingly realistic results. Every architectural design offers distinct advantages in the constantly changing field of deep learning.

3.3.1 Convolutional Neural Networks (CNNs)

They are a type of deep learning algorithm that is particularly efficient in analysing visual input. However, their uses are not limited to just image recognition. CNNs are crucial in intelligent cyber threat detection in modern education systems because they can automatically and flexibly learn spatial hierarchies of attributes from input data. In the following, we will explore the mechanisms of CNNs and their particular suitability for detecting cyber threats.

CNNs are specifically engineered to analyse and categorise complex data with multiple dimensions by utilising a sequence of convolutional and pooling layers, which are then followed by fully connected layers. The basic components of CNNs include the following:

- Convolutional layers utilise convolutional filters to process the input data, extracting local patterns like edges, textures, or more intricate features in succeeding layers. Convolutions aid in lowering the spatial dimensions of the input, enhancing the efficiency of the network while maintaining important properties.
- Pooling layers employ pooling operations, such as min pooling, max pooling, or average pooling, to decrease the dimensionality of the feature maps by summarising the existence of features in certain regions of the input. This contributes to the completion of spatial invariance and the reduction of computational complexity.
- Activation Functions like non-linear activation functions, such as ReLU (Rectified Linear Unit), add non-linearity into the network, allowing it to understand deep patterns and relationships in the data. There are many more activation functions like Leaky Relu which removes the "dying ReLU" issue, softmax for classification problems, sigmoid, and softplus which are used based on the use case.

- Fully connected layers are responsible for combining the acquired features and conducting a final categorization by utilizing the combined information from the preceding levels.

Now let's discuss the CNNs for the detection of cyber threats in education systems that are becoming more dependent on digital platforms, which exposes them to a range of cyber dangers including phishing assaults, malware infections, and unauthorised access. CNNs can be employed for intelligent identification and analysis of cyber threats through various methods:

Network Traffic Analysis: CNNs can examine network traffic data to detect irregularities that may suggest possible cybersecurity risks. CNNs can acquire the ability to identify patterns linked to both regular and malicious behaviour by considering network traffic as a series of data packets. Convolutional layers can detect and extract characteristics such as packet size, frequency, and source/destination addresses. On the other hand, pooling layers aid in condensing and summarising these characteristics over a period of time. Comprehensive analysis of CNN along with recurrent neural networks, long-term short memory, and gate recurrent neural networks has been performed to detect intrusion [21].

Malware Detection: Convolutional Neural Networks (CNNs) can be trained to identify malware by analysing executable files or their binary representations. CNNs can identify unique patterns that distinguish normal software from malicious code by transforming binary code into pictures. This technology utilises the power of Convolutional Neural Networks (CNNs) in identifying visual patterns to improve the ability to detect viruses. The following gives an overview of how malware detection is performed using CNNs. The functioning of CNNs in the context of malware detection.

1. Data Representation: Malware can be expressed in diverse formats, including binary files, byte sequences, or even pictures. Raw binary files can be transformed into grayscale images, with each pixel value representing a byte value. This transformation enables Convolutional Neural Networks (CNNs) to effectively utilise their expertise in picture processing.
2. Feature Extraction: CNNs consist of convolutional layers that utilise filters to extract localised patterns from the input data. Subsequently, pooling layers are added after these layers that decrease the size of the data to lower its complexity and computational requirements. These layers possess the ability to autonomously acquire knowledge to identify significant characteristics, such as recurring sequences of bytes or code arrangements that suggest the presence of malicious software [22].

3. Classification: The retrieved features undergo processing in fully connected layers, resulting in a softmax layer that produces probability for various classes (such as benign or malignant). The end-to-end learning process allows CNNs to accurately differentiate between which is malicious and benign software.

Phishing Detection: Phishing attacks frequently target education systems intending to illegally obtain sensitive information. CNNs have the ability to examine the visual and textual elements of emails, webpages, or URLs in order to identify and flag potential phishing attacks [23]. CNNs can effectively differentiate between legitimate communications and phishing schemes by analysing factors such as email headers, body content, and embedded links.

3.3.2 Recurrent Neural Networks (RNNs)

RNNs are a type of artificial neural network specifically created to handle sequential input and time series data. They are highly effective for tasks that heavily rely on context and temporal dynamics. RNNs are advantageous in intelligent cyber threat detection in modern education systems because they can effectively analyse and learn from sequences of occurrences over time. Long Short-Term Memory (LSTM) and Gated Recurrent Units (GRUs) are enhanced variations of RNNs that include certain changes.

Reasons for using RNNs in the context of Cyber Threat Detection are because they are effective in the following:

- Sequential data handling often involves the analysis of sequences of log entries, network packets, or user actions. RNNs, due to their capacity to retain a hidden state that collects information from preceding inputs, are well-suited for representing these sequences.
- Context awareness refers to RNNs' capacity to understand the context of occurrences. This ability is crucial for differentiating between regular and harmful behaviors. For instance, while one unsuccessful login attempt may not be harmful, a sequence of such attempts could suggest a brute-force attack.
- Temporal analysis is where Numerous cyber risks emerge gradually over a period. RNNs have the ability to capture the sequential patterns in data, which makes them well-suited for identifying abnormalities that occur over long time periods.

Applications of RNNs for cyber threat detection include analyzing logs where they can be trained on sequences of log entries to identify patterns that suggest the presence of cyber threats. Logs from several sources, including application logs, system logs, and network logs, can be analyzed to detect irregularities. The next application includes network traffic monitoring where RNNs can identify abnormal traffic patterns, which could indicate attacks like Distributed Denial of Service (DDoS) or data exfiltration, by analyzing sequences of network packets. The final application includes user behavior analytics where RNNs can acquire knowledge about usual patterns of user behavior and identify any variations that might potentially signify compromised accounts or insider threats. A general framework for how RNNs can be used for cyber threat detection is by data collection, pre-processing, feature extraction, building an RNN model, training model, and evaluating model.

4. An Objective Examination of Deep Learning's Impact, Going Beyond It

Modern education systems extensively depend on digital resources for administration, teaching, and learning, which leads to an increased digital footprint and greater vulnerability to cyber threats. Educational institutions house valuable data, such as personal information of students and staff, financial records, and intellectual property, which makes them attractive targets for hackers. The COVID-19 pandemic has expedited the use of remote and hybrid learning environments, leading to increased reliance on digital platforms. This has expanded the vulnerability to cyber threats by widening the potential targets for attacks. Regulatory compliance for educational institutions is required to adhere to data protection standards, such as FERPA in the United States, which enforce the safeguarding of student data [24]. Efficient identification of potential dangers is crucial for ensuring adherence to regulations.

4.1 Business and Government Institutions' use of Deep Learning for Threat Detection

Several institutions and organizations have implemented deep learning technologies to enhance their cybersecurity capabilities. Here are some notable examples:

1. DARPA (Defense Advanced Research Projects Agency) has initiated several projects that leverage deep learning for cybersecurity. One such program is the "Cyber Grand Challenge," which focuses on developing autonomous systems for cyber defense [25].

2. MIT's Lincoln Laboratory researches applying deep learning techniques for cybersecurity, including anomaly detection and malware analysis.

3. NVIDIA, a well-known silicon company for its GPUs, collaborates with various institutions to implement deep learning for cybersecurity, focusing on areas such as threat detection and response [26].

4. IBM's Watson for Cyber Security utilizes deep learning and NLP to analyze vast amounts of unstructured data, such as threat reports and blogs, to identify and respond to cyber threats and many works have been done using IBM's Watson for cybersecurity [27].

4.2 Advantages and Limitations of Deep Learning Models

Some of the notable advantages include:

- DL models can achieve high accuracy in detecting and classifying cyber threats by learning complex patterns from large datasets.
- Unlike traditional machine learning models, deep learning models can automatically extract relevant features from raw data, reducing the need for manual feature engineering.
- Deep learning models can scale to analyze vast amounts of data, making them suitable for real-time threat detection in large networks.
- These models can adapt to new and evolving threats by retraining on updated data, improving their ability to detect previously unseen attacks.
- Deep learning can improve the detection rates of various cybersecurity tools, such as IDS, antivirus software, and threat intelligence platforms.

There are always going to be obstacles and constraints that need to be considered. Some of them include the following:

- Deep learning models require large amounts of labeled data for training. Acquiring and labeling such data can be challenging and time-consuming.
- Training and deploying deep learning models require significant computational resources, including powerful GPUs and large amounts of memory. Many institutions and students often lack the resources to develop these models.
- Deep learning models are often considered black boxes, making it difficult to understand and interpret their decisions. This can be a barrier in security applications where explainability is crucial. One can overcome this barrier using Explainable AI (XAI) to interpret the results that the black box models produce [28].
- Without proper regularization and validation, deep learning models can overfit the training data, reducing their effectiveness on unseen data.
- Deep learning models can be vulnerable to adversarial attacks, where small disturbances to the input data can lead to incorrect predictions.

5. Practical Implementation

This section focuses on implementing deep learning for cybersecurity that involves several critical steps, from data preprocessing to model training and evaluation, followed by real-world applications shown through case studies. Below is a detailed discussion of each aspect.

5.1 Data Preprocessing for Deep Learning in Cybersecurity

Data preprocessing is an important step in preparing raw data for deep learning models. In cybersecurity or in general ML modelling, this involves handling various types of data, including network logs, system logs, and other digital footprints. The steps typically include the following:

a. Data collection involves gathering data from various sources such as network traffic logs, endpoint security logs, and user activity logs. For educational institutions, this could include data from campus networks, online learning platforms, and administrative systems. It is important to gather data from various places and integrate them while maintaining the consistency of data.
b. Data cleaning involves removing noise and irrelevant data points. This may involve filtering out redundant data, correcting inconsistency, and handling missing values. There are various ways to handle missing values based on the kind of feature and its importance [29].
c. Data transformation involves converting data into a suitable format for deep learning models. A machine learning or deep learning model only understands numbers but not alphabets, it is necessary to follow various techniques (one hot encoding, word to vector, word embedding, etc.,) to convert the features with characters into numbers. For example, network traffic data might be transformed into sequences of packet headers, while malware samples could be converted into byte sequences or binary images.
d. Feature extraction involves identifying and extracting relevant features. It can help distinguish between normal and malicious behavior. For example, in network traffic analysis, features like packet size, protocol type, and time between packets might be relevant.
e. Normalization and scaling involve standardizing data to ensure that it fits within a specific range, which helps in speeding up the convergence of the deep learning models. Data transformation by normalization can also be performed in various techniques such as min-max normalization, z-score normalization, and normalization by decimal scaling [29].

f. Data augmentation involves generating additional training data through techniques such as oversampling, and under sampling, especially when dealing with imbalanced datasets which can cause bias and incorrect predictions. It can lead to a decrease in accuracy and other key metrics.

5.2 Model Training and Evaluation

Once the data is preprocessed, the next step is to train and evaluate the deep-learning models. This process involves several key stages:

a. Model selection involves choosing the appropriate deep-learning architecture based on the problem at hand. Common models include CNNs for image-based data, RNNs for sequence data, and hybrid models for complex tasks. One has to use a tailor-made deep learning model with proper hyperparameter tuning in order to produce accurate predictions.
b. Training the model involves feeding the preprocessed data into the selected model and adjusting the model parameters using optimization techniques like gradient descent, stochastic gradient descent ADAGRAD (short for adaptive gradient), RMSprop (Root Mean Square Propagation), and many more. During training, it's crucial to use a validation set to monitor the model's performance and prevent overfitting.
c. Hyperparameter tuning involves adjusting the model's hyperparameters, such as learning rate, batch size, and the number of layers, to improve performance. These hyperparameters are settings that control the learning process of the model, rather than being learned from the data itself. Some of the famous techniques of hyperparameter tuning techniques are grid search, random search, bayesian optimization, and gradient-based optimization. The impact of hyperparameters on model performance varies and gives priority to fine-tuning those with a higher level of influence. When selecting a tuning approach, it is important to take into account the computational resources that are available. Grid search can incur significant processing costs when dealing with extensive hyperparameter spaces.
d. To evaluate the model, make use of various metrics, such as accuracy, precision, recall, F1 score, and confusion matrix for classification tasks, and Mean Squared Error (MSE) or R-squared for regression tasks. One can make use of a neural network to perform both classification and regression.

e. Implementing cross-validation techniques to ensure the model generalizes well to unseen data. It is a resampling method used to evaluate the performance of a machine learning model on a limited data sample. It involves partitioning the dataset into multiple subsets, training the model on some of the subsets, and validating it on the remaining subset. This process is repeated multiple times, with different subsets used for training and validation in each iteration. Cross-validation is performed to prevent overfitting and to estimate performance and it is often used to select the best hyperparameters for the model. Some of the common cross-validation techniques include K-Fold cross-validation, stratified K-Fold cross-validation, Leave-One-Out Cross-Validation (LOOCV), and hold-out validation. Each one has its pros and own, for instance, LOOCV is expensive for large datasets, stratified K-Fold cross-validation is similar to K-fold but ensures that the class distribution in each fold is approximately the same as the overall dataset which is important for imbalanced datasets and holdout validation is less reliable than k-fold cross-validation for performance estimation.

f. Any model trained and validated is ultimately required to be deployed. It involves deploying the trained model in a production environment where it can analyze real-time data and provide actionable insights that can further help in making the model better over time. It involves several critical considerations and steps. Here's a breakdown:

There are several challenges in deployment, some of the notable ones are education systems demand real-time threat detection for immediate response. Models must process data efficiently without compromising accuracy. Secondly, The model should handle increasing data volumes and user numbers without performance degradation.

- Integration: Seamless integration with existing security infrastructure is essential for effective threat response.
- Model Drift: Cyber threats evolve rapidly, requiring continuous model updates and retraining.
- False Positives and Negatives: Minimizing these is crucial to avoid disrupting educational activities and ensuring efficient threat response.
- Privacy and Security: Protecting sensitive student and institutional data while deploying the model is paramount.

Deployment Strategies include the types presented below.

- Cloud-based Deployment: Offers scalability, flexibility, and access to powerful computing resources. Utilize cloud platforms like AWS, Azure, or GCP for model hosting and serving. Consider serverless architectures for efficient resource utilization.
- On-premises Deployment: Provides more control over data security and privacy. Requires robust hardware and infrastructure. Suitable for organizations with stringent data residency requirements.
- Hybrid Deployment: Combines cloud and on-premises for optimal benefits. Can be used for data preprocessing, model training, and inference in different environments.

Deployment Architecture

- Model Serving: Choose a suitable framework (TensorFlow Serving, TorchServe, etc.) for efficient model serving. Implement REST APIs for model access. Consider load balancing and auto-scaling for handling varying traffic.
- Data Pipeline: Establish a reliable data pipeline to continuously feed data to the model for retraining and inference. Ensure data privacy and security through encryption and access controls.
- Monitoring and Evaluation: Implement robust monitoring to track model performance, detect anomalies, and identify potential issues. Continuously evaluate model accuracy and update as needed.

5.3 Case Study: Malware Detection

In the evolving landscape of modern education systems, the integration of digital technologies has significantly enhanced learning experiences. However, this digital transformation has also increased the vulnerability of these systems to cyber threats, with malware being one of the most prevalent and pernicious. Malware, which includes viruses, worms, Trojans, ransomware, and spyware, can severely disrupt educational operations, compromise sensitive data, and incur significant financial losses. This case study explores the application of deep learning approaches for intelligent malware detection, illustrating how advanced algorithms can fortify educational institutions against such cyber threats.

Educational institutions increasingly rely on interconnected digital platforms to manage administrative functions, facilitate online learning, and store sensitive information. These platforms are attractive targets for cybercriminals aiming to exploit vulnerabilities through malware. Traditional signature-based malware detection methods, which rely on known patterns, are often insufficient against sophisticated, evolving threats. This necessitates the adoption of more advanced techniques capable of identifying novel and complicated malware.

The following deep learning architectures are particularly noteworthy:

- CNNs are originally designed for image recognition, CNNs can be adapted to analyze binary malware files as images. By converting malware binaries into grayscale images, CNNs can identify patterns and anomalies indicative of malicious behavior.
- RNNs are suitable for sequential data, RNNs, and their variants like Long Short-Term Memory networks, can analyze sequences of system calls or API calls made by executables. This temporal analysis helps in detecting malware based on behavior patterns over time.
- Autoencoders are unsupervised learning models that can be used to detect anomalies in network traffic or executable files. By learning to compress and reconstruct normal data patterns, autoencoders can flag deviations that may indicate the presence of malware.

To demonstrate the effectiveness of deep learning in malware detection, consider a modern educational institution deploying a comprehensive cybersecurity strategy. The institution integrates a deep learning-based malware detection system within its network infrastructure, utilizing a combination of CNNs and RNNs to monitor both static and dynamic aspects of software behavior.

By performing data collection the system collects diverse datasets, including known malware samples, benign software, and real-time network traffic. This data is used to train the deep learning models, ensuring they can distinguish between normal and malicious activities. In model training the CNN is trained on binary images of malware and benign executables, learning to identify visual patterns unique to malware. Simultaneously, the RNN is trained on sequences of API calls and system behaviors, enabling it to detect anomalies over time. Once deployed, the system continuously monitors network traffic and executable files within the institution's infrastructure. Suspicious activities are flagged for further investigation, allowing for rapid response to potential threats.

The implementation of deep learning-based malware detection in educational institutions yields significant improvements in cybersecurity. The system successfully identifies and mitigates several previously undetected malware threats, preventing data breaches and operational disruptions. Key outcomes include increased detection accuracy, reduced false positives, and enhanced threat response.

6. Conclusion

In conclusion, the integration of deep learning approaches for intelligent cyber threat detection in modern education systems represents a significant advancement in the ongoing battle against cybercrime. This chapter has highlighted the critical need for adaptive and proactive cybersecurity measures to protect sensitive educational data amidst an increasingly digital learning environment. By leveraging the autonomous learning capabilities of deep learning architectures such as convolutional neural networks (CNNs) and recurrent neural networks (RNNs), educational institutions can effectively identify and mitigate complex cyber threats, from malware detection to the identification of suspicious activities. The practical implementations and case studies presented underscore the transformative potential of these technologies, demonstrating their ability to enhance the resilience of educational infrastructures against evolving cyber threats. Ultimately, this chapter emphasizes the importance of embracing advanced deep learning methodologies to safeguard the integrity and security of modern educational systems, ensuring a safe and secure digital learning experience for all stakeholders.

References

[1] Humayun, M., Niazi, M., Jhanjhi, N., Alshayeb, M. and Mahmood, S. (2020). Cyber security threats and vulnerabilities: A systematic mapping study. *Arab. J. Sci. Eng.*, 45(4): 3171–3189, doi: 10.1007/s13369-019-04319-2.

[2] Sewak, M., Sahay, S.K. and Rathore, H. (2022). Deep reinforcement learning for cybersecurity threat detection and protection: A review, 1549: 51–72, doi: 10.1007/978-3-030-97532-6_4.

[3] Ferrag, M.A., Maglaras, L., Moschoyiannis, S. and Janicke, H. (2020). Deep learning for cyber security intrusion detection: Approaches, datasets, and comparative study. *Journal of Information Security and Applications*, 50: 102419, doi: 10.1016/j.jisa.2019.102419.

[4] Abu-Nimeh, S., Nappa, D., Wang, X. and Nair, S. (2007). A comparison of machine learning techniques for phishing detection. In *Proceedings of the anti-phishing working groups 2nd annual eCrime researchers summit*, in eCrime '07. New York, NY, USA: Association for Computing Machinery, Oct. 2007, pp. 60–69, doi: 10.1145/1299015.1299021.

[5] Yang, P., Zhao, G. and Zeng, P. (2019). Phishing website detection based on multidimensional features driven by deep learning. *IEEE Access*, 7: 15196–15209, doi: 10.1109/ACCESS.2019.2892066.

[6] Munir, M., Siddiqui, S.A., Dengel, A. and Ahmed, S. (2019). DeepAnT: A deep learning approach for unsupervised anomaly detection in time series. *IEEE Access*, 7: 1991–2005, doi: 10.1109/ACCESS.2018.2886457.

[7] Kim, T., Kang, B., Rho, M., Sezer, S. and Im, E.G. (2019). A multimodal deep learning method for android malware detection using various features. *IEEE Transactions on Information Forensics and Security*, 14(3): 773–788, doi: 10.1109/TIFS.2018.2866319.

[8] Goldman, J.J. (2024). *Princeton Moves Culprits in Yale Web Site Hacking*. Los Angeles Times. Accessed: Jun. 25, 2024. [Online]. Available: https://www.latimes.com/archives/la-xpm-2002-aug-14-na-hacker14-story.html.

[9] Eugine Prince, M. et al. (2023). An optimized deep learning algorithm for cyber-attack detection. pp. 465–472. *In*: Bhateja, V., Carroll, F., Tavares, J.M.R.S., Sengar, S.S. and Peer, P. (eds.). *Intelligent Data Engineering and Analytics*, in Smart Innovation, Systems and Technologies. Singapore: Springer Nature. doi: 10.1007/978-981-99-6706-3_39.

[10] Tarun, R. (2024). Threats Impacting Education Cybersecurity | Fortinet. Fortinet Blog. Accessed: Feb. 03, 2024. [Online]. Available: https://www.fortinet.com/blog/industry-trends/threats-impacting-education-cybersecurity.

[11] Cyber Attacks on Schools: Who, What, Why and Now What?. GovTech. Accessed: Feb. 03, 2024. [Online]. Available: https://www.govtech.com/education/k-12/cyber-attacks-on-schools-who-what-why-and-now-what.

[12] Chollet, F. (2021). *Deep Learning with Python, Second Edition*. Simon and Schuster.

[13] McCulloch, W.S. and Pitts, W. (1943). A logical calculus of the ideas immanent in nervous activity. *Bulletin of Mathematical Biophysics*, 5(4): 115–133, doi: 10.1007/BF02478259.

[14] Rosenblatt, F. (1958). The perceptron: A probabilistic model for information storage and organization in the brain. *Psychological Review*, 65(6): 386–408, doi: 10.1037/h0042519.

[15] Werbos, P. and John, P. (1974). Beyond regression: New tools for prediction and analysis in the behavioral sciences.

[16] Pesce, F., Albanese, F., Mallardi, D. et al. (2022). Identification of glomerulosclerosis using IBM Watson and shallow neural networks. *J. Nephrol.*, 35(4): 1235–1242, doi: 10.1007/s40620-021-01200-0.

[17] Bharati, S., Podder, P. and Mondal, M.R.H. (2020). Hybrid deep learning for detecting lung diseases from X-ray images. *Informatics in Medicine Unlocked*, 20: 100391, doi: 10.1016/j.imu.2020.100391.

[18] Buddi, K.K., Anamalamudi, L., Mutupuri, S.S., Madupuri, R., CC, S. and Anamalamudi, S. (2023). Hybrid deep learning approach for information analysis and fake news detection. In *2023 IEEE 15th International Conference on Computational Intelligence and Communication Networks (CICN)*, pp. 1–5. doi: 10.1109/CICN59264.2023.10402146.

[19] Mutupuri, S.S., Preetam, V., Aditya, D., Harishitha, A., Sivarajan, S. and Anamalamudi, S. (2023). Machine learning based malware detection for IoT networks. In *2023 IEEE 15th International Conference on Computational Intelligence and Communication Networks (CICN)*, pp. 298–303. doi: 10.1109/CICN59264.2023.10402231.

[20] Madupuri, R., Vemula, D.R., Chettupally, A.C., Sangi, A.R. and Ravi, P. (2023). Deep learning image-based automated application on classification of tomato leaf disease by pre-trained deep convolutional neural networks. *Mehran University Research Journal of Engineering & Technology*, 42(3): 52–58, doi: 10.3316/informit.264315976515009.

[21] Vinayakumar, R., Soman, K.P. and Poornachandran, P. (2017). Applying convolutional neural network for network intrusion detection. In *2017 International Conference on Advances in Computing, Communications and Informatics (ICACCI)*, pp. 1222–1228. doi: 10.1109/ICACCI.2017.8126009.

[22] Xiao, G., Li, J., Chen, and Li, K. (2020). MalFCS: An effective malware classification framework with automated feature extraction based on deep convolutional neural networks. *Journal of Parallel and Distributed Computing*, 141: 49–58, doi: 10.1016/j.jpdc.2020.03.012.

[23] Aljofey, A., Jiang, A., Qu, Q., Huang, M. and Niyigena, J.-P. (2020). An effective phishing detection model based on character level convolutional neural network from URL. *Electronics*, 9(9): Art. no. 9, doi: 10.3390/electronics9091514.

[24] Family Educational Rights and Privacy Act (FERPA). Accessed: Jun. 29, 2024. [Online]. Available: https://www2.ed.gov/policy/gen/guid/fpco/ferpa/index.html.

[25] Cyber Grand Challenge. Accessed: Jun. 29, 2024. [Online]. Available: https://www.darpa.mil/program/cyber-grand-challenge.

[26] NVIDIA AI Cybersecurity. NVIDIA. Accessed: Jun. 29, 2024. [Online]. Available: https://www.nvidia.com/en-in/industries/cybersecurity/.

[27] Conde Camillo da Silva, M.P., Oliveira Camargo, M., Sanches Quessada, A., Claiton Lopes, J., Diassala Monteiro Ernesto and Pontara da Costa, K.A. (2022). An intrusion detection system for web-based attacks using IBM Watson. *IEEE Latin America Transactions*, 20(2): 191–197, doi: 10.1109/TLA.2022.9661457.

[28] Alejandro Barredo Arrieta, Natalia Díaz-Rodríguez, Javier Del Ser, Adrien Bennetot, Siham Tabik, Alberto Barbado, Salvador Garcia, Sergio Gil-Lopez, Daniel Molina, Richard Benjamins, Raja Chatila and Francisco Herrera. (2020). Explainable Artificial Intelligence (XAI): Concepts, taxonomies, opportunities and challenges toward responsible AI. *Information Fusion*, 58: 82–115, doi: 10.1016/j.inffus.2019.12.012.

[29] Han, J., Kamber, M. and Pei, J. (2012). 3-data preprocessing. pp. 83–124. *In*: Han, J., Kamber, M. and Pei, J. (eds.). *Data Mining (Third Edition)*, in The Morgan Kaufmann Series in Data Management Systems. Boston: Morgan Kaufmann, doi: 10.1016/B978-0-12-381479-1.00003-4.

Chapter 7

Federated Learning-Based Security Analytics Education System

Y Lalitha Kameswari

Cybersecurity education prepares students to navigate the ever-evolving landscape of digital threats. However, traditional teaching methods often lack practical, hands-on experiences and are hindered by data privacy and security challenges. This chapter introduces a pioneering approach to address these concerns by integrating Federated Learning (FL) into a Security Analytics Education System. The system fosters a collaborative and secure learning environment, allowing students to actively contribute to model training without compromising the confidentiality of sensitive data. Federated Learning is presented as a decentralized machine learning paradigm designed to facilitate model training across distributed devices or servers. Its inherent capability to operate without the need for centralized data sharing becomes a cornerstone for addressing privacy concerns. The educational context is elucidated, emphasizing the significance of hands-on experiences in security analytics. Traditional teaching methods are scrutinized for their limitations in effectively addressing data privacy and security concerns. The chapter details the seamless integration of Federated Learning

Assistant Professor, Department of Electrical and Electronics Engineering, MLR Institute of Technology, Hyderabad.
Email: lalithayeluripati2593@gmail.com

into the security analytics education system. Each student's device or server becomes a federated node, participating in collaborative model training without direct sharing of raw security data. Mechanisms ensuring privacy during the model training process are explored. Encryption techniques and secure aggregation methods are highlighted, underlining their role in safeguarding sensitive information. The collaborative nature of Federated Learning is articulated, illustrating how students actively contribute to model improvement. The framework encourages a community of practice, fostering knowledge sharing within a secure environment. Benefits arising from the incorporation of Federated Learning into security analytics education are detailed. Improved model accuracy, real-world applicability, and the development of practical skills emerge as primary advantages. Additional security measures embedded in the system to protect against potential threats are discussed. The system's compliance with data protection regulations and ethical considerations is outlined, ensuring the utmost integrity and security. Attention is devoted to ensuring a seamless and user-friendly experience for both educators and students. Considerations for accessibility in diverse learning environments are meticulously addressed. The chapter explores the scalability and adaptability of the system to different educational settings and cybersecurity curricula. Considerations for future expansion and integration into various learning environments are underscored.

1. Introduction

In the rapidly evolving landscape of education, safeguarding sensitive data and ensuring the security of academic systems have become paramount. The increasing digitization of educational records, the adoption of online learning platforms, and the growing use of data analytics in education highlight the need for robust security measures to protect against cyber threats and unauthorized access [1]. Traditional centralized security approaches, while effective, often face limitations in terms of data privacy, scalability, and real-time threat detection. Federated learning, an advanced approach in the field of machine learning, offers a promising solution to these challenges by enabling collaborative model training across multiple decentralized nodes while preserving data privacy. When combined with security analytics, federated learning can enhance the ability to detect, prevent, and respond to security incidents in educational systems, ensuring a secure and trustworthy learning environment. Federated learning is a machine learning paradigm that allows models to be trained collaboratively across multiple decentralized devices or servers, without requiring centralization of data. Data remains on local devices or servers, only model updates or gradients are shared with a central server or aggregator. This approach minimizes the risk of exposing sensitive data. Multiple participants (e.g., educational institutions, departments, or even individual devices) contribute to the training of a shared model, enhancing its performance without compromising data privacy. Federated learning is designed to handle large-scale deployments, making it suitable for educational systems with numerous data sources and varying data types. Security analytics involves data analysis techniques to detect, prevent, and respond to security threats. Monitoring and analysing access patterns to detect potential breaches or unauthorized attempts to access sensitive academic records [2].

2. Security Analytics Education System

Security analytics is an essential component of modern educational systems, particularly as digital tools and platforms become increasingly prevalent. The integration of security analytics in education aims to protect sensitive information, ensure the integrity of academic records, and safeguard the privacy of students and staff. This section explores the role of security analytics within educational systems, detailing its objectives, methodologies, and the challenges it faces [3].

2.1 Objectives of Security Analytics in Education Systems

1. Protecting Sensitive Data: Educational institutions handle a wide range of sensitive information, including student records, financial details, and research data. Security analytics aims to:

Monitor Data Access: Track who accesses sensitive information and detect unusual or unauthorized access patterns.

Protect Personally Identifiable Information (PII): Ensure that student and staff PII is securely stored and transmitted [4].

2. Preventing and Detecting Cyber Threats: Educational systems are targets for various cyber threats, including phishing, malware, and ransomware. Security analytics helps by:

Identifying Threat Patterns: Analysing network traffic and user behaviour to detect signs of potential threats.

Responding to Incidents: Providing tools and insights for rapid response and mitigation of security breaches [5, 6].

3. Ensuring Compliance: Educational institutions must comply with various regulations, such as the Family Educational Rights and Privacy

Act (FERPA) in the United States or the General Data Protection Regulation (GDPR) in Europe. Security analytics helps institutions by:

Auditing Compliance: Monitoring data practices to ensure adherence to legal and regulatory requirements.

Generating Reports: Creating documentation and reports for compliance audits and reviews.

4. Enhancing Operational Efficiency:

Automated Monitoring: Reducing the need for manual oversight through automated alerts and analysis.

Optimized Resources: Allocating security resources more effectively based on threat intelligence and risk assessments [7, 8].

2.2 Methodologies in Security Analytics

1. Data Collection and Integration: Security analytics relies on the collection and integration of data from various sources, including:

Network Traffic: Monitoring data flows across the institution's network to identify anomalies.

User Activity Logs: Tracking login attempts, file access, and other user activities.

Security Devices: Gathering data from firewalls, intrusion detection systems (IDS), and antivirus software.

2. Threat Detection Techniques: Several techniques are employed in security analytics to detect and analyse threats.

Anomaly Detection: Identifying deviations from normal behaviour patterns that may indicate a security threat.

Pattern Recognition: Using historical data to recognize known attack patterns and signatures.

Behavioural Analysis: Monitoring user and system behaviour to detect suspicious activities.

3. Data Analysis and Visualization: Advanced analytics tools are used to process and visualize security data:

Machine Learning Algorithms: Employing supervised and unsupervised learning methods to detect and predict threats.

Dashboards and Reports: Creating visualizations to help security teams understand and act on data insights.

4. Incident Response and Management:

Automated Alerts: Generating real-time alerts for suspicious activities or breaches.

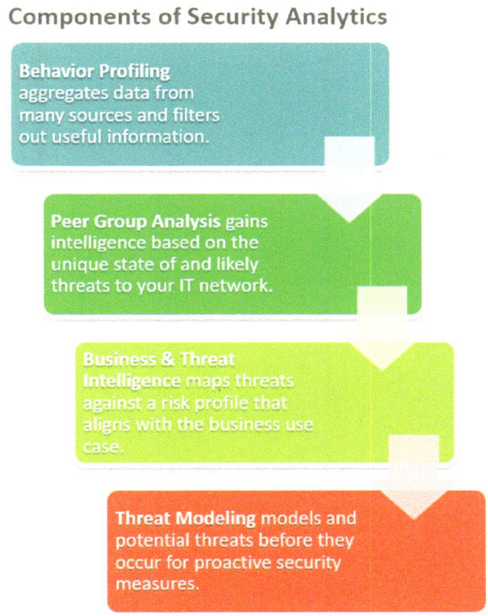

Figure 1. Security analytics components.

Forensic Analysis: Analysing data post-incident to understand the nature of the attack and improve defences.

Response Plans: Developing and executing response strategies based on analytics findings.

2.3 *Challenges in Implementing Security Analytics*

1. Data Privacy and Security: Maintaining privacy while analysing sensitive data is crucial.

Challenges include:

1. Balancing Privacy and Security: Ensuring that security measures do not infringe on user privacy or violate data protection regulations.

Protecting Collected Data: Securing data collected for analysis to prevent unauthorized access or breaches.

2. Integration Complexity: Integrating security analytics tools with existing systems can be complex due to:

Diverse Data Sources: Combining data from different systems and formats.

Legacy Systems: Adapting new security tools to work with outdated or incompatible systems [9, 10].

3. Scalability Issues: As educational institutions grow, so do their security needs. Challenges include:

Handling Increased Data Volume: Managing large amounts of data without compromising performance.

Resource Allocation: Ensuring adequate resources (e.g., personnel, technology) to handle growing security demands.

4. Skill Gaps and Training: Effective security analytics requires skilled professionals. Challenges include:

Shortage of Skilled Personnel: Finding and retaining qualified security analysts.

Continuous Training: Keeping staff updated with the latest security threats and technologies.

2.4 *Future Directions*

1. Integration with Emerging Technologies: Future security analytics in education will likely involve:

Artificial Intelligence (AI): Enhancing threat detection and response through advanced AI and machine learning techniques [11, 12].

Blockchain Technology: Leveraging blockchain for secure data management and verification.

2. Enhanced Privacy Solutions: Developing new methods to protect privacy while conducting security analytics, such as:

Federated Learning: Using federated learning techniques to analyse data without centralizing it.

3. Collaborative Threat Intelligence: Encouraging collaboration between educational institutions and industry partners to share threat intelligence and improve security measures.

4. Adaptive Security Measures:

Implementing adaptive security strategies that evolve based on real-time data and emerging threats.

Introduction to the educational context, focusing on the importance of practical experience in security analytics.

Challenges related to data privacy and security in traditional teaching methods [13].

3. Federated Learning Implementation

Federated learning offers a decentralized approach to machine learning that allows multiple entities to collaborate on model training without

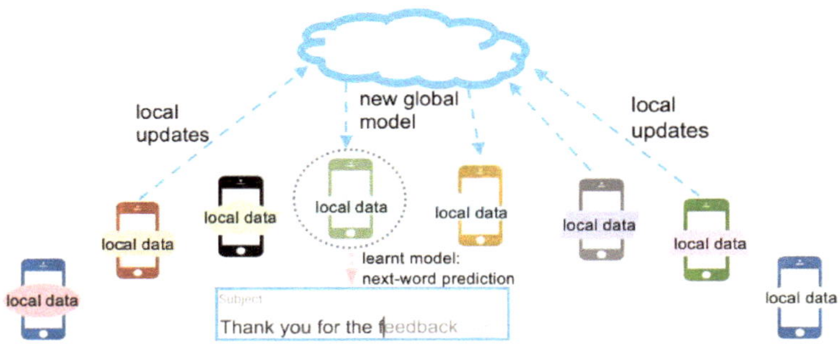

Figure 2. Feedback of federated learning.

sharing raw data. This is particularly beneficial for educational systems, where privacy and security concerns are paramount. Implementing federated learning involves several steps, including system design, data management, model training, and evaluation [14]. This section outlines these steps in detail and discusses key considerations and challenges associated with the implementation.

3.1 System Design for Federated Learning

1. Architecture

The architecture of a federated learning system typically includes:

Local Nodes: Individual devices or servers (e.g., educational institutions, student devices) where data resides and model training occurs.

Central Server (Aggregator): A server responsible for aggregating model updates from local nodes, updating the global model, and distributing the updated model back to the nodes.

Communication Protocols: Secure protocols to facilitate data transfer between local nodes and the central server [15].

2. Data Distribution

Data in federated learning remains decentralized. The system must handle:

Data Diversity: Different nodes may have diverse data types and distributions. The system should accommodate this heterogeneity.

Data Privacy: Implementing privacy-preserving techniques to ensure that sensitive data does not leave local nodes.

3. Model Design

The model should be:

Scalable: Capable of handling inputs from multiple sources without performance degradation.

Compatible: Able to work with the various data types and formats at different nodes.

3.2 Data Management

1. Data Privacy and Security
To protect privacy:

Data Localization: Keep data at the local node and only share model updates with the central server [16].

Encryption: Use encryption methods to secure model updates and communications between nodes and the central server.

Differential Privacy: Implement differential privacy techniques to add noise to model updates, enhancing privacy.

2. Data Pre-processing
Data pre-processing at the local level includes:

Normalization: Ensuring data consistency across different nodes.

Feature Engineering: Extracting relevant features from the data to improve model performance.

3. Compliance
Ensure compliance with data protection regulations such as:

GDPR: Adhering to the General Data Protection Regulation in Europe [17].

FERPA: Complying with the Family Educational Rights and Privacy Act in the United States.

3.3 Model Training

1. Local Training
At each local node:

Train the Model: Perform training using local data to generate model updates.

Optimize Hyperparameters: Adjust model parameters to improve performance based on local data characteristics.

2. Aggregation
The central server performs:

Aggregation of Updates: Combine model updates from all nodes to create an improved global model [18].

Model Averaging: Average the model weights or gradients received from different nodes to update the global model.

3. Communication

Effective communication strategies include:

Update Frequency: Determine how often model updates are sent from local nodes to the central server.

Bandwidth Management: Optimize the use of network resources to handle communication between nodes and the central server efficiently.

3.4 Evaluation and Validation

1. Model Evaluation

Evaluate the global model using:

Cross-Validation: Use techniques such as cross-validation on local data to assess model performance.

Performance Metrics: Track metrics like accuracy, precision, recall, and F1 score to measure model effectiveness.

2. Feedback Loop

Incorporate feedback to:

Refine the Model: Adjust the model based on performance evaluations and real-world use.

Update Training Strategies: Modify training approaches or data preprocessing techniques as needed.

3. Anomaly Detection

Implement mechanisms to:

Detect Outliers: Identify and manage any anomalies in model updates that could indicate issues or malicious activities.

Secure Training Data: Ensure the integrity of training data and model updates.

3.5 Challenges and Considerations

1. Data Heterogeneity

Different nodes may have varying data distributions, leading to challenges in:

Model Convergence: Ensuring that the global model converges effectively despite data variations.

Performance Consistency: Maintaining consistent model performance across different nodes.

2. Computational Resources
Federated learning can be resource-intensive:

Computational Load: Local nodes must handle the computational load of model training.

Resource Constraints: Ensuring that nodes with limited resources can still participate effectively.

3. Scalability
Scalability issues include:

Handling Large Numbers of Nodes: Efficiently managing model training and updates across a large number of nodes.

Communication Overhead: Reducing latency and bandwidth usage in communication between nodes and the central server.

4. Security Risks
Potential security risks involve:

Model Poisoning: Attacks where malicious nodes send harmful updates that compromise the global model.

Data Leakage: Risks associated with unintended data exposure through model updates.

3.6 Future Directions

1. Advanced Privacy Techniques

Homomorphic Encryption: Explore advanced encryption methods that allow computations on encrypted data.

Secure Multi-Party Computation (SMPC): Investigate SMPC techniques for secure collaborative computations.

2. Improved Algorithms

Federated Optimization Algorithms: Develop algorithms specifically designed for federated learning to enhance convergence and efficiency.

Robust Aggregation Methods: Implement methods to improve the robustness of the aggregation process against malicious updates.

3. Integration with Emerging Technologies

Edge Computing: Integrate federated learning with edge computing to enhance performance and reduce latency.

AI-Driven Insights: Utilize AI techniques to improve model training and optimization in federated settings.

4. Regulatory Compliance

Global Standards: Develop and adhere to global standards and best practices for federated learning and data privacy.

4. Privacy-Preserving Model Training

Privacy-preserving model training is crucial for ensuring that sensitive information remains confidential while still enabling the effective training of machine learning models. This is particularly relevant in contexts such as federated learning, where data is decentralized, and maintaining privacy is a priority. This section explores various techniques and methodologies for preserving privacy during model training, including their principles, implementations, and challenges.

4.1 Principles of Privacy-Preserving Model Training

1. Data Privacy

The primary goal is to protect the privacy of data while still allowing for useful model training. Key principles include:

Confidentiality: Ensuring that sensitive information is not exposed during the training process.

Data Minimization: Collecting and using only the data necessary for model training.

Access Control: Restricting access to data and model parameters to authorized entities only.

2. Transparency

Clear Protocols: Defining and documenting privacy-preserving protocols and techniques.

Auditability: Ensuring that privacy measures can be audited and verified to maintain trust.

3. Security

Robust Protection: Implementing robust security measures to protect against data breaches and unauthorized access.

Resilience: Designing systems to be resilient to various types of attacks and privacy threats.

4.2 Techniques for Privacy-Preserving Model Training

1. Differential Privacy
Differential privacy adds noise to the data or model updates to protect individual privacy. Key concepts include:

Privacy Guarantees: Providing formal guarantees that the inclusion or exclusion of a single data point does not significantly affect the outcome of the analysis.

Noise Addition: Adding noise to query results or model updates to obscure individual contributions.

2. Homomorphic Encryption
Homomorphic encryption allows computations to be performed on encrypted data without decrypting it first. Key aspects include:

Encryption and Computation: Encrypting data before sending it for processing and performing computations on the encrypted data.

Decryption: Decrypting the results only after computations are complete to ensure data privacy.

3. Secure Multi-Party Computation (SMPC)
SMPC enables multiple parties to collaboratively compute a function over their inputs while keeping those inputs private. Techniques include:

Secret Sharing: Dividing data into shares and distributing them among participants to perform computations without revealing the data itself.

Protocol Design: Designing protocols that enable secure computations and ensure that no single party has access to the complete data.

4. Federated Learning
Federated learning trains models across multiple decentralized nodes while keeping data local. Privacy-preserving aspects include:

Local Training: Performing model training on local devices and sending only model updates to a central server.

Aggregation: Aggregating updates from multiple nodes to improve the global model without accessing raw data.

5. Privacy-Preserving Data Mining
Data mining techniques that preserve privacy involve:

Secure Query Processing: Conducting data mining operations in a way that protects sensitive information.

Data Anonymization: Techniques such as k-anonymity or l-diversity that modify data to prevent re-identification of individuals.

4.3 Implementing Privacy-Preserving Techniques

1. Frameworks and Tools

Several frameworks and tools support privacy-preserving machine learning, including:

TensorFlow Privacy: A library that integrates differential privacy into TensorFlow models.

PySyft: A framework for privacy-preserving machine learning that supports homomorphic encryption and federated learning.

2. Integration Strategies

Model Integration: Incorporating privacy-preserving techniques into existing model training workflows.

Data Management: Ensuring that data pre-processing and handling comply with privacy requirements.

3. Regulatory Compliance

Data Protection Regulations: Adhering to regulations such as GDPR, HIPAA, and FERPA to ensure privacy compliance.

Best Practices: Following industry best practices and guidelines for privacy preservation.

4.4 Challenges in Privacy-Preserving Model Training

1. Computational Overhead

Performance Impact: Privacy-preserving techniques such as encryption and differential privacy can introduce computational overhead, affecting training performance.

Resource Requirements: Ensuring adequate computational resources to handle the increased complexity of privacy-preserving methods.

2. Model Accuracy

Trade-offs: Balancing privacy guarantees with model accuracy, as adding noise or encryption can impact the quality of the model.

Fine-Tuning: Adjusting privacy parameters to minimize the impact on model performance while ensuring privacy.

3. Scalability

Handling Large Datasets: Scaling privacy-preserving techniques to handle large volumes of data and numerous participants.

Integration with Existing Systems: Ensuring that privacy-preserving methods can be effectively integrated into existing infrastructure.

4. Security Risks

Potential Vulnerabilities: Identifying and addressing potential vulnerabilities in privacy-preserving methods.

Adversarial Attacks: Protecting against adversarial attacks that may exploit weaknesses in privacy-preserving techniques.

4.5 Future Directions

1. Advancements in Privacy Techniques

Enhanced Differential Privacy: Developing more advanced methods for adding noise and providing stronger privacy guarantees.

Efficient Homomorphic Encryption: Improving the efficiency and practicality of homomorphic encryption techniques.

2. Hybrid Approaches

Combining Techniques: Exploring hybrid approaches that combine multiple privacy-preserving techniques for enhanced protection.

Adaptive Privacy Models: Develop models that adapt privacy guarantees based on the sensitivity of the data.

3. Interdisciplinary Research

Collaboration: Encouraging interdisciplinary research to address privacy challenges from technical, legal, and ethical perspectives.

Innovative Solutions: Exploring innovative solutions to privacy challenges in machine learning and data science.

4. User-Centric Privacy

Personalized Privacy Settings: Allowing users to customize privacy settings based on their preferences and requirements.

Transparency and Control: Providing users with greater transparency and control over how their data is used and protected.

5. Collaborative Learning Environment

Federated Learning (FL) enables a collaborative approach where multiple entities, such as students or educational institutions, collectively contribute to the improvement of a shared machine-learning model without needing to centralize their data. This approach is particularly beneficial in educational settings where privacy and data security are crucial. The following illustration outlines how this collaborative nature works in practice.

1. Overview of Federated Learning in Education

In a Federated Learning system within an educational context:

Local Data: Each participating student or institution has access to its own local data (e.g., student performance records, and learning interactions).

Local Model Training: Instead of sending this data to a central server, each participant trains a local model using their data.

Model Aggregation: The central server aggregates the model updates (e.g., weights, gradients) from all participants to improve the global model.

2. Collaborative Process Illustration

Step 1: Initial Model Deployment

Global Model Initialization: The central server initializes a global machine learning model and distributes it to all participating nodes (e.g., students' devices or institutional servers).

Diagram:
rust
Copy code
```
[Central Server] -> [Global Model] -> [Student A's Device]
                    -> [Student B's Device]
                    -> [Institution C's Server]
```

Step 2: Local Model Training

Student A: Trains the global model on their local data (e.g., student quizzes and assessments).

Student B: Trains the global model on their local data (e.g., student engagement metrics).

Institution C: Trains the global model on institutional data (e.g., course completion rates).

Diagram:
rust
Copy code
```
[Student A's Device] -> [Local Model Training]
[Student B's Device] -> [Local Model Training]
[Institution C's Server] -> [Local Model Training]
```

Step 3: Model Update Sharing

Local Updates: Each participant computes updates (e.g., model weights or gradients) based on their local training.

Secure Upload: These updates are encrypted and securely sent to the central server.

Diagram:
rust
Copy code
[Student A's Device] -> [Local Updates] -> [Central Server]
[Student B's Device] -> [Local Updates] -> [Central Server]
[Institution C's Server] -> [Local Updates] -> [Central Server]

Step 4: Aggregation of Updates

Aggregation Process: The central server aggregates the received model updates (e.g., by averaging the weights) to form an improved global model.

Diagram:
[Central Server] -> [Aggregation] -> [Updated Global Model]

Step 5: Distribution of Updated Model

Model Distribution: The updated global model is sent back to all participants for further local training.

Diagram:
rust
Copy code
[Updated Global Model] -> [Student A's Device]
-> [Student B's Device]
-> [Institution C's Server]

Step 6: Continuous Improvement

Iterative Process: This process repeats iteratively, with the global model being continuously refined based on contributions from all participants.

Code:
[Central Server] -> [Global Model] -> [Local Training] -> [Model Updates] -> [Aggregation] -> [Updated Global Model]

3. Benefits of Collaborative Federated Learning

Data Privacy: Sensitive local data remains on individual devices or servers, protecting privacy.

Enhanced Model Performance: Aggregated updates from diverse sources lead to a more robust and generalized model.

Local Relevance: Models can be tailored to reflect the specific contexts and needs of different participants.

Scalability: Enables collaboration across a large number of participants without centralizing data.

4. Practical Example

Imagine a federated learning system in an educational platform where:

Student A in a high school trains the model on their quiz performance data.

Student B in a different high school trains the model on their assignment submissions.

Institution C contributes data from its course evaluations.

The global model, trained collaboratively, can predict student performance trends more accurately and personalize learning experiences without any single institution having access to all the data.

6. Enhanced Cybersecurity Education

Enhanced cybersecurity education is crucial in preparing students and professionals to handle the increasing complexity of digital threats. As cyber threats evolve, so must the strategies and practices used in cybersecurity education. This section explores how modern educational practices can be enhanced to better prepare individuals for the cybersecurity landscape.

6.1 Current Trends in Cybersecurity Education

1. Increasing Complexity of Cyber Threats

Emerging Threats: As cyber threats become more sophisticated, including advanced persistent threats (APTs) and ransomware attacks, education must address these evolving challenges.

Complex Attack Vectors: The rise of multi-faceted attacks involving technical and social engineering elements necessitates a comprehensive understanding.

2. Integration of Real-World Scenarios

Hands-On Training: Incorporating practical exercises and simulations that reflect real-world scenarios helps students gain practical experience.

Cyber Range Exercises: Use of virtual environments where students can practice defending against live cyber-attacks.

3. Interdisciplinary Approach

Collaboration with Other Fields: Combining knowledge from computer science, law, and policy to provide a holistic understanding of cybersecurity.

Legal and Ethical Considerations: Teaching the legal and ethical aspects of cybersecurity to ensure compliance and responsible behaviour.

6.2 Enhancing Cybersecurity Education

1. Leveraging Technology and Tools

Simulation Platforms: Utilizing advanced simulation platforms for hands-on experience in a controlled environment.

Cybersecurity Labs: Setting up labs with the latest tools and technologies used in the industry to provide practical exposure.

Online Learning Platforms: Offering courses and certifications through online platforms to reach a broader audience.

2. Curriculum Development

Up-to-date Content: Regularly updating curriculum to reflect the latest trends, tools, and techniques in cybersecurity.

Skill-Based Training: Focusing on specific skills such as penetration testing, incident response, and network security.

Industry Collaboration: Partnering with industry experts to develop relevant and practical course content.

3. Promoting Critical Thinking and Problem-Solving

Case Studies: Analysing real-world case studies to understand the intricacies of different cyber-attacks and defences.

Scenario-Based Learning: Engaging students in problem-solving exercises that mimic real-life situations.

4. Certifications and Continuous Education

Certifications: Encouraging the pursuit of industry-recognized certifications such as CISSP, CEH, and CompTIA Security+.

Professional Development: Providing opportunities for continuous learning and professional development to keep skills current.

6.3 Implementing Advanced Cybersecurity Education Strategies

1. Integration of AI and Machine Learning

AI for Threat Detection: Teaching how artificial intelligence and machine learning can be used for threat detection and response.

Algorithm Understanding: Providing insights into how machine learning algorithms can enhance cybersecurity measures.

2. Utilizing Federated Learning

Privacy-Preserving Training: Implementing federated learning to train models on decentralized data while preserving privacy.

Collaborative Learning: Leveraging data from multiple institutions to improve threat detection models without centralizing sensitive information.

3. Gamification and Interactive Learning

Gamified Training: Incorporating gamification elements to make learning more engaging and motivating.

Interactive Simulations: Using interactive simulations and role-playing scenarios to enhance learning and retention.

4. Ethical Hacking and Red Team Exercises

Ethical Hacking: Training students in ethical hacking techniques to understand how to find and fix vulnerabilities.

Red Teaming: Conducting red team exercises to simulate attacks and improve defensive strategies.

6.4 *Challenges and Solutions*

1. Keeping Up with Rapid Changes

Continuous Updates: Ensuring that educational content and tools are regularly updated to reflect the latest developments.

Industry Collaboration: Collaborating with industry partners to stay informed about emerging threats and technologies.

2. Resource Constraints

Funding and Access: Securing funding and resources for advanced tools and technologies required for effective training.

Access to Labs: Providing access to high-quality cybersecurity labs and simulation environments.

3. Skill Gaps and Workforce Shortages

Addressing Skill Gaps: Designing programs to bridge skill gaps and prepare students for real-world cybersecurity challenges.

Workforce Development: Developing partnerships with industry to address workforce shortages and create career pathways for students.

6.5 *Future Directions*

1. Enhanced Integration of Cybersecurity Concepts

Cross-Disciplinary Education: Integrating cybersecurity concepts into broader educational programs to raise awareness and understanding.

K-12 Education: Introducing cybersecurity principles early in education to build foundational knowledge.

2. Global Collaboration

International Programs: Developing international collaborations to address global cybersecurity challenges and share knowledge.

Global Standards: Contributing to the development of global standards and best practices for cybersecurity education.

3. Research and Innovation

Innovative Teaching Methods: Exploring new teaching methods and technologies to enhance cybersecurity education.

Cutting-Edge Research: Engaging in cutting-edge research to advance the field and inform educational practices.

7. Conclusion

Integrating Federated Learning (FL) into security analytics education systems represents a significant advancement in how educational institutions handle sensitive data while training machine learning models. Federated Learning offers a decentralized approach where data remains at its source, and only model updates are shared, enhancing privacy and security. This approach is particularly valuable in the field of security analytics, where handling sensitive and potentially confidential data is paramount.

Key Takeaways:

Privacy Preservation: Federated Learning addresses critical privacy concerns by ensuring that data does not leave its original location. This is essential for security analytics, where data often contains sensitive information.

Collaborative Improvement: By enabling multiple institutions or participants to contribute to model training, Federated Learning enhances the robustness and accuracy of security analytics models. This collective effort leads to better threat detection and response capabilities.

Scalability: Federated Learning supports scalability by allowing numerous participants to contribute to the training of security models without centralizing large datasets. This is particularly useful in educational settings where resources and data might be distributed across various locations.

Real-World Relevance: The hands-on experience with Federated Learning and security analytics equips students and professionals with practical skills that are directly applicable in the field. This prepares them to handle complex security challenges and leverage advanced machine-learning techniques in their careers.

8. Future Scope

The application of Federated Learning in security analytics education systems is still evolving, and several areas offer the potential for further development and research:

Enhanced Algorithms and Techniques:

Optimization Algorithms: Development of more efficient federated optimization algorithms to improve model convergence and training efficiency.

Advanced Privacy Techniques: Integration of cutting-edge privacy-preserving technologies such as secure multi-party computation (SMPC) and homomorphic encryption.

Integration with Emerging Technologies:

Edge Computing: Exploring how Federated Learning can be combined with edge computing to enhance real-time security analytics and reduce latency.

AI and Machine Learning Advancements: Incorporating new AI and machine learning advancements into federated models to improve threat detection and response capabilities.

Broader Adoption and Implementation:

Expanding Use Cases: Applying Federated Learning to other domains within security analytics, such as fraud detection, anomaly detection, and cybersecurity threat intelligence.

Industry and Academic Collaboration: Encouraging collaboration between industry and academia to develop and refine federated learning models and applications.

Educational Innovations:

Curriculum Development: Integrating Federated Learning concepts into cybersecurity and data science curricula to provide students with up-to-date knowledge and skills.

Interactive Learning Platforms: Developing interactive and gamified learning platforms that simulate federated learning environments and security analytics scenarios.

Regulatory and Ethical Considerations:

Compliance and Standards: Establishing standards and best practices for implementing Federated Learning in compliance with data protection regulations and ethical guidelines.

Ethical AI Use: Ensuring that Federated Learning models are developed and used ethically , respecting user privacy and data security.

Global Collaboration:

International Research: Promoting international research collaborations to address global security challenges and enhance the effectiveness of Federated Learning models.

Global Standards: Contributing to the development of global standards for Federated Learning and security analytics to ensure interoperability and consistency.

References

[1] Chen, J. and Liu, H. (2021). A survey of federated learning for cybersecurity. *IEEE Access*, 9: 112345–112357. https://doi.org/10.1109/ACCESS.2021.3061234.

[2] Deng, Y., Wang, S. and Liu, T. (2020). Federated learning for privacy-preserving security analytics. *Journal of Cyber Security Technology*, 4(2): 123–137. https://doi.org/10.1080/23742917.2020.1773084.

[3] Gong, Z. and Zhang, Z. (2022). Federated learning in security analytics: Techniques and challenges. *ACM Computing Surveys*, 55(3): 1–33. https://doi.org/10.1145/3491426.

[4] Kairouz, P., McMahan, B. and Rouhani, S. (2019). Advances and open problems in federated learning. *Foundations and Trends® in Machine Learning*, 14(1): 1–210. https://doi.org/10.1561/2200000076.

[5] Li, X., Wu, Y. and Wu, J. (2021). Federated learning with privacy protection in smart security systems. *IEEE Transactions on Information Forensics and Security*, 16: 289–302. https://doi.org/10.1109/TIFS.2020.3033679.

[6] Liu, Y., Liu, S. and Zhao, X. (2020). Privacy-preserving federated learning for security analytics: A survey. *Computer Networks*, 178: 107323. https://doi.org/10.1016/j.comnet.2020.107323.

[7] McMahan, H.B. and Ramage, D. (2017). Federated learning: Collaborative machine learning without centralizing training data. *Proceedings of the 20th International Conference on Artificial Intelligence and Statistics (AISTATS)*, 54, 1–10. http://proceedings.mlr.press/v54/mcmahan17a.html.

[8] Nguyen, T. and Dinh, T. (2021). Federated learning-based anomaly detection in cybersecurity. *Journal of Computer Security*, 94: 103185. https://doi.org/10.1016/j.jocs.2020.103185.

[9] Park, S., Lee, S. and Kim, H. (2020). Federated learning with differential privacy for secure analytics. *IEEE Transactions on Cybernetics*, 50(11): 4315–4327. https://doi.org/10.1109/TCYB.2020.2996763.

[10] Qin, Y., Wang, Y. and Zhang, J. (2021). Leveraging federated learning for privacy-aware security analytics in IoT. *IEEE Internet of Things Journal*, 8(4): 2745–2757. https://doi.org/10.1109/JIOT.2020.3037173.

[11] Rieke, N., Hancox, J. and Li, W. (2020). Federated learning for healthcare: A systematic review. *Nature Communications*, 11(1): 1–13. https://doi.org/10.1038/s41467-020-18516-1.

[12] Sattler, F., Wiedemann, S. and Müller, K.R. (2021). Beyond i.i.d. data: Privacy-preserving federated learning for security analytics. *IEEE Transactions on Neural Networks and Learning Systems*, 32(2): 791–804. https://doi.org/10.1109/TNNLS.2020.3012820.

[13] Shokri, R. and Shmatikov, V. (2015). Privacy-preserving deep learning. *Proceedings of the 22nd ACM SIGSAC Conference on Computer and Communications Security*, 1310–1321. https://doi.org/10.1145/2810103.2813685.

[14] Sun, S., Li, J. and Li, Y. (2021). Enhancing privacy and security in federated learning with data sanitization. *IEEE Transactions on Information Forensics and Security*, 16: 303–316. https://doi.org/10.1109/TIFS.2020.3044576.

[15] Yang, Q., Liu, Y. and Chen, T. (2019). A survey on federated learning systems: Vision, hype, and reality. *IEEE Transactions on Knowledge and Data Engineering*, 34(4): 2334–2350. https://doi.org/10.1109/TKDE.2019.2903986.
[16] Zhao, L., Wu, Y. and Zhao, Z. (2020). Federated learning-based intrusion detection for security analytics. *Proceedings of the 2020 IEEE International Conference on Communications (ICC)*, 1–6. https://doi.org/10.1109/ICC40277.2020.9149318.
[17] Zhou, L., Zhang, L. and Zheng, Y. (2021). Federated learning for privacy-preserving security analytics in edge computing. *IEEE Transactions on Network and Service Management*, 18(3): 2470–2483. https://doi.org/10.1109/TNSM.2021.3086746.
[18] Zhu, H., Chen, C. and Wang, X. (2021). Federated learning with secure aggregation for privacy-preserving security analytics. *Proceedings of the 2021 IEEE Conference on Computer Vision and Pattern Recognition (CVPR)*, 1234–1243. https://doi.org/10.1109/CVPR46437.2021.00127.

Chapter 8

Strengthening Digital Skills for Industry 4.0 and Society 5.0 among Students by Learning Low-code Tools for Intelligent Automation

Damian Kedziora,[a,b,*] *Arkadiusz Jurczuk*[c] and *Julia Siderska*[c]

In the era of intensive digital transformations, dynamic technological development, virtual work dissemination, and business process automation are becoming increasingly common. Hence, skills related to working with these technologies and the ability to collaborate with them will be of key importance. These transitions empower higher education institutions to become leading engines of shaping and developing future digital skills of students – potential employees of Organizations 5.0. The chapter diagnoses the role and impact of educational activities using low-code tools for Intelligent Automation on the development of transversal digital competencies of Polish and Finnish students who study non-technical degrees. The research identified the students' digital competencies developed by building intelligent software robots. Moreover, the study discusses

[a] Lappeenranta Lahti-University of Technology, Mukkulankatu 19, 15210 Lahti, Finland.
[b] Kozminski University, 57/59 Jagiellonska St. 03-301 Warsaw, Poland.
[c] Bialystok University of Technology, 45A, Wiejska Street, 15-351 Bialystok, Poland.
* Corresponding author: Damian.Kedziora@lut.fi

the digital skills that students lack to remain competitive in the labour market and their attitudes toward modern technologies. It was conducted in the context of the current development strategy of European universities and changes in the labour market related to the formulation of Industry 5.0 and Society 5.0.

1. Introduction

One of the boosters of the ongoing digital transformations is the ability to understand and use digital technologies. Their dynamic growth and expansion have been changing our societies, organizations, and workforce and turned former factory workers into knowledge workers [22]. Hence, education of the future needs to supply the labour market with highly skilled, competent, and tech-savvy employees [5]. The changing demands on the skill sets of employees and society at large offer pertinent guidance for education and training. In the past decade, the academic and business debate has shifted from machines as tools to machines as teammates [24, 28]. The development of modern technologies fostering Industry 5.0 and Society 5.0, as well as the ongoing changes in the perception of their role are driving the need for new competencies required to work effectively and sustainably with digital, mainly AI-based and process automation technologies [11]. The transformation that is taking place requires a blend of technical and soft skills, including creativity and critical thinking, with the powerful, intelligent, and high-accuracy machinery of Industry 5.0 [21]. On one hand, digital skills are becoming an essential component of employability in sustainable, resilient organisations and societies, while the awareness of the role and importance of digital technologies for social and economic development is still growing. On the other hand, there are still fundamental challenges and prejudices among many people, such as fear of being replaced by machines, and lack of transparency and understanding of the capabilities of the technologies, which limit their further diffusion and catalyse innovation [31].

Rapidly advancing digitalisation and accompanying changes in the labour market introduce new challenges for Higher Education Institutions (HEIs) [19]. They consequently need to monitor and adapt their curricula to fulfil their societal role and develop new skills for students, preparing them to live and work in the future digital world. The role of HEIs in the development of digital literacy is very clearly stated in the European strategy for universities. Students and staff must be equipped with digital skills for the future and the potential of universities must be harnessed to address emerging new societal and economic challenges. The European Commission [8] points out that the key role of HEIs in the digital transition of society and industry is to address the skills shortage in science, technology, engineering, and mathematics (STEM). This can be achieved by educating in digital domains, including cutting-edge, innovative technologies. Universities need to play a role in analysing the impact of digital technologies on society, as they are significantly changing the way universities operate and deliver their value, i.e., educating students [6, 29]. Moreover, HEIs are expected to make their courses more flexible to keep up with changes in the labour market and to close the digital literacy gap among students [32].

Digital transformation and the inherent requirements of Industry 5.0 imply several significant challenges and questions for the activities of HEIs [11, 32], such as: *What knowledge and skills are required from employees in modern organisations? How should employees be trained and prepared to drive digital transformation? What staff skills would be required to make proper use of digital technologies?* One of the modern technological solutions that support the digital transformation of organisations and that HEIs should include in their competence framework is the automation and robotization of business processes [14, 15].

Low-code solutions, including Robotic Process Automation (RPA) technology, are being successfully adopted by a wide range of organisations [25]. Recent research has shown that low-code skills are very important in the day-to-day execution of business processes [15, 27], as well as a useful tool to support and secure them in unexpected crises , such as the coronavirus pandemic that broke out globally in 2020 [7, 30]. Understanding the process perspective in the complex educational and technological landscape, complemented with the set of transferable and technical skills related to the basics of modelling and robotic automation, can significantly improve the perception of the employee's strength in the future labour market. Therefore, the teaching of digital skills required by Industry 5.0 should be considered a fundamental part of the curricula of today's students. Moreover, given the role of modern technologies in the development of Society 5.0, the training of the skills expected by Industry 5.0 should not only be the domain of technical subjects but also of so-called 'soft studies', such as management and logistics. Hence, this study aims to diagnose the role and impact of low-code solutions for intelligent automation on the development of transversal digital competencies of Polish and Finnish students in non-technical fields of education. The research involved students from two countries representing extreme values of the Digital Economy and Society Index (DESI), i.e., Finland and Poland. Such comparison makes it possible to define directions for the development of specific groups of digital competencies that will ensure the implementation of the goals of the Digital Decade. Finland ranks first in the latest DESI, with 93.1% of its population aged 16–24 having at least basic digital skills. In contrast, Poland ranks 24th out of the 27 EU Member States, with only 68.5% of people in this age group having at least basic digital skills [8].

Low-code tools for intelligent automation of business processes play an important role in Industry 5.0 [34]. Furthermore, the need to develop transversal digital competencies that can benefit from the capabilities of modern technologies is widely emphasized [27]. So far, researchers mainly focused on analysing competencies needed by selected sectors of the labour market [16, 20, 37] or an overall assessment of students' digital competence levels [10, 13]. The role and effect of courses about new technologies on students' development of digital abilities, on the other hand, are not well connected. HEIs need evidence to make informed decisions about upgrading curricula and implementing digitally supported teaching [3, 5, 10]. Since such has to be done through an evidence-based analysis process, our study aimed to address the following research questions:

RQ1: What digital skills can be enhanced by learning low-code tools in non-technical degree courses?

RQ2: Can learning low-code tools be perceived as an effective way to improve the skills needed to succeed in Industry 5.0 and Society 5.0?

2. Literature

The ongoing evolution of technology and turbulent business circumstances, additionally influenced by the COVID-19 pandemic, and other global crises have been leading to new challenges for organisations. We are undoubtedly witnessing the digitisation-oriented 5.0 transformation with a key role to be played by humans, human machine collaboration, and green-oriented development. The concept of Industry 5.0 reflects on these challenges [12]. Industry 5.0 is to acknowledge the power of industry to achieve societal goals beyond jobs and growth and to become a resilient provider of prosperity [35]. Breque et al. [2] recognize Industry 5.0, considering the industry's future as a human-centric, sustainable, and resilient manufacturing/production system. Manufacturing is currently undergoing a future-oriented, societal-driven transition. The European Union makes excellent efforts to achieve Industry 5.0 assumptions, which mostly address "an economy that works for people" [9]. The shift to Industry 5.0 is projected to provide new possibilities and challenges for companies and workers. As machines take on increasingly mundane and repetitive activities, the employees will need to learn new skills, such as adapting to shifting job market needs. As we progress toward a more collaborative working environment, soft skills such as critical thinking and creativity will become increasingly vital [33].

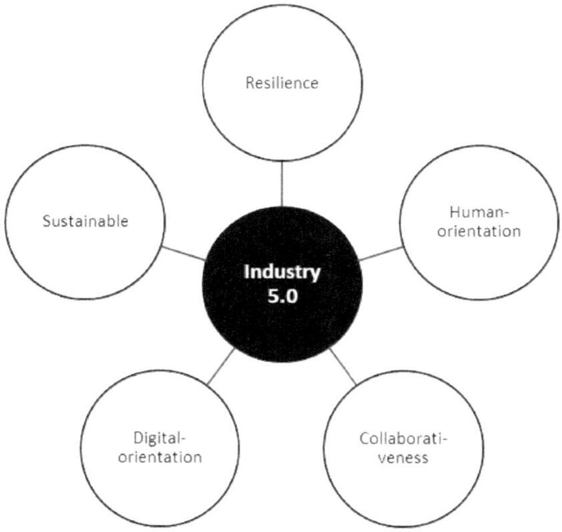

Figure 1. Main aspects of Industry 5.0.
Source: Own elaboration based on the literature review [2, 9, 33, 35].

Academia has been playing a key role since the early stages of Industry 5.0. Having considered the Fifth Industrial Revolution, key trends/ influencing factors that will have a fundamental impact on engineering education, and analysed the skills needs of the next generation, we have identified four strategies that can help higher education institutions (HEIs) redesign their programmes [3, 23]:

- lifelong learning and transdisciplinary education,
- sustainability, resilience, and human-centric design modules,
- hands-on data fluency and management courses,
- human-agent/machine/robot/computer interaction.

The rapidly advancing digitalisation and accompanying changes in the labour market pose new challenges for HEIs. They should therefore monitor and adapt their curricula to fulfil their societal role and develop new skills in their students, preparing them to live and work in a digital world. The role of HEIs in the development of digital literacy is set out in the European strategy for universities [9]. Students and staff must be equipped with digital skills for the future, and the potential of universities must be harnessed to address emerging societal and economic challenges. The European Commission points out that a key role for HEIs in the digital transformation of society and industry is to address the skills shortage in science, technology, engineering, and mathematics (STEM). This can be achieved by providing education in digital fields, including advanced

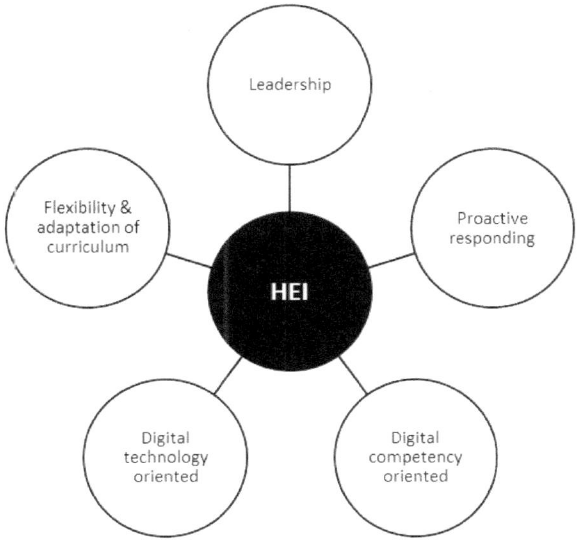

Figure 2. Role of High Education Institutions (HEIs) in the development of digital skills.
Source: Own elaboration based on the literature review [3, 6, 8, 23, 32].

digital technologies [8]. In particular, HEIs also have a role to play in analysing the impact of digital technologies on society. This is because they are significantly changing the way universities operate and deliver their services, i.e., the education of students [6, 29]. HEIs are also expected to make their courses more flexible to keep up with changes in the labour market and to close the digital literacy gap among students [32].

Digital transformation and inherent requirements of Industry 5.0 address several lenses for HEIs, such as: knowledge and skills required by employees in modern organisations, training, and readiness to drive digital transformation. HEIs play an important role in the value chain of digital skills development. As leading institutions in professional development, HEIs should promote and raise awareness of the crucial role of new technologies in the digital economy. HEIs should respond to the needs of future-oriented industries and society, with the development of digital skills through up-to-date technologies as a key element of the curriculum adapted to their needs [6, 8, 23, 32].

One of the modern technological solutions supporting the digital transformation of organisations is the automation and robotization of business processes [14]. Robotic Process Automation (RPA) technology is being successfully deployed in a wide range of organisations [17]. Recent research has shown that low-code skills are very important in the day-to-day execution of business processes [15, 25, 27], as well as being a useful tool to support and secure them in unexpected crises , such as the coronavirus pandemic that will break out globally in 2020 [7, 30]. Understanding the process perspective in the complex educational and technological landscape, complemented with the set of transferable and technical skills related to the basics of modelling and robotic automation, can significantly improve the perception of the employee's strength in the future labour market. Therefore, the teaching of digital skills required by Industry 5.0 should be considered as a fundamental part of the curricula of today's students [31, 34]. Moreover, given the role of modern technologies in the development of Society 5.0, the training of the skills expected by Industry 5.0 should not only be the domain of technical subjects, but also of non-technical majours, such as management and logistics.

3. Research Approach

The exploratory research aimed to identify and understand the competence needs, fears, and challenges of Polish and Finnish students in the area of collaborative work with the use of innovative technological solutions supporting automation and robotization of business processes, in the context of Industry 5.0. The chapter also discusses the digital skills that students most lack to remain competitive in the labour market, and their attitudes towards modern technologies, especially artificial intelligence and process automation.

The research aimed also to diagnose the role and impact of didactic activities in the field of low-code tools for Intelligent Automation on the development of transversal digital competencies of students in non-technical fields of study. The authors chose deliberate sampling as software robots are still in an emerging phase and not many students had a chance to learn how to build them during their studies. The data collection was conducted with a diagnostic survey of Finnish and Polish students, using the Computer-Assisted Web Interview (CAWI) technique. The data was collected from 116 students or graduates of Bialystok University of Technology University of Lodz (Poland) and Lappeenranta Lahti-University of Technology (Finland), who submitted their responses electronically in February–March 2022 and February–March 2023. All students took part in their degree classes in business process automation and acquired practical skills related to the low-code tools for Intelligent Automation. Hence, the limitation of purposive sampling was the difficulty in determining the population of students possessing skills in developing software robots to automate simple manual tasks. The majority of respondents were women (68%), students or recent graduates of logistics (70%), while the rest of them—business processes automation, management, management, and production engineering.

The electronic questionnaire consisted of two parts. The first is related to digital skills and the use of innovative technologies in the workplace. Respondents were asked to indicate the digital skills they use in their professional work or consider important in their future workplace. Using a five-point Likert scale, respondents also rated the importance of employees' advanced digital skills in the labour market and indicated the digital skills they most lack to be competitive in the labour market. In this part of the questionnaire, students were also asked to express their attitudes towards modern technologies, including artificial intelligence, automation, robotization, etc. The second part of the questionnaire consisted of questions about the automation of business processes using software robots and skills related to low-code tools. The students identified the importance of skills related to robotization in the labour market and assessed the difficulty of the tool for building software robots. They also rated their low-code skills for automating simple business activities and indicated which of their digital skills were improved by programming software robots.

To address the aim of the study, the first part of the chapter presents the results of the conducted literature review on issues related to digital competencies and the role of low-code solutions in the establishment of Industry 5.0. The main challenges and recommendations for HEIs regarding the development of digicompetencies nces were also discussed. The research process and methods were then presented. The analysis of the empirical data and its interpretation are described in the results section. The last part of the chapter summarises the research findings and their research contribution. Limitations of the study conducted and potential avenues for future research were also identified.

4. Results

The first part of the questionnaire focused on digital skills and the use of innovative technologies in the workplace. The respondents were asked to indicate digicompetencies they use at their work or consider important at their future workplace. Nearly 90% of responders indicated that they use digital skills while working. The following activities that require digicompetencies were among the most frequently indicated by the respondents: working with spreadsheets (81.6%), database management (52.6%), teamwork in a virtual environment (48.1%), working in ERP/MRP systems (39.1%), process management and process modelling (34.3%), creating digital content (16.2%). With the five-point Likert scale, responders evaluated the importance of employees' advanced digital skills in the labour market. Here, the majority of respondents (85.3%) stated that they are of great and very great importance. The students/graduates indicated also what digital skills they lack the most to be competitive in the labour market. The results are presented in Figure 3.

The respondents perceived a lack of their competencies both in the group of transversal competencies and in the skills directly related to the implementation of software robots. The two dominant areas of specialised (technical) digital skills, i.e., knowledge of programming languages and automation of business processes, are perceived by them as those that can determine their competitiveness in the labour market. Respondents have a relatively good background in design, data security, or working in virtual teams. Skills gaps in these areas were identified by less than 20% of respondents.

The main aim of the second part of the questionnaire was to identify students' skills, fears and challenges in the field of collaborative work with the use of innovative technological solutions supporting automation and robotization of business processes in the context of Industry 5.0, as well as to diagnose their skills of using low-code solutions. Respondents were asked to rate the importance of competencies related to the robotization of simple business processes in the labour market (1-very insignificant, 5-very significant). Almost all respondents consider digital skills to be important in the labour market. Nearly 70% of respondents indicated that these skills are important or very important for the development of their professional competence.

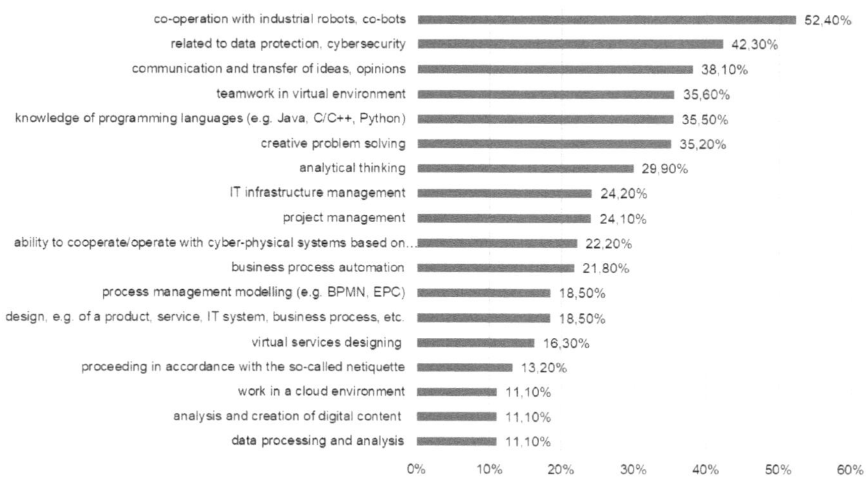

Figure 3. Students' digital skills gaps.
Source: Own elaboration based on the conducted survey [N=116].

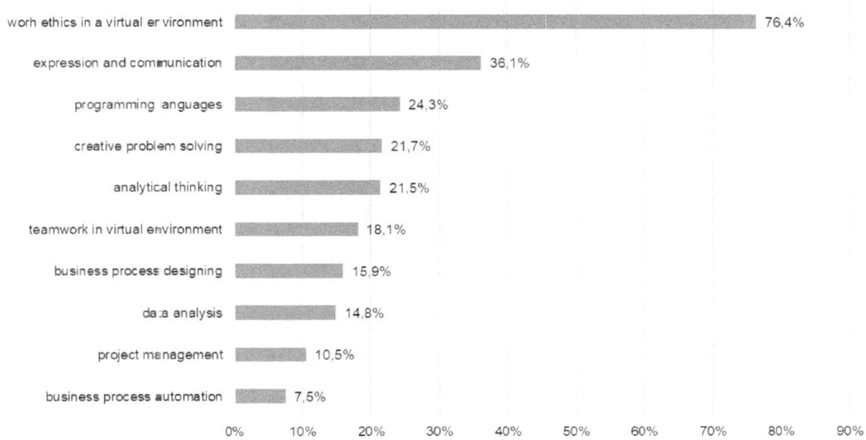

Figure 4. Digital skills of students developed while learning low-code tools.
Source: Own elaboration based on the conducted survey [N=116].

Students were also asked to indicate which of their digital skills were developed/reinforced while learning how to build software robots. The skills most frequently cited by students were those directly related to low-code solutions. It should be noted, however, that some of the respondents recognised that teaching in this area also had an impact on the development of their transversal competencies (Figure 4).

The next objective of the survey was to explore the respondents' attitudes towards low-code tools and their practical skills related to the development of software robots. Almost all students/graduates heard about technology and software robots for the first time during didactic classes at the university. Only a few of them had previously read about such solutions in the trade press or on the Internet. Approximately 60% of the students believe that the automation of business processes is already being implemented or will be widespread in business environments within the next 3–4 years. The study found that a similar proportion of respondents would like to work with software robots in their future workplace. More than 75% of respondents said that the software environments they learned in the course of their studies were a good way to develop/deepen their digital skills. At the same time, almost 80% of them consider the development of software robots to be medium or quite easy. The students pointed out the following business activities for which they believe low-code solutions are useful: data scrapping and analysis (from websites and databases) (74.1%); moving data between IT systems (63%); downloading and saving data from pdf, files, e-mail messages, forms, EPR systems (59.3%); generating invoices (48%); sending/receiving e-mails (44.4%); logging into IT systems (22.2%).

The study showed that low-code tools skills play a significant role in shaping the digital skills of respondents. The vast majority of respondents can identify opportunities to improve their competitiveness in the labour market thanks to their improvement. Students see and understand the mechanisms of improving business processes through the use of modern technologies. Even though the surveyed students perceive the development of software robots as medium or quite easy, a relatively small group of them feel competent to work with the use of modern digital technologies. Moreover, the results of the research showed that there is a significant gap in the area of transversal competencies among the studied group of students. This is undoubtedly one of the major challenges in the educational process of students. According to previous research [15, 3], transversal competencies determine flexibility and interdisciplinarity in the labour market and form the basis for the development of domain-specific digital skills.

Most respondents (81%) emphasised that the acquisition and improvement of digital skills should be a key element of the higher education programme in their field of study (Figure 3). At the same time, almost 70% of them believe that the current number of digital literacy courses in the curriculum should be increased. It is a challenge, but also a responsibility, for universities to adapt their educational programmes to both market trends and students' needs in this area. Students also rated the importance of advanced digital skills of an employee in the labour market, with 1 indicating very low importance and 5 indicating very high importance (Figure 4). The majority of respondents (85%) rated these skills as high and very high in importance. None of the respondents considered these competences to be completely unimportant (1-very low importance).

Respondents were also asked about their attitudes toward modern technologies, in particular artificial intelligence, automation, and robotics (Figure 5). The results are optimistic, with 83.1% of respondents believing that the primary role of innovative technologies is to support people at work, not to replace them. Some 80% of respondents believe that the need for human-machine collaboration will become widespread shortly. In addition, almost half of students (49%) believe that technology will eliminate some jobs while creating new ones. It should also be noted that 38.1% of them are not worried about their jobs. At the same time, only 16.4% of students feel competent and adequately qualified to work with machines and modern technologies, which justifies the need to develop their competencies in this area and to include training in robotics and automation in higher education curricula.

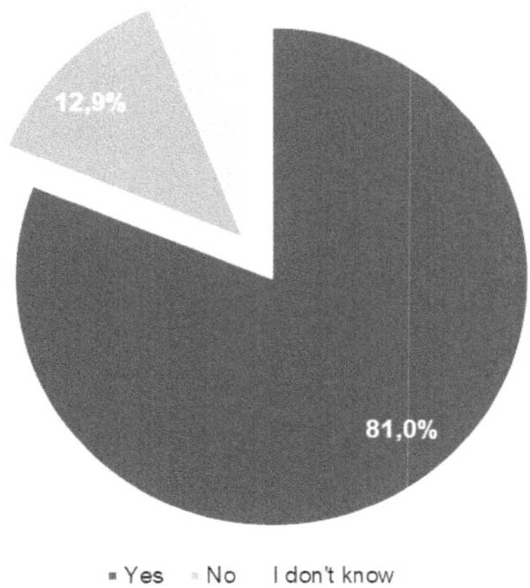

Figure 5. Respondents' opinion on the validity of including digital skills in HEI programs.
Source: Own elaboration based on the conducted survey [N=116].

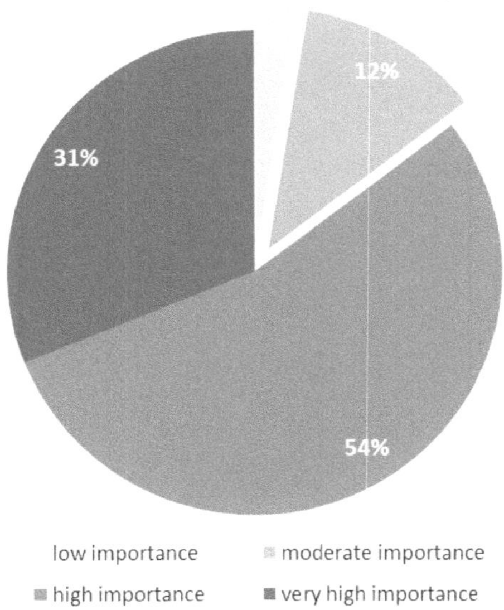

Figure 6. The importance of advanced digital competencies in the labour market in the opinion of students (1-very low importance, to 5-very high importance).
Source: Own elaboration based on the conducted survey [N=116].

It is also worth noting that 66.4% of students think that the current number of classes/curricula in which digital literacy is developed should be increased. Almost three-quarters (73.3%) of them think that the

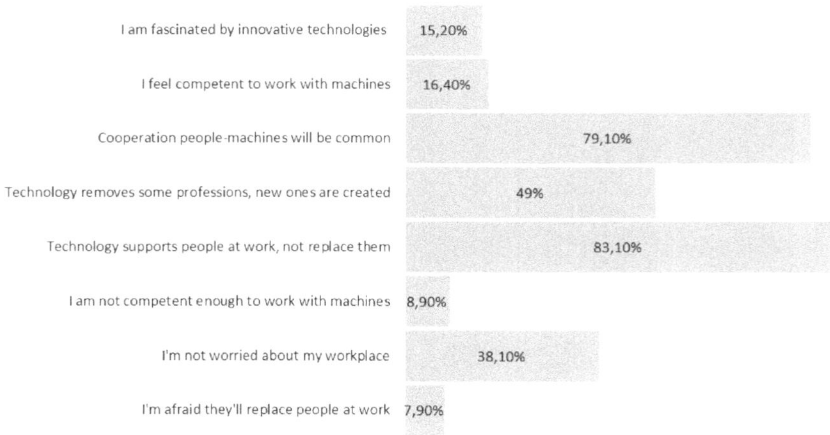

Figure 7. Students' attitude toward modern technologies (artificial intelligence, automation and robotization).

Source: Own elaboration based on the conducted survey [N=116].

automation of business processes using software robots will be common in the working environment in less than 10 years and they would like to work with them in the future.

5. Discussion and Further Research

This exploratory study contributes to science and educational practice from various perspectives. The literature review conducted made it possible to highlight the need to adopt new teaching and learning approaches in education, with a focus on developing transdisciplinary skills and strengthening young people's ability to solve problems and meet the challenges associated with Industry 5.0 and Society 5.0. The chapter discussed the digital skills that students most lack to remain competitive in the labour market and their attitudes towards modern technologies, including artificial intelligence and robotics. Students identified the importance of skills related to the robotization of simple business processes in the labour market and assessed the level of difficulty of developing software robots.

The study contributed by identifying students' digital skills that were deepened by learning how to build software robots. This chapter explores the effectiveness of integrating low-code tools into higher education curricula as a means of enhancing students' digital skills, specifically in the context of intelligent automation. By using low-code platforms, students gain hands-on experience in developing automation solutions, bridging the gap between theoretical knowledge and practical application.

The study examines the impact of such an approach on students' skills development, their adaptability to industry needs, and the effectiveness of low-code tools in preparing them for the evolving landscape of digital work.

As industries continue to embrace Intelligent Automation, the demand for professionals with digital skills is growing. This chapter focuses on the use of low-code tools as a pedagogical strategy to provide students with the skills required for Intelligent Automation. By providing a platform that simplifies the development process, low-code tools offer students the opportunity to engage with automation technologies, fostering a bridge between academia and industry. It may also be interesting to conduct comparative studies between low-code and traditional programming education. Research could explore the strengths and limitations of each approach and shed light on when and how low-code tools may be most beneficial for different learning outcomes.

The limitations of this exploratory study are related to the availability of respondents (students representing three universities from two countries). Therefore, it is recommended to further examine the types and elements of digital skills that can be enhanced by studying low-code tools in other parts of Europe and the world, to compare the results from the perspective of similarities and differences in perceptions stemming from economic and cultural facets. It is also recommended that, in the future, the setting should be explored again, and more qualitative insights should be obtained from people involved in training and studies using other programming tools and technologies. Further research should investigate the effectiveness of specific low-code learning modules in academic programmes. Integrating low-code tools for intelligent automation into the educational framework facilitates a hands-on learning approach, allowing students to apply theoretical concepts in real-world scenarios. Through case studies and practical exercises, students can develop a deep understanding of how Intelligent Automation works in different business contexts, preparing them for the challenges of the digital workforce. Furthermore, low-code tools serve as a gateway for students to delve into the complexities of Intelligent Automation without the need for extensive coding experience. By analysing specific skills such as process modelling, problem-solving, and critical thinking, the study aims to demonstrate how low-code tools contribute to a holistic skill set.

6. Conclusions

The research on the skillset required in the future labour market [26, 27] indicates that digital transformation determines and changes the competency profile of its participants. According to Schlegel and Kraus (2023), over 65% of the surveyed companies are looking for software robot specialists, and nearly 40% require the ability to use one or more tools (Blue Prism, UiPath). Therefore, to meet the current and future expectations of the labour market, systemic changes should be considered. Baker et al. (2021) indicate the need to eliminate the existing gaps between their needs and the profiles of educating students and in-service employee training [4]. The results of the diagnosis of international Master-level programs [4] proved that, despite the universal application of low-code tools, this issue is present in the master's programs only in technical fields (Science/Science Technology). The authors of these studies emphasize that it is necessary to adapt the current and future competence profiles to the requirements related to the implementation of the Industry 5.0 and Society 5.0 concepts. In addition, the results of the studies by Youssef et al.[1] confirm that the use of modern digital technologies positively influences students' performance. They also showed that the development of competencies requires program changes and greater participation of experts representing the business community and certification units.

In response to research questions, our exploratory study proved that learning low-code tools can be perceived as an effective way to improve the skillset required to be successful at Industry 5.0 and Society 5.0. When it comes to digital skills that can be enhanced by learning low-code tools, the responders mainly indicated automation of business processes, creative problem-solving , programming, analytical thinking, and process design. Almost all the respondents acknowledge using digital skills at work, while the majority affirms the great importance of advanced digital skills in the labour market. However, respondents note shortages in transversal competencies as well as low-code and RPA-related skills for Intelligent Automation, emphasizing the significance of programming languages and business process automation. The study emphasizes the role of low-code tools for Intelligent Automation in shaping digital competencies, with students recognizing the opportunities for improving competitiveness. Despite considering software robot development as moderately easy, only a small group feels competent in working with modern digital technologies. Digital and RPA-related skills should therefore be strengthened in the framework of existing and newly introduced training programmes but also kept up to date considering the dynamic nature of technology change [23, 27]. The research also highlights a significant gap in transversal skills, which is a major

[1] Youssef, A.B., Dahmani, M. and Ragni, L. (2022). ICT use, digital skills and students' academic performance: Exploring the digital divide. *Information*, 13: 129.

challenge in the student education process. Almost all respondents were first exposed to low-code technology during their university studies, and 60% believe in the widespread adoption of business process robotics in the next 3–4 years. Respondents emphasised the need for higher education programmes to prioritise digital skills, with 81% emphasising the importance of digital skills and nearly 70% advocating an increase in the number of courses designed to develop digital skills. In light of our research, digitally-based teaching methods should be much more mainstream, which could act as a lever for the development of digital skills. The chapter concludes by highlighting the challenge and responsibility of HEIs to align educational offerings with market trends and student needs in the rapidly evolving digital landscape.

Data Availability Statement

Due to the nature of this research, participants of this chapter did not agree for their data to be shared publicly, so supporting data is not available.

References

[1] Baker, A., Pepe, K., Hutchison, N., Tao, H.Y.S., Peak, R., Blackburn, M. and Whitcomb, C. (2021). Enabling the digital transformation of the workforce: A digital engineering competency framework. In *2021 IEEE International Systems Conference (SysCon)* IEEE, 11–18.

[2] Breque, M., De Nul, L. and Petridis, A. (2021). Industry 5.0: Towards a sustainable, humancentric and resilient European industry, https://msu.euramet.org/current_calls/documents/EC_Industry5.0.pdf.

[3] Broo, D.G., Kaynak, O. and Sait, S.M. (2022). Rethinking engineering education at the age of Industry 5.0. *Journal of Industrial Information Integration*, 25: 100311.

[4] Dellermann, D., Ebel, P., Söllner, M. and Leimeister, J.M. (2019). Hybrid intelligence. *Business & Information Systems Engineering*, 61(5): 637–643.

[5] DIGIFoF. (2019). Report on needs and demands for FoF-design: Findings and recommendations, https://www.digifof.eu/results/d12-report-needs-and-demands-fof.

[6] EIT Digital. (2022). The Future of Education for Digital Skills is part of the EIT Digital Makers & Shapers, https://www.eitdigital.eu/fileadmin/2022/ecosystem/makers-shapers/reports/.

[7] Elgazzar, Y., El-Shahawy, R. and Senousy, Y. (2022). The role of digital transformation in enhancing business resilience with pandemic of COVID-19. In *Digital Transformation Technology: Proceedings of ITAF 2020* (pp. 323–333). Springer Singapore.

[8] European Commission. (2022). The Digital Economy and Society Index (DESI), https://digital-strategy.ec.europa.eu/en/policies/desi.

[9] European Commission. (2021). Industry 5.0. Towards a sustainable, human-centric and resilient European industry, https://op.europa.eu/en/publication-detail/-/publication/468a892a-5097-11eb-b59f-01aa75ed71a1/.

[10] Guillén-Gámez, F.D. and Mayorga-Fernández, M.J. (2020). Quantitative-comparative research on digital competence in students, graduates and professors of faculty education: An analysis with ANOVA. *Education and Information Technologies*, 25, 4157–4174.

[11] Huang, S., Wang, B., Li, X., Zheng, P., Mourtzis, D. and Wang, L. (2022). Industry 5.0 and Society 5.0-Comparison, complementation and co-evolution. *Journal of Manufacturing Systems*, 64: 424–428.

[12] Ivanov, D. (2023). The Industry 5.0 framework: Viability-based integration of the resilience, sustainability, and human-centricity perspectives. *International Journal of Production Research*, 61(5): 1683–1695.

[13] Jara, I., Claro, M., Hinostroza, J.E., San Martín, E., Rodríguez, P., Cabello, T., Ibieta, A. and Labbé, C. (2015). Understanding factors related to Chilean students' digital skills: A mixed methods analysis. *Computers & Education*, 88: 387–398.

[14] Siderska, J., Aunimo, L., Süße, T., von Stamm, J., Kedziora, D. and Aini, S.N.B.M. (2023). Towards Intelligent Automation (IA): Literature review on the evolution of Robotic Process Automation (RPA), its challenges, and future trends. *Engineering Management in Production and Services*, 15(4): 90–103.

[15] Jurczuk, A. and Florea, A. (2022). Future-oriented digital skills for process design and automation. *Human Technology*, 18(2): 122–142.

[16] Kedziora, D. and Hyrynsalmi, S. (2023). Turning robotic process automation onto intelligent automation with machine learning. In *The 11th International Conference on Communities and Technologies (C&T) (C&T '23)*, May 29–June 02, Lahti, Finland. ACM, New York, NY, USA.

[17] Kedziora, D. and Kiviranta, H.M. (2018). Digital sales value co-creation with Robotic Process Automation (RPA) of the finance and accounting industry in Northern and Central Europe. *Management Journal*, 13(2): 161–174.

[18] Kedziora, D., Leivonen, A., Piotrowicz, W. and Öörni, A. (2021). Robotic Process Automation (RPA) implementation drivers: Evidence of selected nordic companies. *Issues in Information Systems*, 22(2): 21–40.

[19] Kedziora, D., Klamut, E., Kärri, T. and Kraslawski, A. (2017). Higher education offshoring as an innovative response to global learning challenges. *International Journal of Management, Knowledge and Learning*, 6(2): 239–260.

[20] Kipper, L.M., Iepsen, S., Dal Forno, A.J., Frozza, R., Furstenau, L., Agnes, J. and Cossul, D. (2021). Scientific mapping to identify competencies required by industry 4.0. *Technology in Society*, 64: 101454.

[21] Maddikunta, P.K.R., Pham, Q.V., Prabadevi, B., Deepa, N., Dev, K., Gadekallu, T.R., Ruby, R. and Liyanage, M. (2022). Industry 5.0: A survey on enabling technologies and potential applications. *Journal of Industrial Information Integration*, 26: 100257.

[22] Moriset, B. (2017). The reputation economy: understanding knowledge work in digital society. *Journal of Urban Technology*, 24(3): 119–122. ff10.1080/10630732.2017.1348879ff. ffhalshs01653903.

[23] OECD. (2019). Learning Compass 2030. Accessed 16 January 2020. http://www.oecd.org/education/2030-project/teaching-and-learning/learning/learning-compass-2030/.

[24] Phillips, E., Ososky, S., Grove, J. and Jentsch, F. (2011, September). From tools to teammates: Toward the development of appropriate mental models for intelligent robots. In *Proceedings of the Human Factors and Ergonomics Society Annual Meeting*, 55(1): 1491–1495. Sage CA: Los Angeles, CA: SAGE Publications.

[25] Elshan, E., Druihin, O., Schmidt, N., Siemon, D. and Kedziora, D. (2024) Unveiling challenges and opportunities in low code development platforms: A StackOverflow analysis. *Proceedings of the 57th Hawaii International Conference on System Sciences (HICSS)*, pp. 4244–4253.

[26] Sari, Y., Muhtarom, A., Nguyen, Q.L.H.T.T. and Nguyen, P.T. Ansir. (2020). Predictors of job performance: Moderating role of conscientiousness. *International Journal of Innovation, Creativity and Change*, 11(6): 135–152.

[27] Schlegel, D. and Kraus, P. (2023). Skills and competencies for digital transformation—A critical analysis in the context of robotic process automation, *International Journal of Organizational Analysis*, 31(3): 804–822. https://doi.org/10.1108/IJOA-04-2021-2707.

[28] Seeber, I., Bittner, E., Briggs, R.O., De Vreede, T., De Vreede, G.J., Elkins, A., Ronald Maier, R., Merz, A.B., Oeste-Reiß, S., Randrup, N., Schwabe, G. and Söllner, M. (2020). Machines as teammates: A research agenda on AI in team collaboration. *Information & Management*, 57(2): 103174.

[29] Sharpe, R., Bennett, S. and Varga-Atkins, T. (2022). Introduction to the handbook of digital higher education. In *Handbook of Digital Higher Education* (pp. 1–12). Edward Elgar Publishing.

[30] Siderska, J. (2021). The adoption of robotic process automation technology to ensure business processes during the COVID-19 pandemic. *Sustainability*, 13: 8020.

[31] Siderska, J., Alsqour, M. and Alsaqoor, S. (2023). Employees' attitudes towards implementing robotic process automation technology at service companies. *Human Technology*, 19(1): 23–40. https://doi.org/10.14254/1795-6889.2023.19-1.3.

[32] Spada, I., Chiarello, F., Barandoni, S., Ruggi, G., Martini, A. and Fantoni, G. (2022). Are universities ready to deliver digital skills and competences? A text mining-based case study of marketing courses in Italy. *Technological Forecasting and Social Change*, 182: 121869.

[33] Suciu, M.C., Plesea, D.A., Petre, A., Simion, A., Mituca, M.O., Dumitrescu, D., Bocaneala, A.M., Moroianu, R.M. and Nasulea, D.F. (2023). Core competence—As a key factor for a sustainable, innovative and resilient development model based on Industry 5.0. *Sustainability*, 15: 7472. https://doi.org/10.3390/ su15097472.

[34] Van Laar, E., Van Deursen, A.J., Van Dijk, J.A. and de Haan, J. (2020). Determinants of 21st-century skills and 21st-century digital skills for workers: A systematic literature review. *Sage Open*, 10(1): 2158244019900176.

[35] Xu, X., Lu, Y., Vogel-Heuser, B. and Wang, L. (2021). Industry 4.0 and Industry 5.0—Inception, conception and perception, *Journal of Manufacturing Systems*, 61: 53–535.

[36] Youssef, A.B., Dahmani, M. and Ragni, L. (2022). ICT use, digital skills and students' academic performance: Exploring the digital divide. *Information*, 13: 129.

[37] Zaragoza-Sáez, P., Marco-Lajara, B. and Ubeda-Garcia, M. (2022). Digital skills in tourism. A study from the Next Tourism Generation (NTG) Alliance. *Measuring Business Excellence*, 26(1): 106–121.

Chapter 9

Transformative Fusion: Leveraging Blockchain and AI for Educational Data Analytics in Modern Education Systems

Oleeviya Babu Poikaryil,[1,*] *Tony Basil Babu,*[2] *Gittil Sagar,*[1] *Vidvath Krishna*[1] and *Saikat Mitra*[1]

The combination of blockchain technology with artificial intelligence (AI) has the potential to transform educational data analytics, providing unprecedented opportunities for improving learning experiences and institutional efficiency in today's education systems.

Blockchain technology creates a decentralized, immutable ledger to assure data integrity, security, and transparency. Using blockchain, educational institutions may securely store and manage sensitive student data, academic records, and learning progress in a tamper-proof manner, increasing stakeholder trust and reducing concerns about data privacy and security breaches.

AI algorithms play a critical role in extracting insights from massive amounts of education data. AI can examine complicated datasets using machine learning, natural language processing, and predictive analytics to detect trends, tailor learning paths, forecast student performance, and enhance teaching tactics. Furthermore,

[1] Otto Von Guericke University, Magdeburg, Germany.
[2] RIT Government Engineering College, Kerala, India.
* Corresponding author: oleeviyazehr@gmail.com

AI-powered adaptive learning systems may dynamically change content delivery based on individual learning styles, preferences, and competence levels, resulting in more personalized and engaging learning experiences.

The combination of blockchain with AI improves the efficiency and effectiveness of educational data analytics but also allows for the creation of novel applications such as credential verification, plagiarism detection, and learning analytics dashboards. Furthermore, blockchain-enabled educational platforms are interoperable, allowing for seamless data sharing and cooperation among a wide range of stakeholders, including students, instructors, administrators, and policymakers.

However, achieving the full potential of blockchain and AI integration in education necessitates overcoming technical, legislative, and ethical barriers. Scalability, interoperability, data standardization, and algorithm bias are critical concerns that must be addressed to promote equal access, inclusion, and fairness in educational data analytics.

Finally, the combination of blockchain and AI creates a breakthrough paradigm for educational data analytics, allowing stakeholders to make informed decisions, optimize learning outcomes, and drive continuous improvement in the modern education system. By adopting this collaborative approach, educational institutions may pave the way for a more adaptable, responsive, and student-centered learning environment in the digital age.

1. Introduction

The landscape of modern education is transforming, driven by the rapid integration of advanced technologies such as blockchain and artificial intelligence (AI). This chapter, "Transformative Fusion: Leveraging Blockchain and AI for Educational Data Analytics in Modern Education Systems," explores the synergistic potential of these technologies in enhancing educational data analytics. The objective is to provide a comprehensive understanding of how blockchain and AI can be harnessed to address current challenges and gaps within the education sector, ultimately leading to more effective, transparent, and personalized learning experiences.

Blockchain, a decentralized digital ledger technology, ensures secure and transparent transactions. In education, it can be utilized for secure record-keeping, credential verification, and protecting academic integrity [1]. AI, on the other hand, refers to the simulation of human intelligence processes by machines, particularly computer systems. Its applications in education include personalized learning, predictive analytics, and automated administrative tasks [2]. Educational data analytics involves data analysis techniques to understand and improve educational processes and outcomes [3].

Despite the growing interest in integrating blockchain and AI in education, significant gaps in the literature remain. Most studies have focused on the individual impacts of these technologies rather than their combined potential. Moreover, concerns about data privacy, ethical implications, and the scalability of these solutions in diverse educational settings continue to be areas requiring further exploration [4].

The significance of this chapter lies in its interdisciplinary approach to addressing these gaps. By examining the combined application of blockchain and AI, this chapter seeks to highlight their complementary strengths. Blockchain's ability to provide secure, immutable records can enhance the transparency and reliability of educational data, while AI's capacity for data analysis can offer deeper insights and more personalized educational experiences [5]. This fusion holds the promise of revolutionizing educational systems, making them more efficient, equitable, and adaptive to individual learner needs [6].

The primary objectives of this chapter are threefold: first, to investigate the current state of blockchain and AI integration in educational data analytics; second, to identify the challenges and opportunities associated with their implementation; and third, to propose a framework for their effective integration within educational systems. This research is driven by the rationale that a combined approach can mitigate the limitations of each technology when used in isolation, thereby maximizing their potential benefits.

To achieve these objectives, a mixed-methods approach is employed, combining qualitative and quantitative data collection and analysis. The structure of the chapter is as follows: the first section reviews the existing literature on blockchain and AI in education; the second section discusses the methodological framework used in this study; the third section presents the findings and analysis; and the final section offers a discussion on the implications of these findings, along with recommendations for future research and practice.

In summary, this chapter endeavours to advance the academic discourse on blockchain and AI in education by providing a nuanced understanding of their integrated potential. Through a thorough examination of their applications, challenges, and opportunities, it seeks to contribute valuable insights that can inform policy, practice, and future research in the field of educational technology.

2. Understanding Blockchain Technology

The disruptive nature of blockchain technology in various sectors including education implies that it is a game changer. The next part will be an introduction to the basic concepts of blockchain, its applications within the educational sector, and descriptions of how it is used in different learning environments around the globe.

At the heart, blockchain is a decentralized and distributed ledger that works through a series of blocks that record transactions. Each block is linked with cryptography to the preceding one, creating an unchangeable and verifiable chain. Its architecture assures transparency and security—any attempt to change any block on a chain will require general agreement of network participants so it will be very safe from fraud or tampering [7].

Apart from security applications, another use of blockchain in education is to provide a superior level of data security. The information that schools have regarding their students is very sensitive, for example, academic performance and grading, and personal information. Rather than storing paper documents of past performance which can be easily manipulated or their digital equivalents which can be hacked into, block-chaining the records will preserve integrity and ensure protection. Every transaction in the blockchain network gets a timestamp with it and is verified by several nodes on the network so there comes out a clear and secure record system [8].

The area where blockchain finds itself being useful is the credential verification process. By the traditional approach, verifying an academic certificate requires long complex procedures that are error-prone as well as susceptible to fraud. Blockchain creates opportunities for the issuance and validation of digital credentials (diplomas, certificates) in a secure tamper-proof way. Issuing institutions can do this on a blockchain as tokens which employers, other educational institutions, or any third party can easily verify without involving intermediaries at any stage [9].

Blockchain has been adopted by many educational institutions across the globe in different matters of credentialing. A case in point is how blockchain will be used in digital diploma issuance only at the Massachusetts Institute of Technology (MIT) through their Digital Diploma program. These digital diplomas are archived on a blockchain making it possible for graduates to have safe and verification proof of their academic accomplishments. This initiative not only improved the processes for verifying employers but also increased the market value of MIT's credentials [10].

Another notable application of blockchain technology is in the recording and maintenance of students' academic records. When compared to traditional paper-based or centralized digital record-keeping systems, the latter may be ineffective and prone to security breaches. Blockchain provides a decentralized substitute whereby academic records are safely stored and can easily be accessed by authorized persons. Universities such as the University of Nicosia/Cyprus employ blockchain technology in the management and authentication of academic records thus ensuring their accuracy, credibility, and reliability system-wide [11].

Unlike mere data security and credential validation, blockchain goes a long way in guaranteeing a transparent and effective administrative system in education setup. The smart contracts are deployed on the networks of blockchain that are programmable self-executing contracts that can do course registration, fee payment, and student admission automation. It is via these smart contracts that preset conditions automatically trigger their execution hence cutting down on manual labor and boosting operational efficiency [12].

In addition, blockchain catapults cooperation amongst educational institutions from one level to another by enhancing information sharing. Blockchain provides a standardized platform for sharing academic records and research data, eliminating intermediaries' trust among affiliated institutions. They could securely exchange information, work together on joint research projects as well, and create a consortium for curriculum development, at the same time safeguarding data integrity and security systems.

Blockchain technology, in brief, has the power to transform the education system for the better by assuring data security – with this one can be sure credential verification will be easier-, digitalizing academic record keeping and eventually administrative systems will be simpler. The use of blockchain in education is not just a fashion but as trends show it is strategically gradually developing into a more honest, open, and available educational environment. While many institutions are beginning to see the benefits of adopting blockchain, the innovation, collaboration, and improved student outcomes promise to uplift the future of education globally [13].

3. Exploring Artificial Intelligence in Education

3.1 Artificial Intelligence

Artificial Intelligence (AI) refers to the simulation of human intelligence in machines that are designed to think and learn like humans. These systems can perform tasks such as visual perception, speech recognition, decision-making, and language translation. AI encompasses a wide range of subfields, each focusing on different aspects of human intelligence and computational capabilities. The goal of AI is not only to mimic human abilities but also to surpass them in various domains, providing innovative solutions and enhancing efficiencies across multiple sectors, including education, healthcare, finance, and more [14].

3.2 Machine Learning

Machine Learning (ML) is a subset of AI that involves the development of algorithms and statistical models that enable computers to learn from and make predictions or decisions based on data. ML algorithms improve their performance on a given task over time without being explicitly programmed. Common applications of ML include recommendation systems, fraud detection, and predictive analytics. ML techniques can be classified into supervised learning, unsupervised learning, and reinforcement learning, each serving different purposes and applications [16].

3.3 Deep Learning

Deep Learning is a specialized subfield of machine learning that focuses on neural networks with many layers (deep neural networks). These networks are capable of learning and extracting features from raw data, making them particularly effective for tasks such as image and speech recognition. Deep learning has led to significant advancements in various AI applications, including natural language processing and autonomous vehicles. The deep structure of these networks allows for the automatic discovery of intricate patterns in large datasets, often surpassing traditional machine learning methods in performance [15].

3.4 Computer Vision

Computer Vision is an AI subfield that enables machines to interpret and make decisions based on visual data from the world. It involves the development of algorithms that can process, analyse, and understand images and videos. Applications of computer vision include facial recognition, object detection, and medical image analysis. This technology is fundamental to advancements in autonomous driving and surveillance systems. By enabling machines to see and understand their surroundings, computer vision is transforming various industries and enhancing automation [18].

3.5 Natural Language Processing

Natural Language Processing (NLP) is the branch of AI that deals with the interaction between computers and humans through natural language. It involves the development of algorithms that can understand, interpret, and generate human language. NLP applications include language translation, sentiment analysis, and chatbots. By enabling more natural and efficient communication between humans and machines, NLP is playing a critical role in improving user experiences and accessibility in technology [14].

3.6 Robotics

Robotics is an interdisciplinary field that integrates AI with mechanical engineering to design and construct robots capable of performing tasks autonomously. Robotics involves perception, manipulation, navigation, and planning, enabling robots to interact with their environment and perform complex tasks. Applications of robotics range from industrial automation and healthcare to service robots and exploration. The integration of AI in robotics enhances the capabilities and flexibility of robots, making them more adaptable to diverse and dynamic environments [17].

4. Artificial Intelligence Applications in Education

4.1 Adaptive Learning

Adaptive learning systems leverage artificial intelligence to tailor educational experiences to individual students' needs, preferences, and learning styles. These systems use data analytics to assess each student's strengths and weaknesses, dynamically adjusting the content and pace of instruction to optimize learning outcomes. By continuously analysing students' interactions and performance, adaptive learning platforms provide personalized pathways that enhance engagement and facilitate mastery of subjects at a comfortable pace for each learner. Research highlights the effectiveness of adaptive learning in improving student retention and performance, as these systems offer immediate feedback and adjust to the learner's progress, thereby creating a more personalized and effective educational experience [19, 20].

4.2 Predictive Analytics

Predictive analytics in education involves the use of AI to analyse historical and real-time data to forecast future academic outcomes. This technology enables educators and administrators to identify at-risk students, predict drop-out rates, and intervene proactively to support students' academic success. By examining patterns and trends in student data, predictive analytics can inform decision-making and help institutions allocate resources more effectively. For example, algorithms can predict the likelihood of a student failing a course or highlight areas where additional support may be needed. This proactive approach not only helps in improving individual student performance but also enhances overall institutional effectiveness [16].

4.3 *Personalized Tutoring*

Personalized tutoring systems powered by AI provide individualized support to students, emulating one-on-one tutoring experiences. These systems utilize natural language processing (NLP) and machine learning algorithms to understand and respond to students' queries, offering explanations, feedback, and additional resources tailored to their specific needs. AI-driven tutors can assess students' learning styles and adapt their teaching methods accordingly, making education more accessible and effective. Intelligent tutoring systems (ITS) have shown significant promise in enhancing learning outcomes by providing continuous, personalized guidance and fostering a deeper understanding of the subject matter. Furthermore, these systems help bridge the gap between students and educators, making learning more flexible and scalable [17].

5. Benefits of AI-Driven Educational Tools and Platforms

AI-driven educational tools and platforms offer a multitude of benefits that enhance both teaching and learning experiences. These advantages span personalized learning, increased accessibility, improved efficiency, data-driven insights, and support for lifelong learning.

5.1 *Personalized Learning*

One of the most significant benefits of AI in education is the ability to provide personalized learning experiences. AI systems can analyse individual students' learning patterns and tailor content to meet their specific needs. This personalized approach helps address different learning styles and paces, ensuring that each student can progress at a comfortable rate. Research indicates that personalized learning leads to better engagement and improved academic outcomes as it keeps students motivated and addresses their unique strengths and weaknesses [25, 26].

5.2 *Increased Accessibility*

AI-powered educational tools significantly improve accessibility for students with disabilities. For instance, speech-to-text and text-to-speech technologies assist students with visual or hearing impairments. Additionally, AI can provide translation and language support for non-native speakers, making education more inclusive. By offering diverse learning formats and assistive technologies, AI helps break down barriers to education, ensuring that all students have the opportunity to succeed [21, 23, 20].

5.3 Improved Efficiency

AI can automate various administrative tasks, such as grading, attendance tracking, and scheduling, thereby freeing up valuable time for educators to focus on teaching and interacting with students. Automated grading systems, for example, can quickly and accurately assess student work, providing timely feedback and reducing the workload on teachers. This increased efficiency enhances the educational process and allows teachers to dedicate more time to personalized instruction and student support [28, 22].

5.4 Data-Driven Insights

AI-driven analytics provide educators with deep insights into student performance and learning behaviors. By analyzing data from student interactions, AI can identify trends and patterns that might not be immediately apparent. These insights enable educators to make informed decisions about instructional strategies, curriculum design, and resource allocation. Predictive analytics, for example, can help identify at-risk students and provide early interventions to support their academic success [24].

5.5 Support for Lifelong Learning

AI-powered platforms facilitate continuous learning beyond traditional classroom settings. Online learning environments and AI-driven courses offer flexible, on-demand education that supports lifelong learning and skill development. These platforms can provide personalized recommendations for further learning based on individual progress and interests, helping learners stay current with new developments in their fields. This flexibility and personalization are crucial for fostering a culture of lifelong learning, which is essential in today's rapidly evolving job market [27, 28].

6. Integration of Blockchain and AI in Educational Data Analytics

Blockchain and synthetic intelligence are two incredibly disruptive technologies. By mixing those two, instructional file analysis can be greatly improved. In doing so, the blockchain provides a consistent and immutable way of storing educational data and progress made by the student, ensuring their integrity. AI is warmly accepted for systems that require record processing, pattern recognition, prediction, and formal recognition. In this way, companies can enhance the validity of their learning processes by leveraging blockchain's security and artificial intelligence analytics capabilities, ensuring transparency, trust, and leakage effectively in developing knowledge across international sectors [30].

The merging of blockchain and AI in educational data analytics gives an important head start on the trust security and transparency frontier. Also by encrypting verifying and recurring educational details on the blockchain, e.g., credentials, attendance, and academic performance both technologies can cooperate effectively on this issue. Issues forecasting student outcomes and personalized delivery of education can be achieved by combining these two technological advances. In such a way AI becomes capable of analysing information that is confirmed by blockchain to make individual learning paths based on the strengths and weaknesses of students which in its turn leads to a more effective learning process Perspective [29].

Blockchain and AI together can play a very significant role in this improvement. Because blockchain is reliable and can't be changed, you can be sure that the information you're reading is correct, and AI's ability to do this will finally help you learn new things. This synergy makes the learning process more individualized as students get pedagogical software with recommendations based on their particular needs and progress. Also, it guarantees that the information is trusted by a greater bank of students, educators, and institutions whose participation should never be interfered with [31].

In the educational sector, integration projects displaying the potential to combine blockchain and AI technologies have already been initiated. One such example is MIT's Digital Diploma system which uses blockchain technology to digitally issue and verify academic certificates; by doing that, it decreases the probability of counterfeit certificates in circulation. At the same time, people are using information on student's performance to adapt learning experiences by suggesting courses and materials based on individual progress and preferences. By taking truth and good information from blockchain ledgers via artificial intelligence systems also relevancy of recommendation receives a big boost that results in being more informative at the end of the day [38].

The use of blockchain and AI not only enhances how individual learners learn but also takes care of the integration of how administrative processes can be streamlined in educational institutions. A good example is that blockchain automates the verification process of student records, this reduces the time taken for manual checks and eliminates the errors that can occur during this process. AI can additionally enhance administrative productivity by trend analysis to foresee information flow for certain layouts, improve supply allocation, and identify areas requiring institutional support. Such a holistic approach serves not only students but also increases the efficient Productivity of informative institutions [33].

In addition, blockchain and AI may be the key to guaranteeing a lifelong learning process and development of professionals. The powerful record-keeping capability makes blockchain a good tool to present an overall picture of a learner's achievements over different stages in their pedagogy and vocation. AI can/will analyze this information, to provide personal recommendations on what/which further learning opportunities, career paths, or skill development he/she should consider. Continuous information-based advice helps individuals to progress through the informational as well as master journeys and also make necessary adjustments to work grocery evolution requirements [32].

Both AI and Blockchain merge to create wonders in the field of education with repositories of this kind. Scholars benefit through the data which is verified by blockchain for doing more accurate and legitimate research on the effectiveness of different teaching methods, student behaviour, and learning outcomes. This can be accomplished by AI which tries to identify structures and provide a storyline that could be educational policies or practices based on evidence. Information at institutional as well as policy levels creates access to learning resources that are driven to make more informed decisions and systemwide instructional approaches are improved [36].

On the other hand, blockchain technology being a worldwide platform can help in achieving wiser education through international collaboration. Blockchain technology could be the answer by creating a standardized and secure platform for recording and sharing educational credentials around the globe to overcome this barrier that is related to credential recognition across borders. AI can process this data from around the world to recognize prevailing approach patterns, as well as upcoming requirements in the sphere of education globally. These insights can catalyze the development of more inclusive and effective educational programs that take issue with widely recognized challenges and opportunities [34].

Even though they have a lot of pros, blockchain and AI unions in education data analysis require an accurate treatment of this issue from the ethical and regulatory side. The most important thing is to guarantee privacy and security of information as educational data usually contains personal information about students. Institutions should adhere to laws like the GDPR in the EU or other relevant laws to safeguard students' rights. Moreover, all ethical issues related to AI use such as bias prevention and fairness should be taken into account for trustful relationships and acknowledgment by all interested parties [37].

The intertwining of blockchain and AI in data analytics for educational purposes not only serves to improve operational efficiency and learning or teaching skills but also to build the spirit of open and responsible sharing of information. Blockchain's irremovable ledger gives a clear past of data transactions and updates so that there can be no future disputes about educational records history. This kind of openness is very important for helping to improve confidence between students, teachers, and education managers since by doing this they can be sure that the information is genuine as well as free from malpractices. In addition to that, it is not only those who are outside part of this transparency like employers or accreditation bodies can vouch for the validity of educational credentials and records [35].

Blockchain as well as AI can open doors for better cooperation and knowledge exchange among educational institutions. Blockchain is a secure, decentralized, and transparent platform that paves the way for the exchange of data among institutions. This allows student information, research data, and academic materials to be easily shared among universities. One beneficiary group is students who transfer between schools or pursue multidisciplinary studies that span various institutions. AI then promotes this collaboration through the analysis of the shared data to find areas where challenges and opportunities are evident, therefore catalyzing collaborative solutions and education innovations [39].

The consolidation of these technologies also pushes the advance of interactive learning modules. AI-powered AL systems can exploit blockchain-verified data to observe and continuously assess learner performance and then, if necessary, adapt instruction content and approach in real-time for personalized learning. The individualized way guarantees that the learners get what they need in terms of difficulty level and scaffolding so their involvement and motivation are increased. In addition, Blockchain by facilitating secure data storage makes it possible to avoid disclosure of important information about a person, which includes such information as results of assessments and personal preferences in the learning process, thus ensuring privacy and integrity of the adaptive learning system [42].

Also combining blockchain with AI technology comes with another key advantage which can improve the credentialing system. It is very significant to consider the fact that traditional methods through which academic qualifications are usually provided can consume a lot of time on one side and on the other side they can be manipulated easily. The operation will make it easier for Blockchain to give out digital badges which are both secure, verifiable as well as easily accessible. Furthermore, AI has the ability to scrutinize badge data aiming at coming up with contradictions or missing skills which later on become part of curriculum development as well as staff training programs. The moment their credentials have lost their value or significance they automatically are disconnected from industry needs [38].

Besides this, blockchain and AI could help boost the transparency and efficiency of learning resource financing and resource allocation at the same time. Blockchain's openness ledger can trace the distribution and application of educational funds, ensuring that resources are spent effectively and properly. AI can analyse funding data to find out trends and optimize resource allocation; hence, financial support is directed towards initiatives that demonstrate a great impact on programs. This data-dependent way of financing and resource management helps achieve better outcomes from educational institutions as well as make the most out of their investments [41].

In general, the application of blockchain technology along with AI into education through data analysis provides a wealth of advantages for the educational sector. The security feature provided by blockchain when incorporated with the analytical capability of AIs results in a reliable, transparent, and efficient system of managing educational data so that there is no manipulation or discreditation on such information. This connectivity also gives room for personalized learning experiences alongside high accuracy and trustworthiness since their launch people from all walks of life including many housewives have taken benefit. however, usually more basic training leads to valuable placements or starting businesses. Successful projects like MIT's Digital Diploma initiative and Coursera's AI-driven platform show the combined strength of these technologies can lead to important improvements in educational outcomes and the overall efficiency of educational institutions [40].

7. Case Studies and Examples

Blockchain as well as AI found their place in the educational sector all over the world and are now rapidly spreading. There have been numerous projects that have used these technologies very effectively which resulted in great progress in the learning of students, institutional efficiency, and management of information. In what follows we will present a number of detailed case studies on such initiatives looking at outcomes, implications/impact, good practices as well as lessons learnt [47].

For instance, let's talk about the Massachusetts Institute of Technology (MIT) and its digital Diploma initiative. MIT has jumpstarted the use of blockchain technology to give out digital diplomas to its graduate students ensuring that academic credentials are authentic and secure. The blockchain-based diplomas cannot be tampered with and it's easy for employers or other schools to verify their authenticity. AI is used for analysing data from these diplomas which have helped improve tracking alumni career advancement and outcomes thus giving useful feedback on the effectiveness of the institution's programs [51].

The results of the MIT Digital Diploma initiative show great success. Graduates are now able to share their verified credentials with employers in an easy way so the time and effort for background checks is reduced. As a result, this development has led to employment at better rates and trust in the qualifications being presented. The analysing of alumni data for the institution provides the ability to further its curriculum development and student support/hence it directly affects student learning outcomes [48].

Coursera is one of the newest ventures. It is an online learning tool that uses AI to make learning more personalized for each person. Coursera employs AI algorithms to analyse the performance data of students and suggest appropriate courses and resources that are customized to the individual's needs and progress. The obverse nature further forces some of these personalized approaches to have higher engagement as well as completion rates among learners since their ways of learning closely match their specific strengths and weaknesses [49].

Coursera uses blockchain technology to secure certificates awarded as credentials. The combination of AI and blockchain not only improves quality but also increases the experience of users, while also ensuring more dependable global recognition for certifications obtained by learners. It is great that you get to know that what you earned is trusted globally so they can be more confident in the value Certification they achieved at end of the program [52].

Besides, The University of Nicosia in Cyprus has taken the lead in incorporating blockchain in education. A university issues its digital certificates for courses on a blockchain so that their authenticity is verified. This step has been a major stop to the fabrication of counterfeit academic achievements. Apart from this, AI is used to scan the performance data of students in order to give personalized feedback and support, thus increasing student outcomes and retention rates [50].

The case of the University of Nicosia brings into sharp focus the critical role played by secure and trustable certificates when it comes to preserving the reputation of an institution. The use of blockchain makes it easier for everyone, including employers and other educational institutions/concerns/organizations, to be able to verify various references while machine learning-derived insights have transformed effectively supporting its students at UNIC. That double method developed improved trust in the quality of programs at UNIC as well as better educational results for learners [53].

Blockchain and AI have been merged by the Open University to introduce a new Analytics Framework which is a typical example of it. It can be made clear how blockchain has introduced its learning analytics framework and at the same time how AI appended it for such purposes through an exemplification provided below. Blockchain keeps student data safe and AI analyses this data to help create personalized learning, tailored to individual students' experiences. Consequently, an approach like this has more closely connected learners with the learning process quite well and has improved both academic results and overall performance in general. Additionally, they have also eliminated waste experienced when managing these kinds of resources and/or support systems [54].

As exemplified above more people at the Open University are now satisfied with their learning progress leading to many people returning or completing their courses. The role of AI in creating personalised learning paths that take into account blockchain-secured data analysis so that students get assignments equal to their abilities as well as receive the required assistance. It resulted in the highest achievement levels for learners and streamlined use of institutional resources [56].

One of the instances that demonstrate this is the cooperation between the National University of Singapore (NUS) and IBM. It resulted in a blockchain-based platform for educational credentials which is made possible by this collaboration. On this platform, academic records can be securely issued, shared, and verified. AI tools deployed on this platform help in analysing the data collected to give insights into student performance and institutional effectiveness [57].

The project IBM-NUS has come up with provides better data management as well as institutional efficacy than before. The process of being able to safely share and certify qualifications has sped up day-today operational routines significantly and lessened the amount of work that had to be done manually. The AI-driven analysis has brought about actionable insights that led to strategic decisions that bear on further improvement in quality teaching offered at the NUS system [46].

Another exciting case is the Central New Mexico Community College (CNM). CNM was one of the first educational institutions to implement blockchain technology into their system for the purpose of issuing digital badges regarding skills and competencies students acquired. The use of blockchain guarantees that these badges are verifiable. AI is also applied to monitor and analyse the data concerning those badges, giving a clear picture of skill development and labour market readiness on a student by student basis [55].

One consequence of the implementation at CNM was that it raised/strengthened motivation and engagement among students. The possibility to gain verifiable badges which can be displayed through having certain skills pushed learners towards continuous learning and skill development. These badges are a credible measure an employer uses in assessing a candidate's competence making the recruitment process less complicated and assuring that the right talent is recruited for a specific role [45].

Among the many institutions that have embraced both blockchain and AI, is the Technical University of Munich (TUM). TUM employs blockchain in the issuance and verification of academic certificates to assure their security and authenticity. Further, AI is used to scan student data in order to spot learning patterns and areas for betterment. The combined use of such technology neither supports students nor increases educational standards at this superior level [58].

The use by TUM of these technologies has made data management more efficient and gave the support to students a big boost. As credentials are safely validated, a university's reputation improves, while AI-powered insights inspire curricular revisions and targeted assistance measures. Consequently, over time student outcomes have been improved and greater institutional efficiency has been achieved [44].

These case studies point out a number of best practices and lessons learned. First and foremost, we must have a clear understanding of the learning challenges that blockchain and AI will address in this industry. The organizations that have achieved remarkable success by applying such technologies did not spare any effort to recognize which areas were most important for these instruments. They cited, for example, credential verification, personalized learning, and data management [59].

Secondly, it is essential to take care of the privacy and security of data. Educational institutions should make sure that using blockchain and AI technologies does not violate any laws or ethical norms. This also includes the protection of personal information about students as well as the prevention of biases in AI algorithms. The way how these two technologies are combined into one whole by those who gained success using them is through the implementation of strict mechanisms that ensure information safety and ethical standards [61].

Thirdly, the significance of regular evaluation and modification processes is an issue that should be taken into account. Organizations must be able to perform the task of continuously monitoring how blockchain and AI implementations are doing by getting feedback from stakeholders so as to make necessary adjustments. This cyclic process through feedback collection guarantees that the applications still meet the student's needs and serve the institution's productivity [43].

At this juncture, we mention that working with technology partners increases the effectiveness of implementing these ventures. Institutions that thrived from joining forces with tech companies like IBM, as well as those in blockchain startups, received resources and expertise from their new partners. Such joint efforts can give the required technical support and innovativeness to implement blockchain and AI solutions on a bigger scale peacefully [60].

8. Challenges and Considerations

8.1 Security and Trust

Blockchain and AI solutions introduce new vulnerabilities and security considerations that must be meticulously addressed. AI-driven systems are prone to adversarial attacks, data poisoning, and inherent model biases, which can compromise their reliability and trustworthiness. Blockchain implementations also face potential security threats, such as smart contract exploits and vulnerabilities within consensus algorithms. Ensuring robust security measures and building trust in these technologies is vital for their successful integration into educational data analytics [68].

8.2 Adoption and Standardization

The adoption of blockchain and AI in education faces significant hurdles due to the lack of standardized protocols and frameworks. The absence of universally accepted standards hampers interoperability and seamless integration across diverse educational systems. Developing standardized guidelines and protocols is essential to facilitate widespread adoption and ensure that blockchain and AI technologies can operate cohesively within the educational ecosystem [69].

8.3 Insufficient Knowledge and Stakeholder Engagement

Implementing blockchain and AI without adequate know-how, training, and understanding can lead to wasted investments and a heightened risk of failure for educational institutions. To promote effective implementation, instructional practices should be applied to all involved stakeholders, ensuring they are well-informed about the technologies. Educating and training individuals on the use of blockchain and AI technology is essential for successful integration into the education sector. This involves developing comprehensive training programs and educational materials that educators, students, and other stakeholders can utilize to learn about the technology and its potential applications in education [72].

8.4 Interoperability and Integration

Implementing blockchain and AI solutions presents significant challenges in achieving interoperability and seamless integration with existing infrastructure and systems. Overcoming these challenges necessitates the development of systems and processes that effectively integrate blockchain technology into current frameworks while preserving the integrity and security of educational data. This requires concerted standardization efforts, careful planning, and investment in middleware solutions to ensure compatibility and smooth operation across diverse educational platforms [71].

8.5 Scalability and Performance Optimization

A significant consideration in leveraging blockchain and AI for educational data analytics is the scalability of these technologies to accommodate the exponentially growing volume of educational data without compromising performance or efficiency. For blockchain, addressing scalability challenges requires optimizing consensus mechanisms, employing advanced optimization techniques, and developing innovative architectures capable of supporting the increasing demands of modern education systems. For AI, ensuring scalability involves improving machine learning algorithms, enhancing data processing capabilities, and utilizing distributed computing frameworks to handle large-scale data efficiently. Together, these efforts ensure that both blockchain and AI can effectively manage the expanding data landscape in education [75].

8.6 Resource Limitations and Availability

The integration of blockchain and AI into educational settings encounterlearner-centered substantial obstacles stemming from financial constraints, insufficient technological infrastructure, and shortages in expertise. Regions in development frequently experience deficits in the resources and technical proficiency necessary to establish and sustain sophisticated technological frameworks. Closing this digital gap and enhancing accessibility necessitate cooperative initiatives involving industry collaborators, governmental bodies, and philanthropic entities. These stakeholders can offer crucial education, financial backing, and technical assistance to foster the uptake and assimilation of cutting-edge technologies within educational environments [74].

8.7 Latency and Cost Optimization

Incorporating blockchain and AI into traditional educational systems encounters hurdles due to the high costs associated with implementation, transactions, and computational processes. Managing extensive student data introduces significant redundancy and complexity, leading to elevated computational expenses. To address these challenges effectively, it is essential to analyse various layers of blockchain and AI technologies comprehensively. This includes assessing their economic impacts and meticulously calculating transaction costs to achieve optimal latency and cost-efficiency. Additionally, optimizing AI algorithms and leveraging distributed computing frameworks can enhance data processing capabilities and mitigate computational burdens, thereby further optimizing overall system performance and cost-effectiveness in educational applications [66].

8.8 Ethics, Policy, and Regulatory Compliance

Addressing ethics, policy, and regulation is crucial when integrating blockchain and AI technologies into educational practices. Ethical considerations such as data ownership, transparency, and algorithmic bias must be carefully managed to uphold fairness, accountability, and equity in educational settings. These ethical challenges are compounded by the complex task of complying with regulatory requirements and data protection laws. Regulations like the General Data Protection Regulation (GDPR) impose stringent obligations to ensure data privacy, consent management, and adherence to regulatory frameworks [73].

Educational stakeholders face navigating an intricate legal landscape, necessitating the establishment of robust governance frameworks to mitigate legal risks and ensure compliance with applicable regulations. Blockchain's decentralized nature, which eliminates the need for centralized authority and enhances activity surveillance, presents unique challenges in regulatory compliance. The dispersal of information across a global network makes it challenging to ascertain jurisdictional boundaries, particularly when international regulations govern the sharing of information across borders [67].

To address these complexities, collaboration with academic institutions is essential to understand internal regulations and ensure full compliance with legal requirements. Establishing clear policies and frameworks that align with ethical standards and regulatory guidelines is paramount to fostering trust and reliability in the adoption of blockchain and AI technologies within education.

9. Future Directions and Implications

The integration of blockchain and AI in educational data analytics heralds a new era of personalized learning expanded blockchain applications, and interdisciplinary collaboration. The future holds significant promise for these technologies to reshape the educational landscape, presenting both opportunities and challenges for various stakeholders. This section explores anticipated trends and developments, their potential impacts on education, and recommendations for further research in this evolving field [64].

10. Advancements in Blockchain Applications

Blockchain technology's role in education is expected to grow beyond credential verification to include a diverse array of applications such as academic record management, e-learning platforms, and digital asset management. The development of interoperability standards and cross-platform integration will enable seamless data exchange across various blockchain networks, enhancing transparency, efficiency, and trust within educational systems.

Future research could explore the potential of blockchain technology to improve educational access and equity, enhance student engagement and collaboration, and support the use of open educational resources. Investigating these areas will be crucial in understanding the full potential of blockchain to create a more inclusive and efficient educational environment [63].

11. Interdisciplinary Collaboration and Ethical Considerations

Future research must prioritize ethical considerations, transparency, and inclusivity to ensure the responsible and equitable deployment of emerging technologies in educational contexts. Proactive engagement with regulatory frameworks and adherence to international standards is essential for fostering trust, interoperability, and compliance in the global educational ecosystem.

Creating a trusted and secure environment for teaching, learning, and collaboration in the digital age requires interdisciplinary collaboration. This collaboration should focus on establishing comprehensive governance frameworks that address the legal, ethical, and societal implications of deploying AI and blockchain in education. By doing so, we can navigate the complexities of these technologies and harness their full potential to transform education [65].

12. AI-Driven Personalized Learning Experiences

Artificial intelligence algorithms are revolutionizing personalized learning by enabling adaptive learning technologies that can dynamically tailor instructional content, pacing, and assessment methods based on real-time student performance data. These AI-driven systems allow educators to gain profound insights into students' learning behaviors, preferences, and challenges, facilitating targeted interventions and personalized support to enhance educational outcomes while safeguarding sensitive information [70].

Moreover, machine learning, in conjunction with blockchain data analysis, has the potential to significantly improve personalized education. By analyzing students' browsing behaviors and interests through blockchain, educators can offer tailored learning materials suited to individual needs, thereby optimizing learning efficiency and increasing student engagement and motivation.

Exploring the future directions of blockchain and AI in educational data analytics is crucial for understanding their long-term implications. For educational stakeholders, including students, educators, administrators, and policymakers, these technologies offer transformative possibilities that can enhance educational outcomes and operational efficiencies. Future research should focus on refining these technologies, addressing ethical and regulatory challenges, and fostering interdisciplinary collaboration to ensure their effective and equitable implementation in education [62].

13. Conclusion

To sum up, the merger of blockchain and AI to do educational data analytics is a great invention for the school system that moves forward. We have gone through how these technologies sweat individually and in harmony, and advance data integrity, personalized learning, and efficiency in institutions as well as overall educational outcomes during the entire chapter [78].

The case studies and examples provided support for said main points. MIT and the University of Nicosia showed one of the important merits of blockchain/AI integrated education: blockchain's application to secure management and verification of academic certificates with authenticity thus reducing fraudulent cases. At the same time, platforms driven by AI such as Coursera have demonstrated how to use AI for analyzing student data so that they can be provided with personal learning paths which eventually result in better engagement and completion rates [81].

The introduction of these technologies has indeed made the processes more efficient however it was not just that but also a rich source of transparency and accountability. The decentralized ledger of blockchain represents trustworthiness through data integrity and an AI's analytical capacity is a way to get usage-ready insights for stakeholders that help to direct strategic decisions as well as improve educational practices [79].

One can determine without much ado that crop education will be done in an innovative environment with technology at its core. Blockchain and AI are used together to make it possible for institutions to create systems that are much faster, transparent, learner centered. This technology devolves learning institutions with tools to, more than ever before, rapidly respond to emerging learners' needs and changes in the world [80].

While we advance, educational leaders and policymakers have a moral responsibility to move with this technology which requires their full support. Such support can be in the form of investment in research, promotion of collaborative practices with technology partners, and creation of acceptable frameworks for ethical use. By combining blockchain and AI, it is possible for institutions to realize the maximum benefit of these innovations. This proactive approach, indeed, ensures not just that the quality of education continues to improve but also that students get ready to live in the era of digital technologies marked by fast technical progress [77].

Finally, the implementation of blockchain and AI into educational data analysises is not merely for technological advancement but a new way of teaching learning and institutional management systems as well. It is mandatory that such innovative tricks should be invented by educational institutions so that they can change and transform themselves and hence each learner will get a personalized, high-quality education that builds them up for succeeding both in the present century as well as after [76].

References

[1] Chen, G., Xu, B., Lu, M. and Chen, N.S. (2018). Exploring blockchain technology and its potential applications for education. *Smart Learning Environments*, 5(1): 1–10.

[2] Grech, A. and Camilleri, A.F. (2017). Blockchain in education. *Luxembourg: Publications Office of the European Union*.

[3] Holmes, W., Bialik, M. and Fadel, C. (2019). Artificial intelligence in education: Promises and implications for teaching and learning. *Boston: Center for Curriculum Redesign*.

[4] Luckin, R., Holmes, W., Griffiths, M. and Forcier, L.B. (2016). Intelligence unleashed: An argument for AI in education. *London: Pearson*.

[5] Siemens, G. and Long, P. (2011). Penetrating the fog: Analytics in learning and education. *EDUCAUSE Review*, 46(5): 31–40.

[6] Tapscott, D. and Tapscott, A. (2016). Blockchain revolution: How the technology behind bitcoin is changing money, business, and the world. *New York: Penguin Random House*.

[7] Blockchain in education: Opportunities, applications, and challenges by Mara-Florina Steiu, DOI: https://doi.org/10.5210/fm.v25i9.10654.

[8] Chakraborty, M., Jana, B., Mandal, T. and Kule, M. (2018). An performance analysis of RSA scheme using artificial neural network. *2018 9th International Conference on Computing, Communication and Networking Technologies (ICCCNT)*, Bengaluru, 2018, doi: 10.1109/ICCCNT.2018.8494032.

[9] George, C. (2017). Bitcoin—A brief analysis of the advantages and disadvantages. Available: http://www.globeco.ro/wpcontent/uploads/vol/split/vol_5_no_2/geo_2017_vol5_ no2_art_008.pdf.

[10] Atul, K. and Arpit, G. (2017). Blockchain: An analysis on next-generation internet. Available: http://dx.doi.org/10.26483/ijarcs.v8i8.4769.

[11] Alhadhrami, Z., Alghfeli, S. and Alghfeli, M. (2017). Introducing blockchains for healthcare. *International Conference on Electrical and Computing Technologies and Applications (ICECTA)*.

[12] Belsis, P. and Pantziou, G. (2014). A k-anonymity privacy preserving approach in wireless medical monitoring environments. *Journal Personal and Ubiquitous Computing*, 18(1): 61–74.

[13] Alammary, A., Alhazmi, S., Almasri, M. and Gillani, S. (2019). Blockchain-based applications in education: A systematic review. *Applied Sciences*, 9(12): 2400.

[14] Jurafsky, D. and Martin, J. (2008). Speech and Language Processing: An Introduction to Natural Language Processing, Computational Linguistics, and Speech Recognition.

[15] Yann, L., Bengio, Y. and Hinton, G. (2015). Deep learning. *Nature*, 521: 436–44. 10.1038/nature14539.

[16] Mitchell, T.M. (1997). *Machine Learning*. McGraw-Hill.

[17] Sabharwal, A., Selman, B., Russell, S. and Norvig, P. (2011). Artificial intelligence: A modern approach, Third Edition. *Artif. Intell.*, 175: 935–937. 10.1016/j.artint.2011.01.005.

[18] Siciliano, B. and Khatib, O. (eds.). (2016). *Springer Handbook of Robotics*. Springer.

[19] Acevedo-Duque, Ángel & Jiménez-Bucarey, Carmen & Prado, Tohtli & Fernández-Mantilla, Mirtha Mercedes & Merino-Flores, Irene, Izquierdo-Marín, Sandra, Valle-Palomino, Nicolás. (2023). Education for sustainable development: challenges for postgraduate programmes. *International Journal of Environmental Research and Public Health*, 20: 1759. 10.3390/ijerph20031759.

[20] Zawacki-Richter, Olaf & Marín, Victoria & Bond, Melissa & Gouverneur, Franziska. (2019). Systematic review of research on artificial intelligence applications in higher education-where are the educators?. *International Journal of Educational Technology in Higher Education*, 16: 1–27. 10.1186/s41239-019-0171-0.

[21] Kabudi, T., Pappas, I. and Olsen, D. (2021). AI-enabled adaptive learning systems: A systematic mapping of the literature. *Computers and Education: Artificial Intelligence*, 2: 100017. 10.1016/j.caeai.2021.100017.

[22] Arici, F., Yildirim, P., Caliklar, S. and Yilmaz, R.M. (2019). Research trends in the use of augmented reality in science education: Content and bibliometric mapping analysis. *Computers & Education*, 142: 103647.

[23] Granić, A. and Mifsud, C. (2019). *Supporting Inclusive Education through AI-based Technology*. Springer Open.

[24] Luckin, R., Holmes, W., Griffiths, M. and Forcier, L.B. (2016). Intelligence unleashed: An argument for AI in education. *Pearson*.

[25] Popenici, S.A.D. and Kerr, S. (2017). Exploring the impact of artificial intelligence on teaching and learning in higher education. *Research and Practice in Technology Enhanced Learning*.

[26] Sampson, D.G., Ifenthaler, D., Spector, J.M. and Isaias, P. (eds.). (2021). *Digital Transformation and Innovation in Chinese Education*. Springer.

[27] Lin, C.-C., Huang, A. and Lu, O. (2023). Artificial intelligence in intelligent tutoring systems toward sustainable education: A systematic review. *Smart Learning Environments*, 10. 10.1186/s40561-023-00260-y.

[28] Wang, T., Lund, B.D., Marengo, A., Pagano, A., Mannuru, N.R., Teel, Z.A. and Pange, J. (2023). Exploring the potential impact of Artificial Intelligence (AI) on international students in higher education: Generative AI, chatbots, analytics, and international student success. *Appl. Sci.*, 13: 6716. https://doi.org/10.3390/app13116716.

[29] Bhaskar, P., Tiwari, C.K. and Joshi, A. (2020). Blockchain in education management: Present and future applications. *Interactive Technology and Smart Education*.

[30] Awaji, B., Solaiman, E. and Albshri, A. 2020. Blockchain-based applications in higher education: A systematic mapping study. In *Proceedings of the 5th International Conference on Information and Education Innovations*, pp. 96–104.

[31] Aria, M. and Cuccurullo, C. (2017). Bibliometrix: An r-tool for comprehensive science mapping analysis. *Journal of Informetrics*, 11(4): 959–975.

[32] Tandon, A., Kaur, P., Mäntymäki, M. and Dhir, A. (2021). Blockchain applications in management: A bibliometric analysis and literature review. *Technological Forecasting and Social Change*, 166: 120649.

[33] Arici, F., Yildirim, P., Caliklar, S. and Yilmaz, R.M. (2019). Research trends in the use of augmented reality in science education: Content and bibliometric mapping analysis. *Computers & Education*, 142: 103647.

[34] Dabbagh, M., Sookhak, M. and Safa, N.S. (2019). The evolution of blockchain: A bibliometric study. *IEEE Access*, 7: 19212–19221.

[35] Nasir, A., Shaukat, K., Khan, K.I., Hameed, I.A., Alam, T.M. and Luo, S. (2021). What is core and what future holds for blockchain technologies and cryptocurrencies: A bibliometric analysis. *IEEE Access*, 9: 989–1004.

[36] Lizano-Mora, H., Palos-Sánchez, P.R. and Aguayo-Camacho, M. (2021). The evolution of business process management: A bibliometric analysis. *IEEE Access*, 9: 51088–51105.

[37] Guan, G., Jiang, Z., Gong, Y., Huang, Z. and Jamalnia, A. (2020). A bibliometric review of two decades' research on closed-loop supply chain: 2001–2020. *IEEE Access*, 9: 3679–3695.

[38] Aria, M. and Cuccurullo, C. (2017). bibliometrix: An r-tool for comprehensive science mapping analysis. *Journal of Informetrics*, 11(4): 959–975.

[39] Van Eck, N. and Waltman, L. (2010). Software survey: Vosviewer, a computer program for bibliometric mapping. *Scientometrics*, 84(2): 523–538.

[40] Buenaño-Fernandez, D., González, M., Gil, D. and Luján-Mora, S. (2020). Text mining of open-ended questions in self-assessment of university teachers: An lda topic modeling approach. *IEEE Access*, 8: 35318–35330.

[41] Nanda, G., Douglas, K.A., Waller, D.R., Merzdorf, H.E. and Goldwasser, D. (2021). Analyzing large collections of open-ended feedback from mooc learners using lda topic modeling and qualitative analysis. *IEEE Transactions on Learning Technologies*, 14(2): 146–160.

[42] Röder, M., Both, A. and Hinneburg, A. (2015). Exploring the space of topic coherence measures. In *Proceedings of the Eighth ACM International Conference on Web Search and Data Mining*, pp. 399–408.

[43] Martins, V., Oyelere, S.S., Tomczyk, L., Barros, G., Akyar, O., Eliseo, M.A., Amato, C. and Silveira, I.F. (2019). A blockchain microsites-based ecosystem for learning and inclusion. In *Brazilian Symposium on Computers in Education (Simpósio Brasileiro de Informática na Educação-SBIE)*, 30(1): 229.

[44] Oyelere, S.S., Qushem, U.B., Jauregui, V.C., Akyar, Ö.Y., Tomczyk, Ł., Sanchez, G., Munoz, D. and Motz, R. (2020). Blockchain technology to support smart learning and inclusion: pre-service teachers and software developers viewpoints. In *World Conference on Information Systems and Technologies*. Springer, pp. 357–366.

[45] Ocheja, P., Flanagan, B., Ogata, H. and Oyelere, S.S. (2022). Visualization of education blockchain data: Trends and challenges. *Interactive Learning Environments*, pp. 1–25.

[46] Tomczyk, Ł., Martins, V.F., Eliseo, M.A., Silveira, I.F., Cibelle, A., Stošic, L. and Oyelere, S.S. (2020). How does the attitude to new media influence the evaluation of a new e-learning platform among current and future teachers?. In *2020 XV Conferencia Latinoamericana de Tecnologias de Aprendizaje (LACLO)*. IEEE, pp. 1–8.

[47] Ocheja, P., Flanagan, B. and Ogata, H. (2019). Decentralized e-learning marketplace: Managing authorship and tracking access to learning materials using blockchain. In *International Cognitive Cities Conference*. Springer, pp. 526–535.

[48] Ocheja, P., Flanagan, B., Oyelere, S.S., Lecailliez, L. and Ogata, H. (2020). A prototype framework for a distributed lifelong learner model. In *28th International Conference on Computers in Education Conference Proceedings, vol. 1. Asia-Pacific Society for Computers in Education (APSCE)*, pp. 261–266.

[49] Eliseo, M.A., Oyelere, S.S., da Silva, C.A., Silveira, I.F., Tomczyk, Ł., Hercovici, M., Cibelle, A., Akyar and Martins, V.F. (2020). Framework to creation of inclusive and didactic digital material for elderly. In *2020 15th Iberian Conference on Information Systems and Technologies (CISTI)*. IEEE, pp. 1–6.

[50] Oyelere, S.S., Tomczyk, L., Bouali, N. and Agbo, F.J. (2019). Blockchain technology and gamification-conditions and opportunities for education. *Adult Education 2018-Transformation in the Era of Digitization and Artificial Intelligence*.

[51] Akyar, Ö.Y., Demirhan, G., Oyelere, S.S., Flores, M. and Jauregui, V.C. (2020). Digital storytelling in teacher education for inclusion. In *World Conference on Information Systems and Technologies*. Springer, pp. 367–376.

[52] Han, M., Li, Z., He, J., Wu, D., Xie, Y. and Baba, A. (2018). A novel blockchain-based education records verification solution. In *Proceedings of the 19th Annual SIG Conference on Information Technology Education*, pp. 178–183.

[53] Brunner, C., Knirsch, F. and Engel, D. (2019). Sproof: A platform for issuing and verifying documents in a public blockchain. In *ICISSP*, pp. 15–25.

[54] Ceke, C. and Kunosic, S. (2020). Smart contracts as a diploma anti-forgery system in higher education-a pilot project. In *2020 43rd International Convention on Information, Communication and Electronic Technology (MIPRO)*. IEEE, pp. 1662–1667.

[55] Liu, D. and Guo, X. (2019). Blockchain based storage and verification scheme of credible degree certificate. In *2019 2nd International Conference on Safety Produce Informatization (IICSPI)*, pp. 350–352.

[56] Alnafrah, I. and Mouselli, S. (2021). Revitalizing blockchain technology potentials for smooth academic records management and verification in lowincome countries. *International Journal of Educational Development*, 85: 102460.

[57] Shah, D., Patel, D., Adesara, J., Hingu, P. and Shah, M. (2021). Exploiting the capabilities of blockchain and machine learning in education. *Augmented Human Research*, 6(1): 1–14.
[58] Bozkurt, A. and Ucar, H. (2021). Blockchain technology as a bridging infrastructure among formal, non-formal, and informal learning processes. In *Research Anthology on Adult Education and the Development of Lifelong Learners*. IGI Global, pp. 959–970.
[59] Richard, S. (2010). *Computer Vision: Algorithms and Applications* (1st. ed.). Springer-Verlag, Berlin, Heidelberg.
[60] Solomos, D., Tsianos, N., Ghodous, P. and Riel, A. (2021). The european chaise initiative to shape the future of blockchain skill qualification and certification. In *European Conference on Software Process Improvement*. Springer, pp. 640–650.
[61] Mingxiao, D., Xiaofeng, M., Zhe, Z., Xiangwei, W. and Qijun, C. (2017). A review on consensus algorithm of blockchain. In *2017 IEEE international conference on systems, man, and cybernetics (SMC)*. IEEE, pp. 2567–2572.
[62] https://www.sciencedirect.com/science/article/pii/S2096720923000404#sec3—Unlocking the power of blockchain in education: An overview of innovations and outcomes.
[63] https://firstmonday.org/ojs/index.php/fm/article/view/10654/9726—The challenges of applying blockchain in the education sector.
[64] https://vtrader.io/news/uncategorized/blockchain-and-ai-in-education-empowering-the next-generation-of-learners/—Challenges and Considerations-AI and blockchain; https://www.researchgate.net/publication/380570990_Educational_Security_Evolution_Blockchain_AI_and_Quantum_Cryptography_Solutions—Educational Security Evolution: Blockchain, AI, and Quantum Cryptography Solutions.
[65] https://link.springer.com/article/10.1007/s10639-022-11399-5—Blockchain in smart education: Contributors, collaborations, applications and research topics.
[66] https://www.researchgate.net/publication/380571131_Securing_Educational_Data_AI_Bloc kchain_and_Quantum_Cryptography_for_Trust—Securing Educational Data: AI, Blockchain, and Quantum Cryptography for Trust.
[67] https://www.researchgate.net/publication/380570898_Building_Trust_in_Education_AI_Blo ckchain_and_Quantum_Cryptography_Integration—Building Trust in Education: AI, Blockchain, and Quantum Cryptography Integration.
[68] Peters, G.W. and Panayi, E. (2016). Understanding modern banking ledgers through blockchain technologies: Future of transaction processing and smart contracts on the internet of money. *In*: Tasca, P., Aste, T., Pelizzon, L. and Perony, N. (eds.). *Banking Beyond Banks and Money. New Economic Windows*. Springer, Cham. https://doi.org/10.1007/978-3-319-42448-4_13.
[69] Peters, G.W., Panayi, E. and Chapelle, A. (2015). Trends in crypto-currencies and blockchain technologies: A monetary theory and regulation perspective, http://dx. doi.org/10.2139/ssrn.2646618.
[70] Pilkington, M. (2016). Does the FinTech Industry Need a New Risk Management Philosophy? A Sequential Blockchain-based Typology for Virtual Currencies and e-Money Services in Luxembourg (March 8, 2016). Available at SSRN: https://ssrn.com/abstract=2744899 or http://dx.doi.org/10.2139/ssrn.2744899.
[71] Ruffing, T., Moreno-Sanchez, P. and Kate, A. (2014). Coinshuffle: Practical decentralized coin mixing for bitcoin. In *Proceedings of European Symposium on Research in Computer Security*. Cham, pp. 345–364.
[72] Sapirshtein, A., Sompolinsky, Y. and Zohar, A. (2015). Optimal selfish mining strategies in bitcoin. *arXiv preprint arXiv:1507.06183*.
[73] Sasson, E.B., Chiesa, A., Garman, C., Green, M., Miers, I., Tromer, E., Virza, M. (2014). Zerocash: Decentralized anonymous payments from bitcoin. In: *Proceedings of 2014 IEEE Symposium on Security and Privacy (SP)*, San Jose, CA, USA, pp. 459–474.
[74] Schwartz, D., Youngs, N. and Britto, A. (2014). The ripple protocol consensus algorithm. *Ripple Labs Inc. White Paper 5.*

[75] Sharples, M. and Domingue, J. (2015). The blockchain and kudos: A distributed system for educational record, reputation and reward. In: *Proceedings of 11th European Conference on Technology Enhanced Learning (EC-TEL 2015)*, Lyon, France, pp. 490–496.
[76] Solat, S. and Potop-Butucaru, M. (2016). ZeroBlock: Timestamp-free prevention of blockwithholding attack in bitcoin. *Technical Report, Sorbonne Universites, UPMC University of Paris*, 6, https://hal.archives-ouvertes.fr/ hal-01310088.
[77] Sompolinsky, Y. and Zohar, A. (2013). Accelerating bitcoin's transaction processing, fast money grows on trees, not chains. *IACR Cryptology ePrint Archive*, 2013(881).
[78] Szabo, N. (1997). The idea of smart contracts.
[79] Tschorsch, F. and Scheuermann, B. (2016). Bitcoin and beyond: A technical survey on decentralized digital currencies. *IEEE Communications Surveys Tutorials*, 18(3): 2084–2123.
[80] Vagata, P. and Wilfong, K. (2014). Scaling the Facebook data warehouse to 300 PB. Tech. rep., https://code.facebook.com/posts/229861827208629/ scaling-the-facebook-data-warehouse-to-300-pb/.
[81] Zheng, Z., Xie, S., Dai, H., Chen, X. and Wang, H. An overview of blockchain technology: Architecture, consensus, and future trends. *In: 2017 IEEE International Congress on Big Data (BigData Congress)*, Honolulu, HI, USA, 2017, pp. 557–564, doi: 10.1109/BigDataCongress.2017.85.

Chapter 10

Exploring the Awareness of Artificial Intelligence in Sustainable Higher Education

Subhra Shankha Chakraborty[1,*] and *Subhankar Ghosh*[2]

In the dynamic intersection of academia and technological innovation, the emergence of Artificial Intelligence (AI) presents a profound opportunity for transformative growth, particularly within higher education's pursuit of sustainability. This chapter explores the integration of AI in higher education at The University of Burdwan, focusing on its potential to promote sustainability. The study investigates postgraduate students' awareness and perception of AI, highlighting the opportunities and challenges of AI adoption. The research methodology includes empirical investigation (including Z-tests and ANOVA) and theoretical frameworks, uncovering nuanced variations in awareness levels across demographics, disciplines, and backgrounds. While the study identified significant differences in awareness levels based on certain factors, such as rural/urban backgrounds, there was no significant difference between male and female students' awareness levels. The

[1] Research Scholar (UGC-JRF), Centre for Education & Technology for Education, Indian Institute of Technology Jodhpur, Rajasthan-342030, India.

[2] Assistant Professor, Department of Education, The University of Burdwan, Golapbag, Purba Bardhaman-713104, West Bengal, India.

Email: sghosh@edu.buruniv.ac.in

* Corresponding author: e.subhrahere@gmail.com

https://orcid.org/0000-0002-5289-4144; https://orcid.org/0009-0004-6230-850X

study suggests strategies for fostering AI literacy, interdisciplinary collaboration, and ethical AI integration in education. It also outlines recommendations for future research, including longitudinal studies, comparative analyses, and investigations into AI's role in lifelong learning and social change. The chapter aspires to provide a comprehensive understanding of AI's pivotal role in shaping the future of sustainable higher education.

1. Introduction

In an epoch brimming with unprecedented possibilities, where the realms of academia intersect with the transformative power of technological innovation, a symphony of infinite potential unfolds—an overture where human ingenuity meets the ethereal symmetries of Artificial Intelligence (AI). This convergence, where the boundaries of learning are redrawn by the elegant strokes of AI's algorithms, heralds a captivating frontier—an uncharted terrain of enlightenment and evolution. In this resonating interplay, higher education becomes a canvas upon which the dynamic brushstrokes of AI paint intricate tapestries of knowledge, where the mind's journey becomes a continuum of exploration into the very heart of sustainable transformation. In the symphony of existence, where the crescendo of human endeavour harmonizes with the cadence of technological marvels, the confluence of Artificial Intelligence (AI) and higher education emerges as a virtuoso composition—a composition that resounds with the notes of innovation, foresight, and sustainable evolution. The path illuminated by AI's brilliance stretches beyond horizons, inviting us to stride forth with wisdom and purpose. It is a path where academia is not an isolated entity but an integral part of the ecosystem, where sustainable enlightenment is not a distant dream but an imminent reality. This expedition of exploration, inquiry, and revelation culminates not in an ending, but in a new beginning—a beginning where the harmonious interplay of AI and higher education becomes the anthem of progress, where the corridors of The University of Burdwan and beyond reverberate with the echoes of transformative growth, sustainability, and the resplendent promise of AI's boundless potential.

Thus, this chapter is a journey towards unravelling intricacies woven at the crossroads of AI and higher education, a journey that captures the ephemeral essence of growth, transformation, and the eternal pursuit of enlightenment. It is a chronicle of boundless potential, a reminder that AI, when harnessed in symbiosis with the ethos of sustainable wisdom, has the power to illuminate the corridors not only of The University of Burdwan but also of the global educational landscape, fostering a harmonious convergence of knowledge, sustainability, and the promise of AI's radiant possibilities. Through this extraordinary odyssey, the path to a harmonious future is lit—a path where AI's brilliance casts its luminance upon the tapestries of sustainable enlightenment, leading humanity towards a future where innovation and wisdom stride hand in hand.

2. Rationale of the Study

In the kaleidoscope of contemporary academia, the confluence of Artificial Intelligence (AI) and higher education has emerged as an enthralling arena of inquiry. As society grapples with the imperatives of sustainability, there is an urgent need to investigate the application and awareness of AI in higher education as a potent catalyst for fostering sustainable practices. Against this backdrop, this chapter sets forth on an intrepid intellectual odyssey, delving into the rich tapestry of AI's integration within the realm of postgraduate education at The University of Burdwan. The intricate interplay between AI and higher education presents a paradigm-shifting opportunity to augment pedagogical approaches, enhance learning outcomes, and cultivate a holistic understanding of sustainability among postgraduate students. The selection of The University of Burdwan as the focal point of this study stems from its unique position as a hub of intellectual excellence and its commitment to fostering sustainable practices. The postgraduate students within this esteemed institution possess a diverse range of academic interests and aspirations, making them an ideal cohort to gauge the awareness and perception of AI's role in promoting sustainability within higher education. Through their perspectives, we hope to gain valuable insights into the current state of AI integration, identify challenges, and unveil novel opportunities for leveraging AI towards sustainable education. By exploring the application and awareness of AI within the context of postgraduate education at The University of Burdwan, we strive to ignite a flame of enlightenment, igniting a profound shift in educational paradigms and fostering a harmonious coexistence between knowledge acquisition and sustainable practices.

3. Significance of the Study

In the vast expanse of human knowledge, where the horizons of innovation and enlightenment meet, there arises an imperious need—a need that echoes with the resonance of transformation, a need that has stirred the foundations of education and beckoned us to the precipice of a new epoch. It is a need that transcends the realms of mere curiosity and extends its hand into the very heart of human sustenance. In the mosaic of contemporary education, where the brushstrokes of technological advancement paint intricate patterns upon the canvas of academia, the need to explore the awareness of Artificial Intelligence (AI) within the sanctums of higher learning stands as a clarion call. It is a call born from the realization that our world, our environment, and our very existence are imperilled by the weight of unsustainable practices. As the sun of human ingenuity rises higher, it casts a long shadow of environmental degradation, resource depletion, and ecological imbalance. Yet, amidst this chiaroscuro, a glimmer of hope emerges—the hope that AI, that brilliant offspring of human innovation, can become a steward of sustainability. The University of Burdwan, a citadel of learning, assumes a role of eminence in this study. It is not merely the locale of investigation; it is the crucible where the alchemy of sustainable enlightenment is being forged. The postgraduate student who traverses its corridors and traverses the landscapes of their intellectual journeys holds within them the seeds of change—seeds that, when nurtured by awareness and understanding, can sprout into a forest of sustainable practices. The significance lies in the potential transformation, in the tapestry of tomorrow woven by the hands of these scholars, in the promise of a brighter, more harmonious coexistence between humanity and its habitat.

4. Operational Definition of Related Terms

- Application: In the context of this study, "application" refers to the practical implementation and use of Artificial Intelligence (AI) technologies and tools in the higher education environment.
- Awareness: "Awareness" refers to the level of knowledge, understanding, and familiarity that PG (Postgraduate) students at The University of Burdwan possess regarding the concepts, capabilities, and potential applications of AI in the context of higher education and sustainability.
- AI: "AI" stands for Artificial Intelligence, which refers to the simulation of human intelligence in machines that are capable of performing tasks and making decisions that would typically require human intelligence.
- Higher Education: "Higher education" encompasses tertiary education institutions such as universities and colleges that offer advanced academic programs beyond the secondary school level, including undergraduate and postgraduate degrees.
- Sustainability: "Sustainability" refers to the concept of meeting present needs without compromising the ability of future generations to meet

their own needs. This study specifically relates to the integration of AI in higher education to promote sustainable practices, strategies, and outcomes.

Delimitation

1. The research work has been confined to one university in West Bengal, named The University of Burdwan.
2. The sample includes the postgraduate students who studied through the regular system at The University of Burdwan.

Review of Related Literature

Brown, L. and Wilson, J. (2018) show the integration of artificial intelligence (AI) in higher education for sustainable development. Yousaf, T.H., Ibrahim, S.M. and Al-Dubai, A.Y. (2020) explore the potential for integrating AI and sustainable development in higher education. This study suggested a framework for integrating AI and sustainability education including the development of courses and programs that address the intersection of AI and sustainability, the establishment of interdisciplinary research teams, and the promotion of industry partnerships. The paper highlights the importance of integrating AI and sustainable development in higher education to prepare students for the challenges and opportunities of the future. Correia, N. and Hill, D.M. (2020) examine the potential of AI in supporting sustainability education in higher education. The authors suggest that AI can be used to enhance student engagement, provide personalized learning experiences, and support data-driven decision-making for sustainability initiatives. Arokiamary, A.R. and Uma, G.V. (2021) examines the opportunities and challenges of using AI in higher education. The authors argue that AI can support personalized learning, improve student outcomes, and reduce costs. Ogwueleka, F.C. and Nwosu, M.J. (2021) found that AI can enhance education quality and efficiency, research capabilities, and sustainability. Skulimowski, A. and Mazzucchelli, P.L. (2020) identified potential benefits and challenges of AI integration in sustainability education, such as the ability to facilitate personalized learning and the need for ethical considerations. Sun, L., Yang, M. and Zhang, X. (2021) explore the opportunities and challenges of using AI-enabled education for sustainability. Ntloedibe-Kuswani, C. K. (2021) shows a valuable resource for understanding the current state of adoption and implementation of AI in higher education in their study. Zhang, X. and Yang, M. (2021) found that AI can be a valuable tool in promoting sustainability in education.

Objectives of the Study

1. To explain the role of AI in achieving sustainable higher education.
2. To study the awareness towards AI applications for learning based on academic discipline.
3. To study the awareness towards AI applications for learning based on locality.
4. To study the awareness towards AI applications for learning based on Gender.

Research Questions

RQ1: How Artificial Intelligence can help in achieving sustainable higher education?

Hypotheses

H01: There is no significant difference in awareness towards AI applications between Arts, Science, and Social Science students regarding AI applications for learning.

H02: There is no significant difference in awareness towards AI applications between rural and urban students regarding AI applications for learning.

H03: There is no significant difference in awareness towards AI applications between male and female students regarding AI applications for learning.

5. Methodology

5.1 Area of Study

A visual representation of the distribution of departments within The University of Burdwan is presented herewith, elucidating their relative positions within the educational tapestry. This map not only situates the study within its academic context but also provides a visual narrative of the institutional backdrop against which the research unfolds. As such, this spatial depiction assumes significance as both a geographical illustration and a symbolic representation of the academic landscape traversed within the study.

Population and Sample

- **Population:**

  This study was conducted at the University of Burdwan in the Purba Bardhaman District of West Bengal. The population of this study

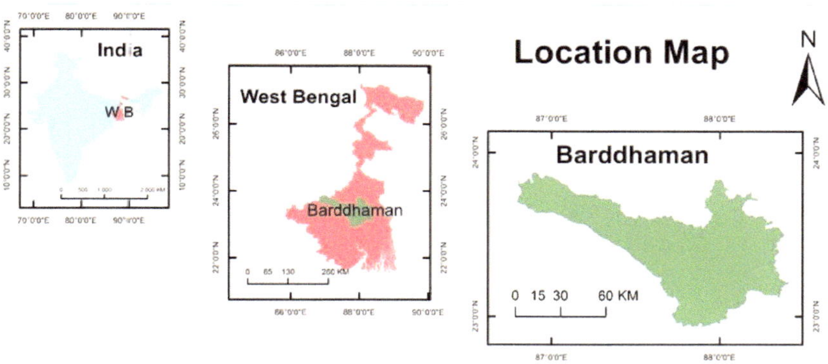

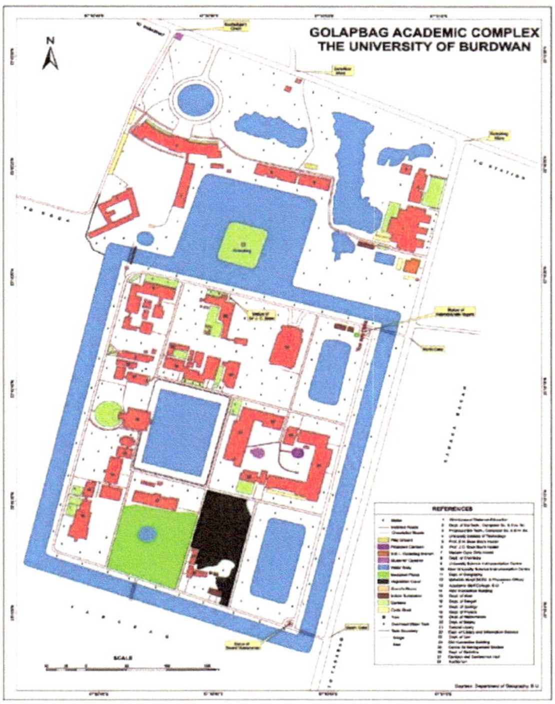

includes P.G. students of all academic disciplines at the University of Burdwan.

- **Sample size:**

  The study covered sixteen departments of The University of Burdwan. The researcher followed a purposive sampling method for conducting the present study. While selecting the departments for the study, the researcher selected Science departments as well as Arts departments at The University of Burdwan. The details of the distribution of the sample are given below:

Distribution of the Sample

Sl. No.	Name of the Departments	No. of Male Students	No. of Female Students
1.	Bengali	4	16
2.	Education	3	7
3.	English and Culture Studies	3	12
4.	Geography	2	9
5.	Library and Information Science	5	4
6.	Philosophy	5	5
7.	Sociology	3	2
8.	Mass Communication	3	4
9.	Computer Science	3	8
10.	Mathematics	6	20
11.	Environmental Science	2	13
12.	Bio-Technology	5	2
13.	Electronics & Communication	3	4
14.	Microbiology	2	3
15.	Statistics	2	7
16.	Chemistry	5	8
	Total sample	56	124

Variables:

Major Variables:

- ➢ Awareness of AI application

Demographic Variables:

- ➢ Gender (Male and Female)
- ➢ Locale (Rural and Urban
- ➢ Academic Discipline (Science, Social Science, and Language)

Tools Used:

The tool which has been used for data collection in this study was-

1. **Awareness of AI Application Questionnaire (AAIAQ)**—have been prepared and validated by the researchers. This questionnaire consisted of 25 items. Each item of the tool includes three options, i.e., Yes (Agree), No (Disagree), Maybe (Neutral). Content Validity has been checked. Raw scores on the test can range from 25 to 75.

Sl. No.	Items	Sl. No.	Items
1.	I have heard the term "Artificial Intelligence".	14.	I use White Noise & Relaxing Music to increase concentration and focus in my study.
2.	I can provide examples of AI that are used in education.	15.	I use various entertainment streaming apps like Netflix, Spotify, etc., in my daily life.
3.	I am familiar with terms like Siri, Alexa, Google Assistant, etc.	16.	I am aware that if & when I play any game, I am using AI.
4.	I can use Alexa to play audiobooks & convert speech to text.	17.	I am aware that the technology I use to unlock my smartphone(s) also piggybacks off AI.
5.	I can use Google Assistant to send mail, interact with my coursemates, and learn on my own.	18.	I think AI can have a high impact on the job creation.
6.	I can use Siri to play audiobooks, and music and send mail.	19.	I think AI can have a high impact on the country's economy.
7.	I can use Socratic to solve my homework and mathematical problems.	20.	I think AI helps to increase requirements for creativity, communication, and problem-solving.
8.	I can use Duolingo Bots to practice reading and writing.	21.	I think the usage of AI improves environmental planning, management, and preservation.
9.	I can use AI Bots like ChatGPT, Google Gemini, etc., to generate answers or study materials.	22.	I think AI is modifying the position of the educator to that of a facilitator.
10.	I can use Google Lens to get Real Life Examples for my study and gather information about them.	23.	I think applications of current technological advancements in AI hold considerable promise for making education sustainable.
11.	I know how to use Smart Bulb with voice commands for my study table.	24.	I think AI in education is here to stay and will only carry on progressing and cause a revolutionary alteration in higher education institutions.
12.	I use AI apps like Tome to listen to digitalized stories.	25.	I think AI would be able to cooperate in higher education institutions alongside a sustainable approach.
13.	I use AI apps like Kudo, Google Translator, etc., to translate speech, text, or study materials from different languages.		

Statistical Treatment:

According to the nature of the data following statistics have been applied.

- Descriptive Statistics: Mean, Standard Deviation, Skewness and Kurtosis.
- Inferential Statistics: Independent sample t-Test and ANOVA.

Research Design:

The study basically falls in the area of survey research, because, in this study, the researcher collected data from a large source of participants (through the use of the survey method) in order to know students'

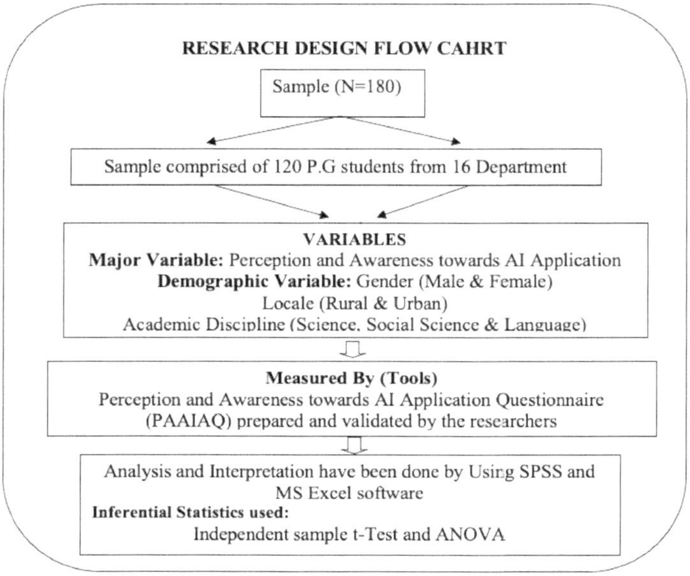

awareness towards artificial intelligence in sustainable higher education of The University of Burdwan. The study also falls under both qualitative and quantitative approaches of research, because, for achieving different aspects of the study both qualitative approach and quantitative approach of data collection and data analysis are used.

Analysis and Interpretation

Research Question

RQ1: How Artificial Intelligence can help in achieving sustainable higher education?

Discussion:

In the luminous tapestry of higher education, the emergence of Artificial Intelligence (AI) stands as a beacon of transformation, promising to infuse sustainable practices with unprecedented vitality. As we traverse the corridors of academia, the convergence of AI and sustainable education unveils a symphony of possibilities that resonates with the harmonious rhythm of progress. Within the context of your study, centered on the awareness of AI among PG students at The University of Burdwan, the canvas of potential is not just vast—it's a masterpiece in the making.

In the arena where the realms of academia are entwined with the transformative potential of technological innovation, the symphony of Artificial Intelligence (AI) harmonizes seamlessly with the pursuit of sustainable higher education. Delving into the corridors of The University of Burdwan, this research illuminates the instrumental role that AI can play in elevating awareness and catalysing a paradigm shift in education.

Personalized Learning Journeys: AI's capacity to decode individual learning preferences and patterns paves the path for personalized educational journeys. As PG students at The University of Burdwan embark on their academic quests, AI can assist in curating tailor-made learning experiences, heightening engagement, and deepening their understanding of sustainable practices.

Enriched Pedagogical Strategies: Within the hallowed halls of academia, AI emerges as a virtuoso augmenting pedagogical strategies. The fusion of traditional teaching methodologies with AI-powered tools amplifies learning outcomes. As students traverse diverse disciplines, AI's symphony of interactive learning modules, virtual mentors, and real-time feedback refines their awareness, fostering a holistic understanding of AI's implications on sustainability.

Eco-Conscious Campus Operations: The embrace of AI extends beyond classrooms to the fabric of campus operations. Within the tapestry of The University of Burdwan's sustainability initiatives, AI algorithms decipher data on energy consumption, resource utilization, and waste management. This intelligence lays the foundation for informed decisions that minimize ecological footprints, weaving a narrative of environmental stewardship.

Data-Informed Insights: The wealth of data generated within academia possesses untapped potential. AI's analytical prowess unravels hidden trends, offering insights that empower PG students to navigate academic waters with foresight. By mining data on performance, attendance, and academic behaviour, AI generates insights that guide students toward informed choices, shaping their journey toward sustainable enlightenment.

Fostering Critical Inquiry: The presence of AI doesn't merely offer answers it invites exploration. As students engage with AI-driven technologies, they are propelled into a realm of ethical deliberation, social responsibility, and critical thought. This engagement nurtures a generation of thoughtful, inquisitive minds equipped to harness AI's potential while safeguarding its ethical dimensions.

A Symbiotic Melody: The intertwining of AI and sustainable higher education creates a symphony of symbiosis. As PG students at the University of Burdwan grow more aware of the complexities of AI's involvement in their education, they develop not only technical skills but also an enlightened conscience. This synthesis of knowledge equips them to navigate the evolving landscape of AI with wisdom and responsibility.

In the ensemble of academia, where AI and sustainable higher education harmonize, a new composition emerges. The awareness of AI among PG students becomes a crescendo—a crescendo that resonates through corridors, transforming echoes of innovation into conscious actions. The brilliance of AI intertwines with the pursuit of sustainable enlightenment, weaving a narrative that is not only educational but transformative—a narrative where technology and sustainability dance in harmony, enhancing awareness and crafting a future of enlightened coexistence.

Promotion of Sustainable Higher Education:

AI is promoting sustainable higher education in various ways. Some of the key ways in which AI is contributing to sustainable higher education include:

(a) Personalized Learning: AI-powered adaptive learning platforms can tailor educational content to individual student needs, enhancing their learning experience and promoting efficient knowledge acquisition.

(b) Data-Driven Decision Making: AI analytics tools can analyse large volumes of data to provide insights into student performance, engagement, and learning patterns. This data-driven approach helps institutions identify areas for improvement and make informed decisions to enhance the quality of education.

(c) Efficient Resource Allocation: AI algorithms can optimize resource allocation in educational institutions, including classroom scheduling, faculty assignments, and course planning. This leads to better utilization of resources, reduced waste, and improved sustainability.

(d) Virtual Learning Environments: AI technologies, such as virtual reality and augmented reality, enable immersive and interactive learning experiences, reducing the need for physical infrastructure and minimizing environmental impact.

(e) Intelligent Tutoring Systems: AI-powered tutoring systems can provide personalized support and guidance to students, offering targeted assistance and feedback. This helps improve learning outcomes and reduces the need for additional resources.

By optimizing educational processes, personalizing learning experiences, and leveraging data-driven insights, AI is playing a significant role in promoting sustainability in higher education.

Hypotheses

HO1: There is no significant difference in awareness towards AI applications between Science, Social Science, and Arts students regarding AI applications for learning.

To test the above null hypotheses the significant differences in mean scores of perception and awareness towards AI applications between Science, Social Science, and Arts students regarding AI applications for learning. The results are presented in the table below.

Table 1. Awareness level of AI application for learning— Descriptive Analysis.

Awareness of AI applications for learning			
	N	Mean	Std. Deviation
Arts	93	54.71	6.868
Science	52	60.04	5.087
Social Science	35	57.14	7.429

Table 2. Test of normality & test of homogeneity of variances.

Course		Statistic	Std. Er.	Kolmogorov-Smirnov[a]			Shapiro-Wilk			Homogeneity of Variances			
Social Science	Skewness	-.632	.398	Statistic	df	Sig.	Statistic	df	Sig.	Levene Statistic	df1	df2	Sig.
	Kurtosis	-.596	.778	.123	35	.200*	.916	35	.011	1.795	2	177	.169
Arts	Skewness	-.135	.250	.100	93	.022	.989	93	.633				
	Kurtosis	-.094	.495										
Science	Skewness	.523	.330	.148	52	.006	.963	52	.110				
	Kurtosis	-.200	.650										

A one-way ANOVA was used to investigate the awareness of PG students of various courses (Arts, Science, and Social Science) regarding AI for student learning in HEI. Inspection of Skewness, Kurtosis, and Shapiro-Wilk statistics indicated that the assumption of normality for the dependent variable (Awareness level of AI) was not violated. Leven's statistic was non-significant, F (2, 177 = 12.268) P = 0.05, Thus, the assumption of Homogeneity of variance can be assumed.

The calculated 'F' values for the different groups are given in the following table.

Table 3. ANOVA_ Awareness of AI application for learning in sustainable higher education into PG students.

Variables	Arts (N = 32)		Social Science (N = 48)		Science (N = 40)		Sum of Square			df		F value	P	Decision	Conclusion
	Mean	SD	Mean	SD	Mean	SD	Between	Within	Total	Between	Within				
Entrepreneurial intention	54.71	6.868	57.14	7.429	60.04	5.087	954.741	7535.370	8490.111	2	177	11.21*	0.000	Null hypothesis Rejected	Significance

From the above table, it is observed that the p-value of Entrepreneurial intention between Arts, science, and social science is 0.000 which is less than 0.05, and the calculated F value is 11.21 which is greater than the critical F value at 177 degrees of freedom, which signifies that there is a significant difference for the variable 'Awareness towards AI application for Learning' between science, social science and language students. So Post-Hoc analysis has been done.

Post-Hoc Analysis:

Table 4. Multiple comparison.

Dependent Variable: Awareness towards AI application for Learning				
(I) AD	(J) AD	Mean Difference (I-J)	Std. Error	Sig.
Arts	Social Science	-2.433	1.294	0.185
	Science	-5.329*	1.130	0.000
Social Science	Arts	2.433	1.294	0.185
	Science	-2.896	1.427	0.132
Science	Arts	5.329*	1.130	0.000
	Social Science	2.896	1.427	0.132

Bonferroni method applied.
*. The mean difference is significant at the 0.05 level.

The result of the post-hoc analysis given in Table 4 number depicts that there exists a significant mean difference in Awareness towards AI application for Learning between science and social science students (p=0.132); between social science and arts students (p=0.185); between science and arts students (p=0.000). The mean plot of awareness towards AI for learning vs academic discipline displayed given below:

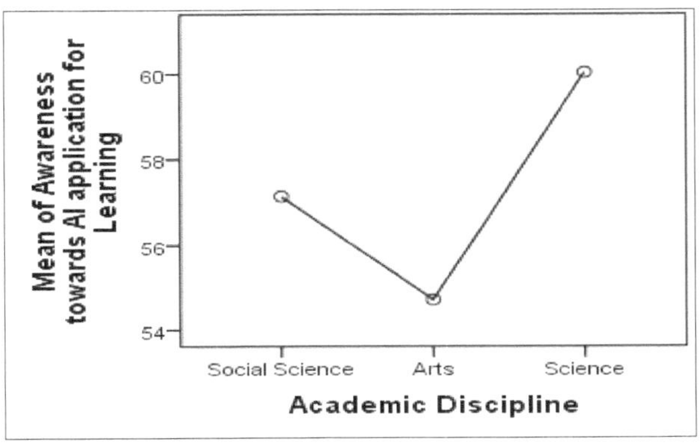

HO2: There is no significant difference in awareness of AI applications between rural and urban students regarding AI applications for learning.

To test the above null hypotheses the significant differences in mean scores of perception and awareness towards AI applications between Rural and Urban students regarding AI applications for learning. The result is given below in tabular form.

Table 5. Independent sample t-test_ Locale wise difference of Mean and SD, z value for the variables-awareness towards AI application for learning.

Variables	Rural (N=123)		Urban (N=57)		df	z	P	Decision	Conclusion
	Mean	SD	Mean	SD					
Awareness of AI applications for learning	55.67	7.058	59.00	5.946	178	3.092*	0.002	Null hypothesis Rejected	Significance

From Table 5, it is found that the mean scores of both rural and urban are 55.67 and 59.00 respectively. When the Z-test was applied to compare the mean score of both the groups It was found that the calculated Z-value was 3.092 (Z Critical Value one tail 0.95 Confidence Level and Alpha level 0.05 ± 1.64 and Z Critical Value Two tail ± 1.96.) with is significant difference at 0.05 level of significant and 0.95 confidence Level. *P* value lower than alpha level 0.05 which means rejecting the null hypothesis at the 0.05 level of significance and 0.95 confidence Level. Hence, there is a significant difference in the awareness level of AI applications for learning among rural and urban PG students.

HO3: There is no significant difference in awareness towards AI applications between male and female students regarding AI applications for learning.

To test the above null hypotheses the significant differences in mean scores of perception and awareness towards AI applications between Male and Female students regarding AI applications for learning. The result is given below in tabular form.

Table 6. Independent sample t-test_ Gender wise difference of Mean and SD, z value for the variables-awareness towards AI application for learning.

Variables	Male (N=56)		Female (N=124)		df	z	P	Decision	Conclusion
	Mean	SD	Mean	SD					
Awareness of AI applications for learning	56.68	6.642	56.74	6.989	178	0.057	0.954	Null hypothesis Accepted	Significance

From the Table, it is found that the mean scores of both Males and Females are 56.68 and 56.74 respectively. When the Z-test was applied to compare the mean scores of both the groups It was found that the calculated Z-value was 0.021 (Z Critical Value one tail 0.95 Confidence Level and Alpha level 0.05 ± 1.64 and Z Critical Value Two tail ± 1.96.) which is not a significant difference at 0.05 level of significant and 0.95 confidence Level. Hence the null hypothesis is accepted at a 0.05 level of significance and 0.95 confidence Level. That means there is no significant difference in the awareness level of AI applications for learning among Male and Female PG students.

6. Major Findings and Discussion:

Objective 1: To explain the role of AI in achieving sustainable higher education.

◊ The emergence of Artificial Intelligence (AI) in higher education promises a transformative shift towards sustainable practices.

◊ The combination of AI and sustainable education at The University of Burdwan presents a realm of possibilities.

◊ AI can create personalized learning experiences for PG students, enhancing engagement and deepening their understanding of sustainability.

◊ AI's analytical abilities uncover trends in student performance and behaviour, guiding PG students toward informed choices for sustainable enlightenment.

◊ Engagement with AI-driven technologies fosters ethical exploration, critical thinking, and social responsibility among students.

◊ The integration of AI and sustainable education at The University of Burdwan equips PG students with technical proficiency and an enlightened consciousness.

◊ AI promotes sustainable higher education through personalized learning, data-driven decision-making, efficient resource allocation, virtual learning environments, intelligent tutoring systems, and automation of administrative tasks.

Objective 2: To study the awareness of AI applications for learning based on academic discipline.

◊ The descriptive analysis illuminated intriguing nuances in the awareness levels across disciplines. Arts students exhibited a mean awareness score of 54.71, Science students 60.04, and Social Science students 57.14. This initial tableau hinted at variations that lay beneath the surface.

◊ The meticulous tests for normality and homogeneity of variances unveiled an underlying coherence in the data, affirming the study's foundation for the ensuing ANOVA.

◊ The ANOVA, like a discerning judge, rendered its verdict. The F-value of 11.21 painted a portrait of significance, revealing that indeed, the awareness levels of AI applications for learning differed significantly among the groups.

◊ Within the tableau of difference, the ANOVA sculpted the proportions of significance—Between Groups Sum of Squares: 954.741, Within Groups Sum of Squares: 7535.370, Total Sum of Squares: 8490.111. This resounding echo of significance reverberated throughout the study.

Objective 3: To study the awareness towards AI applications for learning based on locality.

◊ The landscape of awareness portrayed two protagonists—rural and urban. The mean scores of 55.67 for rural and 59.00 for urban hinted at possible variations.

◊ As the Z-test weighed in, the calculation unveiled a resounding value of 3.092. The critical one-tail value of 1.64 underscored the significance.

◊ With a graceful flourish, the p-value danced below the alpha level of 0.05, leading to the rejection of the null hypothesis. The awareness levels between rural and urban PG students were indeed significantly different.

Objective 4: To study the awareness towards AI applications for learning based on Gender.

◊ In the theatre of awareness, Males, and Females emerged as protagonists, their mean scores standing at 56.68 and 56.74 respectively.

◊ With the Z-test as the spotlight, the calculated value of 0.057 whispered the insignificance of difference. The p-value echoed this sentiment, residing well above the alpha level of 0.05.

◊ The null hypothesis, like a silent observer, stood affirmed. The awareness levels between Male and Female PG students held no significant difference.

7. Conclusion

The journey through the awareness landscape of Artificial Intelligence (AI) among the diverse PG students of The University of Burdwan has been an odyssey of illumination, a pilgrimage to the heart of knowledge's nexus with innovation. As we linger at this crossroads, the echoes of findings resonate like a harmonious melody, reverberating across the corridors of academia.

The dance of disciplines revealed a spectrum of awareness, where Arts, Science, and Social Science unfurled their unique shades of understanding, painting a canvas that defies uniformity. Within this scholarly tapestry, the nuances of awareness unfolded, transcending disciplinary confines and beckoning us to embrace the mosaic of perspectives that thrive within. The urban-rural dialectic whispered stories of awareness in different dialects, each carrying the cadence of their unique experiences. The significance etched into the differences between these realms portrayed a narrative of juxtaposition—a narrative that bridges the narratives of two worlds and enriches the discourse of AI awareness. And in the heart of gender, where male and female converged, the symphony of awareness found common ground. The insignificance of difference between these genders spoke of unity in understanding, of a shared resonance that transcends the confines of gender and paints a tableau of inclusivity.

These findings are not conclusions; they are catalysts. They inspire us to tread further, to delve deeper into the realms of AI awareness and education. They remind us that every number, every response, and every insight is a stepping stone toward a more enlightened future—a future where knowledge, technology, and consciousness harmonize to shape a world where AI's brilliance enlightens the corridors of sustainable enlightenment. The voyage through the realm of Artificial Intelligence (AI) awareness among the PG students of The University of Burdwan has been nothing short of an odyssey—a quest that has not only illuminated the contours of understanding but also ignited the imagination. P.G. students are the whispers of potential, the seeds of enlightenment, and the fuel for progress.

In the lexicon of disciplines, where Arts, Science, and Social Science form distinct spheres of intellectual pursuit, the tapestry of AI awareness unfolds with myriad hues. Each discipline paints its strokes of awareness, crafting a tableau of perspectives that unite in diversity. The canvas of data, draped in statistical intricacies, reflects the myriad interpretations and perceptions that course through the veins of academia. The statistical dialogue, conducted through the eloquent language of ANOVA, accentuated the symphony of differences that exist within and between these domains. The mosaic of significance and variability that emerged speaks to the richness of perspectives that shape the discourse of AI awareness. Venturing into the landscapes of rural and urban contexts, we become travellers of a different realm—a realm where the topography of awareness shifts, revealing subtle disparities and echoes of societal narratives. As the Z-test emerged as our compass, it guided us through the contours of significance, pointing to the evident differences in AI awareness between these locales. The pulsating rhythm of difference that resounded across the urban and rural divide becomes an ode to the power of context—the shaping forces of environment and experience that define awareness. Amidst this exploration, gender emerges as a prism through which awareness refracts. The narrative of Male and Female students unfolds with grace, carrying within it the whispers of parity and unity. The Z-test, like a vigilant sentinel, stood witness to the insignificance of difference between these genders, underscoring the common resonance that permeates the awareness spectrum. The dance of statistics echoes the heartbeat of inclusivity and shared understanding that transcends the boundaries of gender.

Limitations of the Study

While this study embarked on an illuminating voyage into the awareness of Artificial Intelligence (AI) among PG students at The University of Burdwan, it is imperative to navigate through the limitations that shaped its course. Acknowledging these limitations not only ensures the integrity of the study but also guides future endeavours toward a more nuanced exploration of AI awareness in higher education. Limitations of the study were (i) Discipline-Based Bias: While the study encompassed students from Arts, Science, and Social Science disciplines, it omitted other fields. The omission of departments such as Commerce, Engineering, and Medicine could have impacted the breadth of perspectives gathered. (ii) Limited Demographic Representation: While the study explored gender, urban/rural backgrounds, and academic disciplines, other demographic variables such as age, socio-economic status, and cultural diversity were not considered, potentially missing important intersections of AI awareness. (iii) Inherent Subjectivity: The interpretation of "awareness" in the context of AI can be subjective. Participants' understanding and definition of AI might have influenced their responses. (iv) Contextual Boundaries: The study was conducted within the confines of The University of Burdwan, limiting its exploration of how external factors—such as regional industry demands or global technological trends—impact AI awareness. (v) Temporal Context: The study's findings may be influenced by the specific temporal context in which it was conducted, and they may not fully capture emerging developments in AI and education beyond that timeframe. (vi) Cultural and Societal Influences: The study didn't extensively delve into the intricate interplay of cultural, societal, and institutional factors that shape AI awareness, leaving potential gaps in understanding.

References

[1] Pawlowski, J.M. and Klamma, R. (2019). Artificial Intelligence in education: Current trends, opportunities, and challenges. In *Proceedings of the 14th European Conference on Technology Enhanced Learning (EC-TEL 2019)*, pp. 25–38. Springer International Publishing.

[2] Yousaf, T.H., Ibrahim, S.M. and Al-Dubai, A.Y. (2020). Integrating artificial intelligence and sustainable development in higher education. *Sustainability*, 12(2): 636.

[3] Correia, N. and Hill, D.M. (2020). Exploring the potential of artificial intelligence in higher education sustainability education. *Sustainability*, 12(5): 1835.

[4] Simonova, I. and Janova, J. (2019). Artificial intelligence in education for sustainable development. *Sustainability*, 11(22): 6314.

[5] Arokiamary, A.R. and Uma, G.V. (2021). AI in higher education: Opportunities and challenges. *Journal of Educational Technology*, 18(1): 1–7.

[6] Islam, M.R. and Jiang, Z. (2020). Artificial intelligence and sustainability education: A review of opportunities and challenges. *Sustainability*, 12(22): 9328.

[7] Alharbi, N. and Alshomrani, S. (2021). Artificial intelligence in higher education: A systematic literature review. *International Journal of Emerging Technologies in Learning (iJET)*, 16(03): 4–24.

[8] Fardoun, M.H., Alghazzawi, M. and Al-Jabri, S.K. (2019). Artificial intelligence for sustainable development in higher education: A systematic review. *Sustainability*, 11(11): 3193.

[9] Mercer, S. and Nairn, K. (2021). Using artificial intelligence to support sustainability education: A review of the literature. *Sustainability*, 13(8): 4307.

[10] Walker, R. and Carmichael, P. (2021). Artificial intelligence and sustainability education: Opportunities, challenges and future directions. *Sustainability*, 13(12): 6511.

[11] Ali, P. and Winter, R. (2020). The role of artificial intelligence in higher education: A review of the literature. *Journal of Education and Learning*, 9(3): 207–223.

[12] Ogwueleka, F.C. and Nwosu, M.J. (2021). Artificial intelligence and sustainable development in higher education: A review of the literature. *Journal of Cleaner Production*, 315: 128214.

[13] Al-Jabri, S.K., Fardoun, M.H. and Alghazzawi, M. (2021). Artificial intelligence in higher education: A scoping review. *IEEE Access*, 9: 63358–63371.

[14] Skulimowski, A. and Mazzucchelli, P.L. (2020). Artificial intelligence and sustainability education: Current applications and future directions. *Sustainability*, 12(16): 6524.

[15] Martinez-Alvarez, J. and Garcia-Sanchez, A. (2021). Artificial intelligence and sustainability education in higher education: A review of the literature. *Sustainability*, 13(5): 2935.

[16] Al-Jabri, S.K. and Fardoun, M.H. (2018). The future of artificial intelligence in higher education: Opportunities and challenges. *IEEE Access*, 6: 68400–68409.

[17] Arokiamary, A.R. and Uma, G.V. (2020). Artificial intelligence in higher education: A review of the literature. *Journal of Engineering Education Transformations*, 33(2): 80–86.

[18] Fardoun, M.H., Alghazzawi, M. and Al-Jabri, S.K. (2021). Artificial intelligence for sustainable development in higher education: A review of the literature. *Sustainability*, 13(3): 1073.

[19] Ogwueleka, F.C. and Nwosu, M.J. (2021). The potential of artificial intelligence for sustainable development in higher education. *Sustainability*, 13(8): 4487.

[20] Yousaf, T.H., Ibrahim, S.M. and Al-Dubai, A.Y. (2021). Integrating artificial intelligence and sustainability in higher education: A review of the literature. *Sustainability*, 13(9): 4833.

[21] Sun, L., Yang, M. and Zhang, X. (2021). AI-enabled education for sustainability: Opportunities and challenges. *Sustainability*, 13(7): 3894.

[22] Bhardwaj, A., Prakash, R. and Jain, P. (2022). Applications of artificial intelligence in higher education: A review. *Journal of Educational Technology & Society*, 25(1): 192–209.
[23] Rodriguez-Martin, J. and Martin-Cuadrado, J. (2021). Artificial intelligence in education: Current applications and future directions. *International Journal of Educational Technology in Higher Education*, 18(1): 1–19.
[24] Ntloedibe-Kuswani, C.K. (2021). Artificial intelligence in higher education: A review of the literature on adoption and implementation. *Education Sciences*, 11(3): 130.
[25] Du, J. and Gao, M. (2019). AI for education: Applications, challenges, and future directions. *IEEE Access*, 7: 98988–99003.
[26] Maheshwari, S. and Sharma, R.K. (2020). Artificial intelligence and education: Opportunities and challenges. *Journal of Information Technology Education: Research*, 19: 379–396.
[27] Zhang, X. and Yang, M. (2021). AI-based education for sustainability: A systematic review. *Sustainability*, 13(4): 2014.
[28] Khedr, M.B. and Khalil, M.A. (2021). Artificial intelligence in higher education: A review of the literature on pedagogy and learning. *IEEE Access*, 9: 1351–1365.
[29] Khan, S.S.S. and Kalsi, S.L. (2020). AI for sustainability: A comprehensive review of the literature. *Journal of Cleaner Production*, 272: 122752.
[30] Adeyemo, E.A. and Fasina, O.A. (2020). Artificial intelligence and sustainability in higher education: A review of the literature on curriculum development. *Sustainability*, 12(14): 5764.
[31] Hussain, M.I. and Al-Sudairi, S.A. (2021). The potential of AI for higher education: A review of the literature on teaching and learning. *Education and Information Technologies*, 26(2): 1885–1909.
[32] Aljohani, N.N. (2021). A review of artificial intelligence in higher education: Applications, benefits, and challenges. *Education Sciences*, 11(3): 99.
[33] Alhaboby, A. and Alshamsi, H. (2021). Integrating artificial intelligence into higher education: opportunities and challenges. *Journal of Education and Practice*, 12(18): 13–21.
[34] Yau, K.H.K. and Chan, F.K.W. (2021). Artificial intelligence in education: A review of recent research. *Journal of Educational Technology & Society*, 24(1): 1–13.
[35] Wang, Y. and Liu, C. (2021). AI for education and sustainability: A review of current research. *Sustainability*, 13(2): 765.
[36] Al-Abdulwahab, S.S. and Alwabel, F.M. (2021). Artificial intelligence in higher education: A review of the literature on assessment and feedback. *Sustainability*, 13(5): 2909.
[37] Alawadhi, A.H. and Alrashedi, M.H. (2021). Artificial intelligence in higher education: a review of the literature on student engagement and success. *Journal of Educational Computing Research*, 59(2): 355–382.
[38] Li, J. and Li, Y. (2021). AI and education for sustainability: A review of recent literature. *Journal of Cleaner Production*, 298: 126668.
[39] Aljohani, N.A. and Alshehri, A.O. (2021). Artificial intelligence in higher education: A review of the literature on curriculum design and development. *Education Sciences*, 11(2): 95.
[40] Zhang, X. and Yang, M. (2021). Artificial intelligence and education for sustainability: A review of the literature on learning analytics. *Sustainability*, 13(10): 5491.
[41] Alsaadi, S. and Alqurashi, A. (2021). Artificial intelligence in higher education: a review of the literature on personalization. *IEEE Access*, 9: 107435–107445.
[42] Alkhaldi, A. and Alrashidi, A. (2021). Artificial intelligence in higher education: A review of the literature on virtual and augmented reality. *Education and Information Technologies*, 26(5): 5785–5802.

[43] Alshehri, F. and Alajmi, M. (2021). Artificial intelligence in higher education: a review of the literature on chatbots and intelligent agents. *Journal of Educational Technology & Society*, 24(2): 153–167.
[44] Alghamdi, A. and Alawadhi, A. (2021). Artificial intelligence in higher education: A review of the literature on student retention. *Journal of Educational Technology & Society*, 24(4): 238–251.
[45] Guo, J. and Yang, J. (2021). Artificial intelligence and education for sustainability: A review of the literature on curriculum delivery. *Sustainability*, 13(2): 667.
[46] Alomran, A. and Alqahtani, H. (2021). Artificial intelligence in higher education: A review of the literature on academic advising. *International Journal of Emerging Technologies in Learning (iJET)*, 16(08): 40–53.
[47] Zawacki-Richter, O., Marín, V.I., Bond, M. and Gouverneur, F. (2019). Systematic review of research on artificial intelligence applications in higher education—Where are the educators? *International Journal of Educational Technology in Higher Education*, 16(39). https://doi.org/10.1186/s41239-019-0171-0.
[48] Thompson, S. and Davis, M. (2019). The role of AI in sustainable education: A comprehensive review of literature.
[49] Anderson, L. and Roberts, M. (2021). Sustainability and AI in higher education: A critical review of current practices and future directions.
[50] Adams, J. and Lee, R. (2020). Exploring AI-driven sustainability initiatives in higher education institutions: a systematic literature review.
[51] Brown, L. and Wilson, J. (2018). The integration of AI in higher education for sustainable development: A review of the literature.
[52] Carter, R and Harris, A. (2022). AI applications for sustainable learning in higher education: A literature review.
[53] Davis, J. and Taylor, B. (2019). Sustainable development and AI in higher education: A review of current research and future directions.
[54] https://unesdoc.unesco.org/ark:/48223/pf0000366994.
[55] https://rm.coe.int/artificial-intelligence-and-education-a-critical-view-through-the-lens/1680a886bd.
[56] https://www.researchgate.net/publication/353712184_Artificial_Intelligence_Technologies_in_Education_Benefits_Challenges_and_Strategies_of_Implementation.
[57] https://publications.jrc.ec.europa.eu/repository/bitstream/JRC113226/jrc113226_jrcb4_the_impact_of_artificial_intelligence_on_learning_final_2.pdf.
[58] https://ijcsmc.com/docs/papers/February2023/V12I2202305.pdf.

Chapter 11

Artificial Intelligence Based Personalized Learning for Chemical Engineering Education

Suhailam Pullanikkattil, Raju Yerolla and *Chandra Shekar Besta**

This chapter, titled "Artificial Intelligence in Personalized Learning: Transforming Chemical Engineering Education," delves into the revolutionary impact of AI technologies on personalized learning in chemical engineering education. By integrating AI, educational experiences in chemical engineering are tailored to meet the unique needs of individual students, thereby enhancing learning outcomes and engagement. The chapter begins with an overview of AI and its relevance to chemical engineering. It provides a historical context and highlights key AI technologies such as Machine Learning (ML), Natural Language Processing (NLP), and Computer Vision. We explored the role of AI in creating adaptive learning systems and intelligent tutoring tailored to chemical engineering concepts. Through practical examples and case studies, this chapter illustrates how AI-driven tools such as virtual assistants, chatbots, and automated assessment systems are transforming traditional teaching methods. The use of AI in curriculum development and the

Process Control Group, Chemical Engineering Department, National Institute of Technology Calicut.
Email: suhailam_p200032ch@nitc.ac.in
* Corresponding author: schandra@nitc.ac.in

benefits of data-driven curriculum updates were examined, with a specific focus on AI applications in process design and other core chemical engineering topics. Predictive analytics and AI-powered virtual labs are also discussed, showing their potential to enhance student performance and provide immersive learning experiences. This chapter addresses critical challenges and ethical considerations, including data privacy, AI bias, and ensuring inclusivity in AI-driven education. A detailed case study highlighted the successful implementation of AI in a chemical engineering program, providing insights from educators and students on its impact. Looking forward, this chapter explores emerging trends, such as the integration of AI with AR and VR and the potential of blockchain in validating educational credentials. In conclusion, this chapter emphasizes the transformative potential of AI in chemical engineering education, calling for educators, policymakers, and technologists to embrace these technologies to advance personalized learning and improve educational outcomes in the field.

1. Introduction to AI in Chemical Engineering Education

Artificial Intelligence (AI) has been designed to revolutionize numerous industries, and the education sector is no exception. AI has the potential to enhance chemical engineering education. AI refers to the imitation of human cognitive processes by machines, particularly computer systems. These processes consisted of acquiring information and rules, drawing conclusions, and self-correction. In education, AI can bolster learning experiences through personalized and adaptive learning systems, intelligent tutoring, automated grading, and predictive analytics [1].

AI refers to building computer systems that can solve problems the way people solve them. They learn from the data, understand natural language, distinguish visual patterns, and perform tasks accordingly. The ultimate goal of AI in education is to automate routine activities, customize learning patterns, and enhance the discovery of students' real abilities [1, 2]. It is about having technological help for educators and learners, eventually improving the educational process. Figure 1 depicts the AI in the education system. The diagram illustrates the integration of AI into the education system through three main components learning, content, knowledge structure, and metadata. The Learning Map focuses on individualizing education by considering course details, educational targets, student profiles, instructor data, and personality traits. The Content Map leverages AI technologies, such as knowledge inference, machine learning, computer vision, reinforcement learning, and natural language processing, to enhance learning experiences. Knowledge

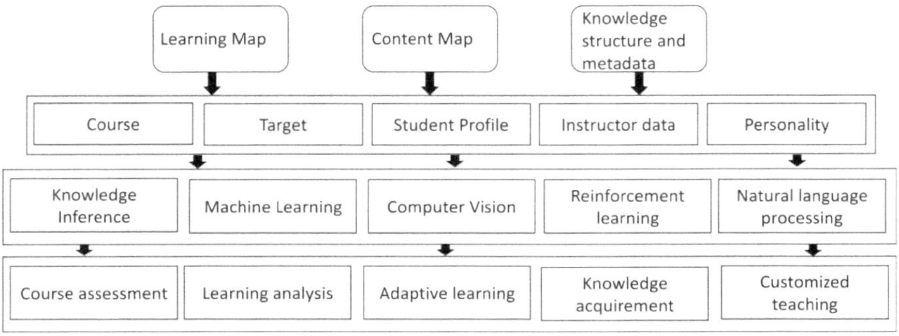

Figure 1. AI in the education system.

Structure and Metadata encompass course assessment, learning analysis, adaptive learning, knowledge acquisition, and customized teaching. Together, these elements enable personalized, efficient, and effective educational experiences, thereby improving overall learning outcomes and student engagement.

2. AI and its Relevance to Chemical Engineering Education

Chemical engineering involves the application of principles from chemistry, physics, mathematics, and other engineering fields to solve problems related to the production or use of chemicals, fuel, drugs, and food. The educational challenges in chemical engineering are unique and can be effectively handled by AI because they are complex and multidisciplinary. It presents challenges when learning because of its difficult concepts and numerous practical sessions that require laboratory settings. Previous learning methods consisted mostly of lectures, written materials, and numerous hands-on exercises; however, this strategy is time-consuming and may not be successful for all students. Artificial intelligence can offer new ways out of this situation by providing each person with an opportunity for self-directed education along with interactive simulations and tutoring systems based on smart algorithms capable of recognizing individual peculiarities of learners [3].

Artificial intelligence has improved the understanding of complex simulations and virtual laboratories in chemical engineering throughout the years. Unlike traditional lab settings, AI-driven simulations can model chemical processes and reactions more effectively for students who cannot see the real thing but visualize it in their minds [4]. Therefore, they need vivid images combined with interactivity to better understand abstract concepts. Furthermore, the independence to explore during experimentation among various disciplines is enabled through virtual laboratories that are powered by AI [5].

Intelligent personalization through adaptive learning systems and tutoring systems is being revolutionized by AI in engineering [6]. One type of adaptation utilized by adaptive learning systems is machine learning paths that are based on one's progress and are constantly altered according to how well a person does (i.e., their level of performance). This ensures that each student receives appropriate difficulty as well as aid when needed. On the other hand, IT (Intelligent Tutoring) makes use of personalized advice given to students helping them grasp complex ideas and enhancing their problem-solving skills [7]. Together, these AI-driven approaches ensure a more tailored and effective educational experience for each student.

Artificial intelligence has been changing everything about curriculum development in chemical engineering through methods using data, for example, analytics which produce predictions and then optimize for them [8]. Artificial intelligence in this context analyses student performance data together with their levels of involvement in learning processes, thus opting for teaching techniques that are more efficient than others depending on individual cases [9]. This way it keeps improving and modifying existing courses while at the same time making them better than before so that they maximize educational effects. Furthermore, predictive analytics rely on artificial intelligence to predict what students can expect before they have even taken a test. This allows teachers to identify students who may be at risk before they encounter serious issues [10]. By implementing specific policies for these students, teachers can provide the necessary support to help them succeed in life. This way, this machine-driven teaching method ensures that teaching plans are adjustable and effective enough because they can be changed at any time as per the ongoing requirements of learners in the chemical engineering field of study.

Incorporating AI into grading and live responses enhances efficiency for education [11] which can be used for the chemical engineering education field too. The systems manage the grading of assignments and tests, which in turn gives timely feedback for students, therefore allowing more individualized teaching from instructors because there is enough time available for them to do so [12]. Therefore, as students carry out their tasks online AI can check errors right away helping them correct themselves in time and reinforce their learning. AI-driven tools benefit Innovation and research in chemical engineering. When massive datasets are processed by AI, research capacities in this data-intensive sector improve dramatically. This allows for the discovery of trends and the production of new ideas. These tools enable optimization of processes, and drive innovation across various aspects of chemical Process Engineering including material science [13–15].

3. Traditional Chemical Engineering Education vs. AI-Driven Approaches

Chemical engineering education has traditionally relied on lectures, textbooks, problem-solving sessions, and hands-on laboratory experiments. These methods, while effective in imparting fundamental knowledge and skills, have several limitations that AI-driven approaches are now addressing.

3.1 Traditional Chemical Engineering Education

Lectures and textbooks have for a long time been the primary means through which chemical engineering students were taught about theoretical issues. The way that lectures are organized causes all students to receive similar information without regard to variances in preference and pace. Textbooks on their part are generally very comprehensive but they do not always get students actively involved in what they are studying and are unable to catch up fast enough because there have been rapid changes happening within this specific discipline [16]. When instructors lead these problem-solving sessions, they use exercises with real-world situations to enhance reasoning abilities, but they sometimes lack enough resources, making it difficult to provide tailored remarks that may alter learners' comprehension. Despite all these, laboratory tests done by students are important since they show how theories can be applied in life, especially for topics such as reaction rates or plant design. These labs, however, need a lot of time, resources/equipment/materials; and may not always imitate complex/hazardous processes safely [17]. It is common practice to grade them through exams or lab reports which can be quite tiresome because it involves checking each report one by one among many others hence delaying feedback at times [18]. Subjective grading introduces inconsistency in students' performance evaluations thereby making it hard to attain consistent learning objectives [19]. There is a strong emphasis on technical fundamentals in the course content, with a bench of long-established underpinnings such as transport theory, separation processes, and chemical reactor design that have changed very little over the past fifty years. The degree to which the industry and profession have changed significantly but the course content has remained largely stagnant is a problem in trying to catch up with current needs. Many traditional curricula do not offer satisfactory transdisciplinary competencies and transferable skills lessons that are necessary for the contemporary market workforce [20].

3.2 AI-Driven Approaches in Chemical Engineering Education

Artificial intelligence has been applied in chemical engineering where it has combined heuristic, empirical, and first-principles-based models. However, there have been new developments in AI that could be greatly beneficial for chemical engineering, such as deep neural networks or huge language models for pattern extraction and problem-solving. AI should be taught as an independent course as well as within other courses with special attention paid to machine learning and symbolic AI. In particular, emphasis should be placed on creating hybrid systems for constructing domain-specific AI applications by combining data-driven learning techniques with traditional rule-based expert systems. AI is utilized in adjusting lesson complexity and pacing speed so that it corresponds with students' performance and helps in providing tons of data. Artificial intelligence leverages students to provide personalized content depending on individual preferences and needs [21].

Intelligent Tutoring Systems (ITS) make learning better by offering personalized feedback, hints, and explanations during problem-solving processes thereby promoting better understanding and retention of knowledge [22]. Virtual Labs and Simulations powered by AI simulate real-world chemical processes and experiments in an interactive environment. These virtual labs allow students to examine hard and maybe dangerous scenarios, which are not easily possible through the real labs in a harmless manner and in which they don't have to invest much money [23]. By monitoring student performance patterns predictive analytics use Artificial Intelligence to alert teachers about students who might not do well so that they put preventive measures to improve performance through personalized interventions [24–26].

Automated Assessment and Feedback mechanisms streamline grading processes for assignments, quizzes, and exams, offering instant and consistent feedback to students while saving instructors valuable time. AI-enhanced curriculum Development optimizes teaching strategies and content through educational data in a continuous fashion. This data-driven approach ensures that the curriculum remains current, relevant, and aligned with industry standards and research advancements, enhancing the overall quality of chemical engineering education.

AI-driven strategies are revolutionizing education by solving major problems with conventional methodologies. One of the main benefits is personalization. AI excels at meeting varied learning demands by tailoring information and pacing to each student, whereas traditional education finds it difficult to match these needs. By ensuring that every student receives the right amount of challenge and assistance, this customized method maximizes their learning experience. Furthermore, AI fosters active participation and a deeper understanding of complex concepts through interactive simulations and intelligent tutoring systems that give prompt feedback. Education resources can be accessed by a large number of students effectively and personally without losing quality; and this is an area in which AI seems particularly competent—scable. Through automating grade giving and feedback provision, AI not only is a timesaver for lecturers but also gives a bit of timely and uniform advice required for student improvements. Moreover, through continuous analysis of data and research for updates in the content, it becomes current and applicable ensuring learners acquire innovation promotion along with preparedness for relevant information and abilities vital for their areas.

4. Key AI Technologies Utilized in Chemical Engineering: Machine Learning (ML), Natural Language Processing (NLP), and Computer Vision

Artificial intelligence (AI) is changing chemical Engineering education by increasing the quality of the learning process and increasing the use of advanced teaching techniques. More specifically, AI-incorporated machine learning, natural language processing (NLP) and computer vision mechanisms ensure that chemical engineering students can use individual studying materials that suit them best; also, these mechanisms help in optimizing the existing methods of learning among university scholars in chemical sciences. Figure 2 outlines how various AI technologies enhance

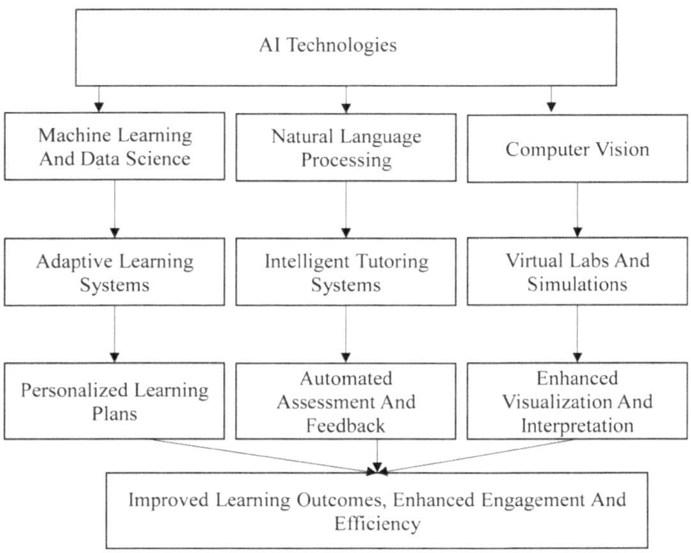

Figure 2. AI-driven approaches in chemical engineering education.

Chemical engineering education. Key technologies include Machine Learning and Data Science, Natural Language Processing, and Computer Vision, which power Adaptive Learning Systems, Intelligent Tutoring Systems, and Virtual Labs and Simulations. These technologies enable Personalized Learning Plans, Automated Assessment and Feedback, and Enhanced Visualization and Interpretation. Together, they contribute to improved learning outcomes, increased student engagement, and greater efficiency in educational processes.

4.1 Machine Learning (ML)

Machine Learning (ML) which is a subset of AI has led to a transformation in education related to chemical engineering by allowing machines to get knowledge from information and choose based on what they have learned without human beings telling them what to choose. The use of ML comes along with multiple uses that improve techniques used in imparting and acquiring knowledge. Machine Learning (ML) is becoming increasingly important in chemical engineering, aiding in the production and characterization of biomass, polymers, and petroleum products [27]. Additionally, ML has been integrated into mechatronics lab activities for measuring mechanical vibrations, which enhances undergraduate mechanical engineering students' understanding and application of ML [28]. It has also been applied to tackle challenges in chemistry and chemical engineering, including improving computational chemistry and modeling pollutant removal processes [29].

Chemical engineering departments are addressing the skills gap by introducing elective courses in ML. These courses cover a wide range of ML models, emphasizing their motivations, derivations, and training algorithms, and applying them to chemical engineering-related data sets [30]. ML techniques have revolutionized the fields of chemical and materials science, enabling accelerated and highly efficient discoveries in the design, synthesis, manufacturing, characterization, and application of novel functional materials, particularly at the nanometer scale [31].

ML technology has been utilized to predict students' performance and identify those at risk of failure, with algorithms such as Logistic Regression, Decision Tree, and Random Forest being applied for this purpose [32]. ML algorithms look into the notes concerning school achievements which are used to point out how students learn along with what they need hence coming up with customized ways of learning that change in accordance to the speed of each learner as well as how fast they can read and understand. Enhanced student engagement and learning outcomes are enabled when these customizations provide content that suits each individual and specific task, hence making engagement interesting.

For instance, if the decision is made to identify those students who are likely to perform poorly, it may help implement appropriate timely interventions hence there will be higher chances of remaining in school and performing well in academics [33]. Furthermore, by giving input parameters, ML optimizes experiments' design and performance within virtual laboratories. This means that a learner can easily consider various options while still narrowing down the scope of research to get more ideas on how chemical processes work in practice. For example, ALEKS uses machine learning to continuously assess the students' understanding and offer personalized questions that fill knowledge gaps [34] hence adding a lot of value during mastering chemical engineering courses.

Figure 3 shows how the ALEKS system enhances chemical engineering education through its integrated components. Students interact with an online platform where the ALEKS assessment engine evaluates their knowledge and maps out their understanding of chemical concepts. Adaptive algorithms create personalized learning pathways in subjects like process design and thermodynamics. Continuous progress monitoring and real-time feedback help tailor the educational experience, while course content and assessments in areas such as chemical reactions and fluid mechanics ensure comprehensive learning. Detailed student performance reports aid educators in tracking progress and adjusting teaching strategies, leading to improved learning outcomes and personalized education.

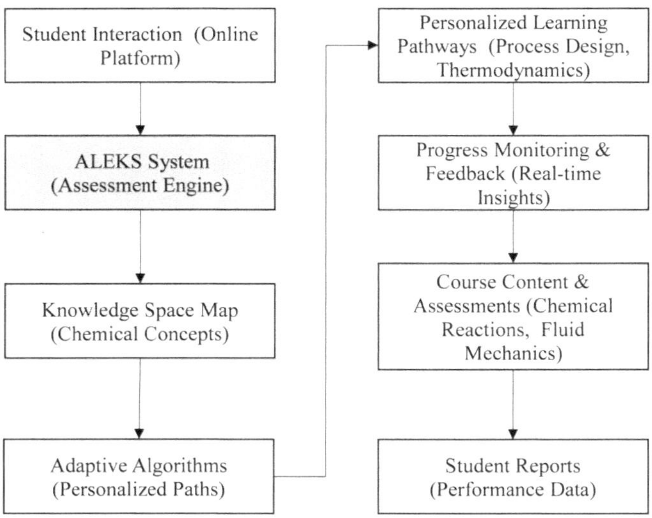

Figure 3. The role of ALEKS in enhancing chemical engineering education.

4.2 Natural Language Processing (NLP)

The primary goal of natural language processing is to forge a tight bond between computers and human beings by employing human languages. So, machines can comprehend, interpret, and assimilate human languages through NLP [35]. In this system, Intelligent Tutoring Systems (ITS) use NLP to interpret and answer academic questions asked by students in their languages. The students can get personalized tutoring through these systems which offer explanations, tips, and feedback that are customized to every student's requirement. Intelligent Tutoring Systems (ITS) enhance learning effectiveness by assisting students in understanding complex ideas and improving problem-solving skills [36]. Virtual Assistants and Chatbots driven by AI use NLP to help students when traditional classroom hours are over. These tools are available at any time to help them with assignments, clear up any confusion, or give them helpful information on their studies. One can learn all the time because they always have a chance to make inquiries about whatever academic or related issues they have in mind. Using natural language processing for analyzing data based on language provides a way through which relevant facts can be gotten from large amounts of printed information including lab reports and science papers. This function ensures that both learners and academics are notified of advances in the field of chemical engineering hence making it easier for schools to manage data.

IBM Watson Tutor, which is an AI system utilizing NLP for chemical engineering learning improvement, is a notable case study. The platform includes question-and-answer services, detailed explanations, and even accurate grading of short-answer responses to help students. It is an amazing tool that provides immediate support based on personal learning requirements while making the studying process more effective [37–39].

Figure 4 illustrates the integration of IBM Watson Tutor in chemical engineering education, highlighting its key components and benefits. IBM Watson Tutor leverages machine learning and natural language processing to personalize content and provide intelligent tutoring. The system includes a content personalization engine and student performance analytics to tailor educational experiences and monitor progress. These AI-driven technologies enable the creation of personalized learning plans and automated assessment and feedback mechanisms, resulting in improved student outcomes and enhanced teaching efficiency. By incorporating IBM Watson Tutor, chemical engineering education can be significantly enhanced through adaptive learning, real-time feedback, and efficient use of instructional resources.

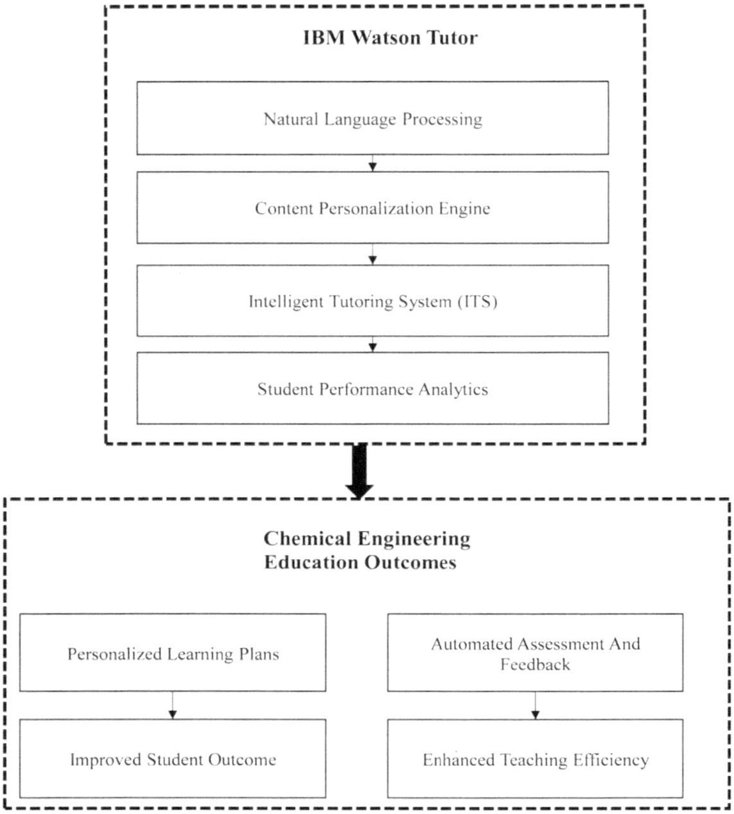

Figure 4. Integration of IBM Watson Tutor in chemical engineering education.

4.3 *Computer Vision*

Computer Vision is an area of "AI" that allows computer systems to interpret and process visual data coming from the real world just like human beings do with their eyes, this includes methods for capturing images and videos, analyzing them as well as understanding such videos too [40]. For the education sector in chemical engineering, learning experiences have been drastically changed by Computer Vision technologies, through a variety of applications. Computer Vision-powered Virtual Labs and Simulations mimic actual chemical engineering experiments in an online setup [41]. Student interactions with virtual equipment through this technology are monitored to make sure they stay on the right track. Students can carry out experiments, master skills, and understand difficult chemical processes better using virtual labs because they are cheaper and safer [42]. Computer Vision systems which facilitate the Automated

Grading of Lab Reports, are capable of analyzing the visual components of lab reports including graphs and experimental setups, ensuring objectivity and stability when awarding grades [43]. By increasing personal feedback between teacher and learner in the classroom context, this new approach eliminates time wastage by teachers marking papers while they could instead be giving individualized attention to the student's performances in a class.

The use of "Virtual Reality (VR) and Augmented Reality (AR)" enhanced interactive learning tools in chemical engineering education leads to greater participation and better spatial comprehension. Through Computer Vision, for instance, students can view in detail, the complex molecular structures as well as perform chemical reaction simulations within a fully 3D world. Such an experience makes concrete those concepts which may otherwise seem vague thereby leading to better understanding both theoretically or practically [44–47]. One notable case study is Labster Virtual Labs, where Computer Vision has been integrated to give an engaging educationist's experience [48]. In virtual settings, experiments can be done, equipment manipulated, and at the same time immediate responses. This approach significantly improves practical learning outcomes through hands-on experiences, as well as, traditional labs that are very effective, because they both operate together. These examples underline that the transformation of chemical engineering education by Computer Vision is done through practical learning that is more enriched, streamlined evaluation processes, and engagement is increased by innovative, interactive learning tools [49].

5. AI-Enhanced Personalized Learning in Chemical Engineering

Personalized learning is a teaching approach that tailors the learning experience to individual learners' needs, goals, and skills [50]. It is very important to have tailored learning in engineering education because it identifies and caters to the different modes of learning and rates of individual students. Different from the traditional one-size-fits-all ways, tailored customized education adjusts by taking into consideration the student`s strengths, weaknesses, interests, and preferred style of learning. A Three-Stage Approach (TSA) has been proposed to enhance personalized education for chemical engineering. This approach includes a professional tutorial system, open experimental projects, and individualized education modules [51].

Advanced algorithms and data analytics make AI vital in allowing customized learning in the education of chemical engineering. Modern algorithms employ AI to process data and determine how students learn based on numerous performance measures and learning preferences. This way the teachers will be able to use the information for each student to have an understanding of what works or does not work for them based on their performance metrics and learning preferences. AI aims to ensure personalized learning experiences for each student as much as possible through the implementation of customized learning pathways and content delivery methods. The use of AI-enhanced personalized learning methodologies has been shown to yield good results in the performance of engineering students, particularly in the context of active learning pedagogy [52]. AI-powered personalized training programs in chemical engineering that come up with interactive simulations as well as virtual laboratories. These systems can modify configurations for exercise simulations in real-time as a function of how students interact with them or perform in real-life scenarios. Individuals participating in such activities can take part in experiments within the context of a computer, work out problems that require problem-solving abilities, and acquire tailored responses immediately after their completion to guide them accordingly. This approach not only enhances practical learning experiences but also fosters critical thinking and problem-solving skills essential in the field of chemical engineering. A famous illustration is the Labster Virtual Labs which uses AI to come up with real virtual situations where pupils can practice experiments, handle things, and see different chemical responses. Such simulations help students to discuss hard principles and situations in an inexpensive way that they can access.

Figure 5 outlines a personalized recommendation system tailored for chemical engineering education, leveraging AI. The system begins by categorizing students based on their skill levels and preferences, recognizing strengths in areas such as fluid dynamics or places for improvement in process control. Students with similar skills are grouped using hierarchical clustering, aiding in targeted support. AI-based analysis evaluates performance metrics through lab reports and quizzes, recognizing learning patterns. Teaching content is then customized, offering adaptive learning modules such as interactive simulations for process safety. Continuous teaching evaluation through quizzes and lab feedback ensures regular assessment and personalized feedback, refining course content and recommendations. This AI-driven approach enhances chemical engineering education by catering to individual student needs and keeping the curriculum current and effective.

5.1 Importance of Personalized Learning in Engineering Education

When engineering education learning is individualized, it involves an educational style that customizes the way of teaching, the course material,

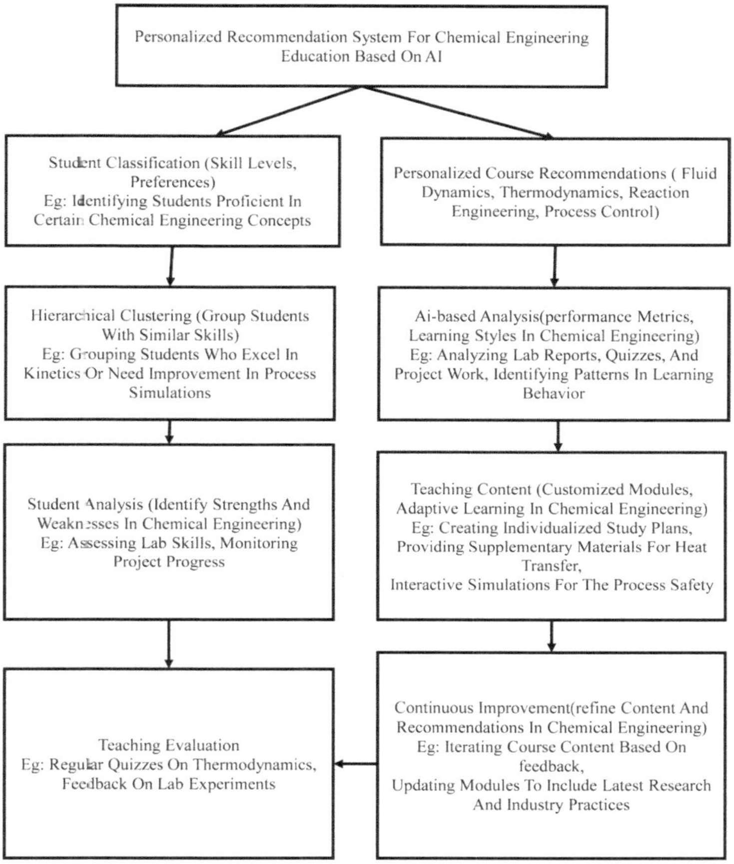

Figure 5. Personalized recommendation system for chemical engineering education based on AI.

and the intervals at which the student learns to meet the specificities of each student's unique characteristics such as needs, interests, preferences, or learning style. Unlike other traditional methods that take the shape of one size fitting all instructions, personalized schooling considers it important that all learners are born unique with different abilities which could be both strengths and weaknesses at any moment depending on how hard they have tried in life. This is the purpose of this approach to learning, to make learning deeper in terms of engagement, improve people's understanding of issues, and make any person learn by themselves.

There is an importance for personalized learning within engineering education which makes it possible for different kinds of students [53].

Making such modifications based on other people's academic profiles does a good job of boosting students' being guided by their work; thus, making sure that they succeed even without supervision provided these instructions are deposited into their memories. It is a way through which they quickly learn whatever they know while taking their sweet time in places of the syllabus that are hardest for them. In engineering, actively participating, thinking critically, and solving problems, and this is possible due to such flexibility. In addition, personalized education teaches pupils in a way that is similar to the real world such that they can apply the knowledge acquired to solve real-life problems, work with others as team players, and keep on studying throughout their lives. This partnership makes schooling in line with the demands of the labour market where technical specialists are required who know how to handle multi-faceted issues caused by rapid technological transformations. As a result, personal enlightenment at colleges enhances grades and helps turn out globally adaptable graduates who can produce something on a large scale.

5.2 *How AI Tailors Learning Experiences to Meet Individual Student Needs in Chemical Engineering*

AI tunes learning practices in the field of synthetic biology and utilizes distinctive algorithms and data interpretation methods to grasp each student's requirements. By monitoring how students communicate, their results, and preferred learning methods, it becomes easier for AI to know the areas where a particular student has excelled and those that he/she is not good at [54]. This helps to readjust reading materials, speed, and modes of delivery to improve. Adaptive learning systems that use machine learning algorithms are one of the ways artificial intelligence improves individualized learning. They work by monitoring how students are doing while engaged in educational materials like interactive simulations plus virtual laboratories and more importantly, they track progress during real-time interactions with students like a virtual tutor [55]. By doing so, It can change the complexity of questions; recommend additional sources for further study through hyperlinks; and give immediate feedback on specific mistakes made by learners because it realizes where learners are basing on the presented content. AI can, for example, identify when a student does not understand a certain concept and give them more practice problems that are connected or explain it again until they master it.

AI-powered intelligent instructional systems (ITS) in chemical engineering enable students to learn through human-like conversations, offering custom-made explanations, clues, and feedback. These platforms are used to study answers and conduct changes to tutoring techniques that are responsive as well as dynamic for every student who receives assistance to help him/her pass.

The AI-driven adaptive learning system for chemical engineering education integrates various components to create a personalized and interactive learning experience. Figure 6 shows an AI-driven adaptive learning system. Central to the system are the Learning Content Management and Learner Data Management modules, which handle educational materials and student data, respectively. Virtual Lab Modules offer simulated environments for hands-on practice, while the Learner Profile & Analytics component analyzes student performance. The Assessment Engine evaluates knowledge through quizzes and exams, and the Simulation Engine ensures realistic lab simulations. The Adaptive Learning Engine uses AI to tailor content based on individual learner profiles, providing customized instruction. Immediate, personalized feedback is delivered through the Feedback System, all accessible via a user-friendly interface. This cohesive system aims to enhance learning outcomes by adapting to each student's needs.

On a broader note, artificial intelligence has transformed the conventional approaches to education in chemical engineering by tailoring educational resources and communication to the particular needs and learning modes of each student. Were it not for the introduction of personalization through AI, student engagement and understanding would not have been so heightened while at the same time providing critical capabilities for future engineers in a world that is moving ever so fast.

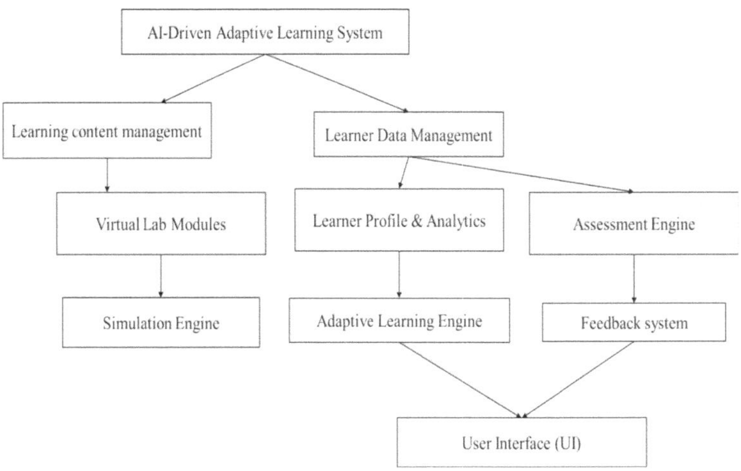

Figure 6. AI-driven adaptive learning system.

5.3 AI-driven Adaptive Learning Systems and Platforms used in Chemical Engineering Education

Chemical engineering education is being revolutionized by AI-powered adaptive learning systems and platforms that offer new methods for improving the educational process. Here are examples of such systems and how they are used

5.3.1 Labster Virtual Labs

Labster uses artificial intelligence to create immersive virtual laboratory environments that allow users to experiment, interact with apparatus, and monitor real-time chemical changes. These artificial environments can mimic elaborate situations that pose significant replication difficulties for conventional platforms primarily due to expense and complexity [56, 57]. Based on student performance and interaction in Labster, difficulty and complexity are adapted automatically which means that learners have a unique way of studying. Consequently, they get immediate responses and conduct experiments severally to understand and master the concepts better.

5.3.2 ALEKS (Assessment and Learning in Knowledge Spaces)

ALEKS uses artificial intelligence to measure what a student knows and then provides them with instruction tailored to their specific needs [58]. This software is used by college professors who teach chemical engineering. It can change its lessons when each student demonstrates understanding or misunderstanding of any given topic area like stoichiometry, etc., hence students receive unique sets of study materials for themselves. The system is always refreshed by updating each student's knowledge profile and adjusting the difficulty of questions in order to make sure they move on well in learning. Educators themselves are given comprehensive reports and analytics by ALEK that make it possible for them to know where a student might need some help [59].

5.3.3 ChemCollective Virtual Lab Simulation

ChemCollective Virtual Lab Simulations serve as a powerful alternative to in-person labs to assist student learning in chemical engineering courses, such as the introduction to chemical engineering and junior-level chemical engineering laboratory, where students design and test prototypes and carry out experiments [60]. These simulations have been integrated into the curriculum to provide early exposure to process simulation software, bridging theory and practice, and supporting new chemical engineering programs where labs may not be fully operational [41, 61]. The use of virtual lab simulations has been found to increase student engagement, learning, motivation, autonomy, interest, and confidence [60, 62]. Students have reported gaining a deeper understanding of concepts, practical skills, and real-world applications through virtual lab experiences [41, 61]. Virtual lab simulations have been shown to enhance students' knowledge retention, understanding of chemical processes, and practical skills, leading to a more favorable learning experience compared to traditional labs [42, 63]. They provide opportunities for learning through the amount of agency and consequential decisions they allow students to make, potentially enhancing student learning experiences [60]. In a comparative study, virtual lab simulations were reported to outperform traditional labs in terms of knowledge retention and learning experience, indicating a more favorable learning experience with virtual labs [42]. While virtual lab simulations have been recognized as potential replacements for traditional labs, they are often preferred as preparatory material for practical sessions, suggesting that they complement traditional labs effectively [62].

5.3.4 Smart Sparrow

Smart Sparrow is an adaptive e-learning platform that enables educators to create and deploy interactive, personalized learning experiences. The platform focuses on delivering tailored educational content that adapts to the needs of individual learners, providing real-time feedback and support [64]. Smart Sparrow has been instrumental in enhancing chemical engineering education through several innovative approaches. Laboratory-based courses designed using Kolb's experiential learning theory and Vygotsky's zone of proximal development have successfully ensured a satisfactory learning experience for students of varying abilities [65]. A project focusing on the Master's program in "Physicochemical Foundations of Innovative Technologies for Supermolecular Systems" aims to develop training courses in smart materials, nanotechnology, and biotechnology, specifically catering to engineering students, including those in chemical engineering [66]. An interdisciplinary curriculum, known as Intelligent Chemical Engineering (ICE), has been developed to equip students with the skills to apply automation and computer knowledge in solving complex industrial problems, thereby enhancing their interdisciplinary thinking and problem-solving abilities [67]. Addressing the lack of industry-relevant examples in the undergraduate core curriculum, a project aims to integrate contemporary industry problems into coursework, fostering student engagement with industry and faculty and improving workforce readiness [68, 69]. Additionally, product-based learning strategies and circular bioeconomy concepts are being integrated into chemical engineering education to help students develop solutions that meet societal demands, promoting creativity and entrepreneurship [54].

6. Intelligent Tutoring Systems (ITS) for Chemical Engineering Concepts

Artificial Intelligence (AI) has been taking center stage across various industries recently and as a result, there has been a significant transformation in the manner in these sectors operate as well as in the way professionals engage in their professions. In of chemical engineering, AI-supported tools are rapidly changing conventional theoretical and practical knowledge. These tools rely on machine learning, natural language processing (NLP), computer vision, and data analytics such that they make educational experiences better by optimizing processes.

AI has brought innovative means for chemical engineering students to interact with theoretical concepts and practical applications. These means range from virtual laboratories that emulate complex experiments to adaptive learning systems that adjust educational content according to the learning style of each student; in this way, AI-driven tools are leading the road toward more personalized, efficient, and effective learning environments. The discussion will explore some of the major AI technologies that have been facilitating innovation in Chemical engineering education.

Intelligent tutoring systems (ITSs) have been developed in various engineering domains, including chemical engineering, where they integrate multiple software tools to facilitate student learning through simulations of real-world applications [70]. These systems are designed to provide adaptive and personalized tutoring based on individual student needs and preferences, aiming to maximize learning gains and improve student engagement [71, 72]. The use of artificial intelligence techniques in ITSs significantly enhances the performance of simulations and helps manage reasoning under uncertainty, a major concern in student model design [73]. A specific example of an ITS in chemistry, known as Chem Tutor, demonstrates how a multi-methods approach in design can lead to significant learning gains in chemistry knowledge [74]. These AI-driven tutoring systems mimic human-like intelligence to offer customized tutoring and feedback, which is particularly beneficial in specialized domains like chemical engineering, where a deep understanding of reaction rates, heat transfer processes, and other core areas is crucial. Personalized intelligent tutors specifically designed for chemical engineering studies have shown substantial improvements in students' comprehension and application of these fundamental concepts.

7. Conclusions

The integration of Artificial Intelligence (AI) into chemical engineering education marks a significant advancement in the way students interact with both theoretical concepts and practical applications. Traditional methods, while foundational, often lack the personalization and adaptability that modern educational paradigms demand. AI-driven approaches, on the other hand, offer tailored learning experiences through technologies like machine learning, natural language processing, and computer vision. These innovations enable the creation of virtual laboratories, adaptive learning systems, and intelligent tutoring systems that cater to individual learning styles and needs. By automating routine educational activities, AI frees educators to focus more on personalized student engagement and complex problem-solving. The benefits are twofold: students receive a more customized, effective, and efficient learning experience, and educators gain powerful tools to enhance instructional methods and student outcomes. AI's role in chemical engineering education is transformative, providing tools that not only enhance learning but also better prepare students for the evolving demands of the engineering profession. As AI technologies continue to evolve, their integration into educational frameworks will likely deepen, fostering an environment where continuous improvement and innovation drive both teaching and learning. The future of chemical engineering education, thus, lies in the seamless fusion of traditional pedagogies with cutting-edge AI technologies, promising a new era of enhanced educational outcomes and professional preparedness.

References

[1] Chen, L., Chen, P. and Lin, Z. (2020). Artificial intelligence in education: A review. *IEEE Access*, 8: 75264–75278. Available: https://ieeexplore.ieee.org/abstract/document/9069875/.

[2] Pedro, F., Subosa, M., Rivas, A. and Valverde, P. (2019). Artificial intelligence in education: Challenges and opportunities for sustainable development. Available: http://repositorio.minedu.gob.pe/handle/20.500.12799/6533.

[3] van der Vorst, T. and Jelicic, N. (2019). Artificial intelligence in Education: Can AI bring the full potential of personalized learning to education. Available: https://www.econstor.eu/handle/10419/205222.

[4] Back, S., Aspuru-Guzik, A., Ceriotti, M., Gryn'ova, G., Grzybowski, B., Gu, G.H., Hein, J., Hippalgaonkar, K., Hormázabal, R., Jung, Y. and Kim, S. (2024). Accelerated chemical science with AI. *Digital Discovery*, 3(1): 23–33. Available: https://pubs.rsc.org/en/content/articlehtml/2024/dd/d3dd00213f.

[5] Forbus, K.D., Whalley, P.B., Everett, J.O., Ureel, L., Brokowski, M., Baher, J. and Kuehne, S.E. (1999). CyclePad: An articulate virtual laboratory for engineering thermodynamics. *Artificial Intelligence*, 114(1-2): 297–347. Available: https://www.sciencedirect.com/science/article/pii/S0004370299000806.

[6] Rane, N., Choudhary, S. and Rane, J. (2023). Education 4.0 and 5.0: Integrating artificial intelligence (AI) for personalized and adaptive learning. *Available at SSRN 4638365*, 2023. Available: https://papers.ssrn.com/sol3/papers.cfm?abstract_id=4638365.

[7] Burns, H.L. and Capps, C.G. (2013). Foundations of intelligent tutoring systems: An introduction. In *Foundations of Intelligent Tutoring Systems*, Psychology Press, pp. 1–19.

Available: https://www.taylorfrancis.com/chapters/edit/10.4324/9780203761557-1/foundations-intelligent-tutoring-systems-introduction-hugh-burns-charles-capps.

[8] Somasundaram, M., Latha, P. and Pandian, S.S. (2020). Curriculum design using artificial intelligence (AI) back propagation method. *Procedia Computer Science*, 172: 134–138. Available: https://www.sciencedirect.com/science/article/pii/S1877050920313430.

[9] Namoun, A. and Alshanqiti, A. (2020). Predicting student performance using data mining and learning analytics techniques: A systematic literature review. *Applied Sciences*, 11(1): 237. Available: https://www.mdpi.com/2076-3417/11/1/237.

[10] Gardner, J., O'Leary, M. and Yuan, L. (2021). Artificial intelligence in educational assessment: Breakthrough? Or buncombe and ballyhoo?. *Computer Assisted Learning*, 37(5): 1207–1216, doi: 10.1111/jcal.12577.

[11] González-Calatayud, V., Prendes-Espinosa, P. and Roig-Vila, R. (2021). Artificial intelligence for student assessment: A systematic review. *Applied Sciences*, 11(12): 5467. Available: https://www.mdpi.com/2076-3417/11/12/5467.

[12] Hill, R.C. and Parvini, Y. (2018). Automated grading with a software-checking program in the system dynamics and control curriculum. In *2018 Annual American Control Conference (ACC)*, IEEE, 2018, pp. 345–351. Available: https://ieeexplore.ieee.org/abstract/document/8431462/.

[13] da Silva-Júnior, E.F. (2023). You've got the Body I've got the Brains—Could the current AI-based tools replace the human ingenuity for designing new drug candidates?. *Bioorganic & Medicinal Chemistry*, 94: 117475. Available: https://www.sciencedirect.com/science/article/pii/S0968089623003231.

[14] Schweidtmann, A.M., Esche, E., Fischer, A., Kloft, M., Repke, J.U., Sager, S. and Mitsos, A. (2021). Machine learning in chemical engineering: A perspective. *Chemie Ingenieur Technik*, 93(12): 2029–2039, doi: 10.1002/cite.202100083.

[15] Ashraf, C., Joshi, N., Beck, D.A.C. and Pfaendtner, J. (2021). Data science in chemical engineering: Applications to molecular science. *Annu. Rev. Chem. Biomol. Eng.*, 12(1): 15–37, doi: 10.1146/annurev-chembioeng-101220-102232.

[16] Cussler, E.L. (2015). The future of the lecture. Available: https://experts.umn.edu/en/publications/the-future-of-the-lecture.

[17] Towler, G. and Sinnott, R. (2021). *Chemical Engineering Design: Principles, Practice and Economics of Plant and Process Design*. Butterworth-Heinemann, 2021.

[18] Riegel, K. (2021). A scaffolded approach to laboratory report writing for non-major and introductory physics classes. *The Physics Teacher*, 59(6): 488–490. Available: https://pubs.aip.org/aapt/pte/article/59/6/488/153006.

[19] Morgan, K. (2023). Evaluation of improvements to the student experience in chemical engineering practical classes: From prelaboratories to postlaboratories. *J. Chem. Educ.*, 100(12): 4597–4607, doi: 10.1021/acs.jchemed.3c00455.

[20] Chintalapati, P., Evans, G., Gladwin, D., Jamieson, M. and Ellis, N. (2024). Shaping futures: A dialogue on chemical engineering education. *Can. J. Chem. Eng.*, 102(5): 1688–1704, doi: 10.1002/cjce.25205.

[21] Tan, S. (2023). Harnessing Artificial Intelligence for innovation in education. In *Learning Intelligence: Innovative and Digital Transformative Learning Strategies*, Singapore: Springer Nature Singapore, pp. 335–363, doi: 10.1007/978-981-19-9201-8_8.

[22] Gounder, N., Faniran, I.V.T. and Faloye, S.T. (2024). Integrating adaptive Intelligent tutoring systems into private higher educational institutes. In *2024 IST-Africa Conference (IST-Africa)*, IEEE, pp. 1–13. Available: https://ieeexplore.ieee.org/abstract/document/10569565/.

[23] Kuntz, A. and Wilson, A.K. (2022). Machine learning, artificial intelligence, and chemistry: How smart algorithms are reshaping simulation and the laboratory. *Pure and Applied Chemistry*, 94(8): 1019–1054, doi: 10.1515/pac-2022-0202.

[24] Corrigan, O., Smeaton, A.F., Glynn, M. and Smyth, S. (2015). Using educational analytics to improve test performance. pp. 42–55. *In*: Conole, G., Klobučar, T., Rensing, C., Konert, J. and Lavoué, E. (eds.). *Design for Teaching and Learning in a Networked World*, in Lecture Notes in Computer Science, vol. 9307. Cham: Springer International Publishing, doi: 10.1007/978-3-319-24258-3_4.

[25] Qazdar, A., Qassimi, S., Hafidi, M., Hasidi, O. and Abdelwahed, E.H. (2023). Artificial neural network with learning analytics for student performance prediction in online learning environment. pp. 788–801. In: Kacprzyk, J., Ezziyyani, M. and Balas, V.E. (eds.). *International Conference on Advanced Intelligent Systems for Sustainable Development*, in Lecture Notes in Networks and Systems, vol. 637. Cham: Springer Nature Switzerland, doi: 10.1007/978-3-031-26384-2_70.

[26] Dwivedi, D.N., Mahanty, G. and Dwivedi, V. nath. (2024). The role of predictive analytics in personalizing education: tailoring learning paths for individual student success. In *Enhancing Education with Intelligent Systems and Data-Driven Instruction*, IGI Global, pp. 44–59. Available: https://www.igi-global.com/chapter/the-role-of-predictive-analytics-in-personalizing-education/341140.

[27] Mafat, I.H., Surya, D.V., Sharma, S.K. and Rao, C.S. (2024). Exploring machine learning applications in chemical production through valorization of biomass, plastics, and petroleum resources: A comprehensive review. *Journal of Analytical and Applied Pyrolysis*, 180, doi: 10.1016/j.jaap.2024.106512.

[28] Kim, J., Choi, J. and Kim, J. (2023). Introducing machine learning in undergraduate mechanical engineering mechatronics classes. *Presented at the ASME International Mechanical Engineering Congress and Exposition, Proceedings (IMECE)*, doi: 10.1115/IMECE2023-112655.

[29] Taoufik, N., Boumya, W., Achak, M., Chennouk, H., Dewil, R. and Barka, N. (2022). The state of art on the prediction of efficiency and modeling of the processes of pollutants removal based on machine learning. *Science of the Total Environment*, 807, doi: 10.1016/j.scitotenv.2021.150554.

[30] Pilario, K.E. (2024). Teaching classical machine learning as a graduate-level course in chemical engineering: An algorithmic approach. *Digital Chemical Engineering*, 11, doi: 10.1016/j.dche.2024.100163.

[31] Xi, Z. (2022). Functional nanomaterials design in the workflow of building machine-learning models. *Lecture Notes in Networks and Systems*, 439: 370–383, doi: 10.1007/978-3-030-98015-3_25.

[32] Almehaiza, F., Jaafar, L., Alatoom, I.A.M. and Hewahi, N.M. (2022). Investigation on machine learning algorithms to predict high school students performance at risk of failure. *Presented at the 2022 International Conference on Data Analytics for Business and Industry*, ICDABI 2022, pp. 77–82. doi: 10.1109/ICDABI56818.2022.10041554.

[33] Adnan, M., Alarood, A.A.S., Uddin, M.I. and Rehman, I.U. (2022). Utilizing grid search cross-validation with adaptive boosting for augmenting performance of machine learning models. *PeerJ Computer Science*, 8, doi: 10.7717/PEERJ-CS.803.

[34] Matayoshi, J. and Cosyn, E. (2018). Identifying student learning patterns with semi-supervised machine learning models. *Presented at the ICCE 2018—26th International Conference on Computers in Education, Main Conference Proceedings*, pp. 11–20.

[35] Patil, C.S. and Patil, A.P. (2023). Machine learning in natural language processing—emerging trends and challenges. In *Data Science with Semantic Technologies: New Trends and Future Developments*, pp. 131–144. doi: 10.1201/9781003310785-7.

[36] Li, S., Tong, Y., Tembo, S. and Han, B. (2022). Overview of intelligent tutoring system. In *Artificial Intelligence in Education and Teaching Assessment*, pp. 281–291. doi: 10.1007/978-981-16-6502-8_25.

[37] Ventura, M., Chang, M., Foltz, P., Mukhi, N., Yarbro, J., Salverda, A.P., Behrens, J., Ahn, J.W., Ma, T., Dhamecha, T.I. and Marvaniya, S. (2018). Preliminary evaluations

of a dialogue-based digital tutor. *Lecture Notes in Computer Science (including subseries Lecture Notes in Artificial Intelligence and Lecture Notes in Bioinformatics)*, 10948: 480–483, doi: 10.1007/978-3-319-93846-2_90.

[38] Murtaza, S.S., Lak, P., Bener, A. and Pischdotchian, A. (2016). How to effectively train IBM watson: Classroom experience. *Presented at the Proceedings of the Annual Hawaii International Conference on System Sciences*, pp. 1663–1670, doi: 10.1109/HICSS.2016.210.

[39] Afzal, S., Dempsey, B., D'Helon, C., Mukhi, N., Pribic, M., Sickler, A., Strong, P., Vanchiswar, M. and Wilde, L. (2019). The personality of AI systems in education: Experiences with the watson tutor, a one-on-one virtual tutoring system. *Childhood Education*, 95(1): 44–52, doi: 10.1080/00094056.2019.1565809.

[40] Ballari, S.O., Srinivas, A., Gupta, M., Dhobal, K., Akabarkhan, P.S. and Reddy, D.V. (2023). A critical analysis of applying computer vision in building an intelligent system. *Presented at the 2023 3rd International Conference on Advance Computing and Innovative Technologies in Engineering*, ICACITE 2023, pp. 562–566, doi: 10.1109/ICACITE57410.2023.10182958.

[41] Le, H.M., Nguyen, G.H., Huynh, V.T., Le, M.K., Tran, M.T., Nguyen, T.V. and Tran, T.N.D. (2022). Chemisim: A web-based VR simulator for chemistry experiments. *Presented at the Proceedings—2022 IEEE International Symposium on Mixed and Augmented Reality Adjunct*, ISMAR-Adjunct 2022, pp. 850–854, doi: 10.1109/ISMAR-Adjunct57072.2022.00183.

[42] Naz, Z., Azam, A., Khan, M.U.G., Saba, T., Al-Otaibi, S. and Rehman, A. (2024). Development and evaluation of immersive VR laboratories of organic chemistry and physics for students education. *Physica Scripta*, 99(5), doi: 10.1088/1402-4896/ad3024.

[43] Wang, D., Bischof, L., Lagerstrom, R., Hilsenstein, V., Hornabrook, A. and Hornabrook, G. (2016). Automated opal grading by imaging and statistical learning. *IEEE Transactions on Systems, Man, and Cybernetics: Systems*, 46(2): 185–201, doi: 10.1109/TSMC.2015.2427776.

[44] Solmaz, S., Dominguez Alfaro, J.L., Santos, P., Van Puyvelde, P. and Van Gerven, T. (2021). A practical development of engineering simulation-assisted educational AR environments. *Education for Chemical Engineers*, 35: 81–93, doi: 10.1016/j.ece.2021.01.007.

[45] Alrige, M., Bitar, H., Al-Suraihi, W., Bawazeer, K. and Al-Hazmi, E. (2021). MicroWorld: An augmented-reality arabian app to learn atomic space. *Technologies*, 9(3), doi: 10.3390/technologies9030053.

[46] Ferrell, J.B., Campbell, J.P., McCarthy, D.R., McKay, K.T., Hensinger, M., Srinivasan, R., Zhao, X., Wurthmann, A., Li, J. and Schneebeli, S.T. (2019). Chemical exploration with virtual reality in organic teaching laboratories. *Journal of Chemical Education*, 96(9): 1961–1966, doi: 10.1021/acs.jchemed.9b00036.

[47] Zhou, Z., Oveissi, F. and Langrish, T. (2024). Applications of augmented reality (AR) in chemical engineering education: Virtual laboratory work demonstration to digital twin development. *Computers and Chemical Engineering*, 188, doi: 10.1016/j.compchemeng.2024.108784.

[48] Stauffer, S., Gardner, A., Duprez, D., Kencana Ungu, D.A. and Wismer, P. (2018). *Labster Virtual Lab Experiments: Basic Biology*, p. 64, doi: 10.1007/978-3-662-57999-2.

[49] Kumar, V. (2019). The inescapable effects of virtual laboratory and comparison of traditional laboratory with virtual laboratory. *Presented at the Communication and Computing Systems—Proceedings of the 2nd International Conference on Communication and Computing systems*, ICCCS 2018, pp. 509–512.

[50] Shemshack, A., Kinshuk and Spector, J.M. (2021). A comprehensive analysis of personalized learning components. *Journal of Computers in Education*, 8(4): 485–503, doi: 10.1007/s40692-021-00188-7.

[51] Zhao, F.-Q. (2016). Personalized education approaches for chemical engineering and relevant majors. *Presented at the MATEC Web of Conferences*, doi: 10.1051/matecconf/20166820003.

[52] Rajesh, K., Sivapragasam, C. and Dargar, S.K. (2024). AI-enhanced personalized learning practices in higher engineering institutes. *Journal of Engineering Education Transformations*, 37(2): 887–892, doi: 10.16920/jeet/2024/v37is2/24136.
[53] Clark, Q.M. and Clark, J.V. (2018). Personalized learning tool for thermodynamics. In *2018 IEEE Frontiers in Education Conference (FIE)*, IEEE, pp. 1–5. Available: https://ieeexplore.ieee.org/abstract/document/8658758/.
[54] Marquez, R., Barrios, N., Vera, R.E., Mendez, M.E., Tolosa, L., Zambrano, F. and Li, Y. (2023). A perspective on the synergistic potential of artificial intelligence and product-based learning strategies in biobased materials education. *Education for Chemical Engineers*, 44: 164–180. Available: https://www.sciencedirect.com/science/article/pii/S1749772823000222.
[55] Colchester, K., Hagras, H., Alghazzawi, D. and Aldabbagh, G. (2017). A survey of artificial intelligence techniques employed for adaptive educational systems within E-learning platforms. *Journal of Artificial Intelligence and Soft Computing Research*, 7(1): 47–64, doi: 10.1515/jaiscr-2017-0004.
[56] Verawati, N.N.S.P., Rokhmat, J., Sukarso, A.A., Harjono, A. and Makhrus, M. (2024). Utilizing interactive labs technology resources in science learning: A literature review. *International Journal of Essential Competencies in Education*, 3(1): 47–76. Available: https://journal-center.litpam.com/index.php/ijece/article/view/1865.
[57] Zinopoulou, M. (2019). *A Framework for Improving Engagement and the Learning Experience through Emerging Technologies*. Ph.D. Thesis, University of Southampton. Available: https://eprints.soton.ac.uk/447746/.
[58] Alam, A. (2023). Intelligence unleashed: An argument for AI-enabled learning ecologies with real world examples of today and a peek into the future. In *AIP Conference Proceedings*, AIP Publishing. Available: https://pubs.aip.org/aip/acp/article-abstract/2717/1/030001/2899678.
[59] Murphy, R.F. (2019). Artificial intelligence applications to support K-12 teachers and teaching. *Rand Corporation*, 10: 1–19. Available: https://www.jstor.org/stable/pdf/resrep19907.
[60] Santos, F. and Van Gerven, T. (2020). Aspen Hysys–Unity interconnection. An approach for rigorous computer-based chemical engineering training. *Computer Aided Chemical Engineering*, 48: 2053–2058, doi: 10.1016/B978-0-12-823377-1.50343-8.
[61] Zaldívar, M.A.B., Intriago, S.N.G., Gorozabel, B.P.L., Palacio, G.L.S., Pachay, P.V.L., Vélez, M.A.F. and Ruperti-Montesdeoca, J.P. (2024). Didactic strategy for the virtual experimental teaching of chemistry. *Presented at the AIP Conference Proceedings*, doi: 10.1063/5.0187702.
[62] Kong, Z.Y., Omar, A.A., Lau, S.L. and Sunarso, J. (2024). Introducing process simulation as an alternative to laboratory session in undergraduate chemical engineering thermodynamics course: A case study from Sunway University Malaysia. *Digital Chemical Engineering*, 12, doi: 10.1016/j.dche.2024.100167.
[63] Al-Nakhle, H. (2022). The effectiveness of scenario-based virtual laboratory simulations to improve learning outcomes and scientific report writing skills. *PLoS ONE*, 17(11), doi: 10.1371/journal.pone.0277359.
[64] Kaw, A., Clark, R., Delgado, E. and Abate, N. (2019). Analyzing the use of adaptive learning in a flipped classroom for preclass learning. *Comp. Applic. in Engineering*, 27(3): 663–678, doi: 10.1002/cae.22106.
[65] Chen, W., Shah, U.V. and Brechtelsbauer, C. (2019). A framework for hands-on learning in chemical engineering education—Training students with the end goal in mind. *Education for Chemical Engineers*, 28: 25–29, doi: 10.1016/j.ece.2019.03.002.
[66] Development of "smart materials" master's degree program module for chemical engineers. *Presented at the Education Division 2018—Core Programming Area at the 2018* AIChE Annual Meeting, 2018, pp. 121–122.

[67] Zhang, W., Zheng, J., Wang, J., Dong, J. and Cheng, Y. (2023). Design and implementation of the interdisciplinary curriculum for intelligent chemical engineering program at Taiyuan University of Technology. *Education for Chemical Engineers*, 42: 1–6, doi: 10.1016/j.ece.2022.10.002.

[68] Bilgin, B., Isa, H.N., Seriruk, E. and Mischel, C.W. (2023). Board 253: Developing professional identity: Integrating academic and workplace competencies within engineering programs. *Presented at the ASEE Annual Conference and Exposition, Conference Proceedings*, 2023.

[69] Bilgin, B., Pellegrino, J.W., Mischel, C.W. and Wedgewood, L.E. (2022). Developing professional identity: Integrating academic and workplace competencies within engineering programs. *Presented at the ASEE Annual Conference and Exposition, Conference Proceedings*, 2022.

[70] Stan, C. and Oprea, M. (2022). Virtual learning simulator of a flexible manufacturing line using Petri NET toolbox. *Presented at the Proceedings of the International Conference on Virtual Learning*, pp. 101–108. doi: 10.58503/icvl-v17y202208.

[71] Sani, S. and Aris, T.N.M. (2015). Computational intelligence approaches for student/tutor modelling: A review. *Presented at the Proceedings—International Conference on Intelligent Systems, Modelling, and Simulation*, ISMS, pp. 72–76. doi: 10.1109/ISMS.2014.21.

[72] Jakobsche, C.E., Kongsomjit, P., Milson, C., Wang, W. and Ngan, C.-K. (2023). Incorporating an intelligent tutoring system into the discoverOchem learning platform. *Journal of Chemical Education*, 100(8): 3081–3088, doi: 10.1021/acs.jchemed.3c00117.

[73] Sani, S.M., Aris, T.N.M., Mustapha, N. and Sulaiman, M.N. (2015). A fuzzy logic approach to manage uncertainty and improve the prediction accuracy in student model design. *Journal of Theoretical and Applied Information Technology*, 82(3): 366–377.

[74] Rau, M.A., Michaelis, J.E. and Fay, N. (2015). Connection making between multiple graphical representations: A multi-methods approach for domain-specific grounding of an intelligent tutoring system for chemistry. *Computers and Education*, 82: 460–485, doi: 10.1016/j.compedu.2014.12.009.

Chapter 12

Modern Higher Education System with Blockchain-based Infrastructure Focusing on Improving the Efficacy of Financial Operations

*Neethu Tressa** and *C Priya*

Blockchain technology has been rapidly evolving by creating applications beyond Cryptocurrencies and adapting to the changes in the modern world concerning areas like Supply Chain Management, Agriculture, Healthcare, E-Governance, and so on. The higher education sector is yet another field where the emergence of Blockchain has enormous contributions. Secured financial transactions have become an inevitable requirement today. Modern Education Systems also need to get upgraded with secured financial practices against fraud, data breaches, cyber security threats, etc as these systems heavily rely on financial transactions on a day-to-day basis including tuition fees, grants, scholarships, employee salaries, research funding, donations, endowments, and many more. This

Dr. M.G.R. Educational and Research Institute, Tamil Nadu, India.
https://orcid.org/0000-0002-5687-8598.
https://orcid.org/0000-0003-1809-5274.
* Corresponding author: neethutressa89@gmail.com

book chapter is intended to propose a framework that can elucidate the influence of Blockchain Technology on the education area to optimize financial operations with technology-driven security measures. The upcoming sections of the chapter begin with an introduction on merging Blockchain Technology with financial activities focusing on security and optimized operations followed by a thorough study of current research works on the same. Further, it elaborates on the proposed framework for more secure as well as blockchain-based financial activities concluding with future scope for framework enhancements.

1. Introduction

Modern higher education is a complicated financial structure with numerous economic events that are critical to its operation and progress. At the root of these institutions are universities and colleges that provide education along with research facilities, which are, in turn, funded by intricate financial structures [1]. Tuition revenues represent one of the main sources of income for these institutions that support essential services including faculty salaries, campus maintenance, and academic programs. The sudden increase in tuition fees always reflected the increased expenses towards high-quality education as well as the high requirement for state-of-the-art facilities and educational resources. Public universities receive significant financial support from both their state (or, in some cases, federal) governments. This financial aid assists in reducing the tuition fee and supports hefty research projects. Grants—both public and private—are crucial in driving scientific research and innovation allowing institutions to conduct revolutionary studies that serve as a boon for society. Endowments are an essential component of financial sustainability within higher education institutions. These are investment dollars, provided by alumni and certain donors of university funds that have been collected over the years to produce an annual cash flow on which a bit more can be delivered back. Endowments can fund scholarships, resource persons, research projects, and various academic initiatives. This money needs proper management to make the best out of it in the long run. Scholarships and financial aid play an important role in ensuring that persons from low-income families can pursue higher education. There are a lot of different financial supports out there - some merit-based, and others need-based for the students. Another significant financial area is that of operational expenses which include environmental support systems across campus (heating, cooling, etc.), maintaining facilities on the premises (office space and similar), utilities (all other infrastructure costs) information technology services throughout the university community, administrative functions, student support activities, etc., to keep up-to-date with actions in place through student-related action initiatives. Collaborations can also help to establish additional revenue streams, such as research contracts and joint ventures, which are an important source of commercial activity for academic ideas. It is a great financial variable for the institution and students towards student loans. For many students, borrowing to pay for college is a necessity which makes student debt management and loan repayment major concerns, not just in terms of financial planning but also in long-term post-graduation achievements. Hence, the contemporary higher education system is supported by multiple important financial activities. Having good control of tuition fees, state finances, endowments, scholarships, and operational expenses are all important variables in the financial management for institutions' long-term sustainability to continue offering a quality education capable of generating innovations that sustainably allow access to broad layers of society.

Introduced as a novel P2P system for cryptocurrency transactions, blockchain technology is now considered to be one of the most important fundamental technologies in real-world financial applications [2]. It works as a decentralized digital ledger that records transactions across many computers so the record cannot be altered retroactively. It solves major problems for the financial industry, with security and fraud prevention as its most notable benefits. In conventional financial systems, transactions need to be verified by central entities such as banks or clearinghouses, which makes them slower and more expensive. The usage of blockchain technology removes these intermediaries and allows for direct peer-to-peer transactions that are verified through a consensus mechanism. This accelerates the whole transaction process along with the decreased cost of transferring funds from A to B upwards or downwards in seconds, without any hidden intermediary margins involved. Cross-Border Payments, one of the most common uses for Blockchain in Finance for traditional methods are slow and expensive, getting repeated for days while high costs also apply. This has made blockchain technology conduct fast and low-fee transactions, which could then streamline both accuracy and access - something extremely beneficial in remittances where migrant workers send their earnings back home. And this is where blockchain creates a perfect solution for transparent and secure financial transactions. In the blockchain, all transactions are recorded on a public ledger that is visible to everyone in the system which minimizes chances of fraud and creates trust. There is no way to change the records thanks to blockchain immutability which guarantees a secure and tamper-proof audit trail of transactions. Blockchain technology changes asset trading beyond just payments. Blockchain platforms can also facilitate trading in security tokens, which are ownership rights to real-world assets, such as real property or corporate shares. The tokenization further provides a method to increase liquidity and enable fractional ownership, allowing more investors the opportunity to invest. Moreover, blockchain allows for the implementation of smart contracts—self-executing contracts with predetermined rules written into code. The thing about these contracts is that they enforce themselves automatically whenever the predefined conditions are met without any third-party intervention (legal intermediaries) so, it speeds up the contractual process tremendously. Well, blockchain technology has completely transformed how we do financial transactions and it provides faster reliable methods to send money cheaply. But it is also a key imagining of the future of finance for its capacity to make things easier, more transparent, and cheaper.

So, taking into consideration the modern higher education system in which financial activity and diverse administrative processes are involved, blockchain technology is a great solution. A secure, transparent, and efficient decentralized digital ledger aimed at solving many of the key challenges in this sector is illustrated in Figure 1.

1. Improved Data Security: Blockchain protects the privacy of student data like academic records and financial information by using its security aspects; Data stored on the blockchain is immutable and it cannot be corrupted or altered in any capacity - which guarantees data integrity, preventing fraud, and detection of unauthorized access. This is a key feature of the verification of academic credentials.
2. Simplifying Administrative Processes: Many standard administrative tasks in education (crediting student accounts, processing requests for records or documentation) are manual and slow, meaning that there is ample room to automate. Smart Contracts using the blockchain can also automate these processes by executing predetermined actions when certain conditions are met. This helps to reduce administrative overhead, improve accuracy, and increase effectiveness.

Figure 1. Benefits of blockchain technology in modern higher education system.

3. Improved Transparency and Traceability: This is one of the greatest advantages that Blockchain gives in financial transparency by monitoring tuition payments, scholarship disbursements, and funding allocations in real-time ensuring better accountability with lesser financial mismanagement risks. This level of transparency improves confidence in students, parents, and donors as well as the various educational institutions.
4. Academic Credential Verification: Most employers and other educational institutions require their academic background to be verified, this can allow the verified credentials to be stored on a tamper-proof and easily accessible, immutable ledger (Blockchain) hence reducing the time needed for verification while preventing spoofing or fraudulent claims.
5. Funding and Collaboration in Research: Blockchain acts as a shared ledger for tracking research grants, and ensures that funds are used where it has been mentioned. It also enables secure and transparent collaboration between institutions and researchers, encouraging innovation and knowledge exchange.
6. Better Student Experience: Through the use of blockchain, students now have a better way to take charge of their academic records and access appropriate certifications. This technology can also support more efficient financial aid distribution and simplify student loan management, potentially easing students' financial burdens.

This chapter aims to propose a framework enabled with Blockchain Technology to be deployed in modern higher education systems that can enhance the security, performance, and user experience of the existing methodologies. The further sections of the chapter are organized into a literature review, proposed system, proposed system architecture, challenges in its implementation, conclusion to the study, and directions for future research work.

2. Literature Review

This section describes the very recent works similar to the proposed one which show the advancements that happened in the field of Blockchain Technology when integrated in education systems specifically. For the review, articles published in the years 2023 and 2024 were considered, and a precise review has been done and elaborated as follows:

The article [1], examines how blockchain can revolutionize the education sector by presenting a detailed framework demonstrating how blockchain can improve security, transparency, and efficiency in managing financial and academic processes. It discusses applications such as secure financial transactions, credential verification, and the use of smart contracts. While a deeper analysis of implementation challenges and real-world examples would enhance the discussion, the paper lays a strong foundation for future research and practical use of blockchain in educational institutions.

The work [2] thoroughly investigates the impact of blockchain on educational practices. It takes deep into the different projects, products, and applications out there and it expands on the pluses while also throwing some light on how blockchain can be a nightmare from an educational perspective. It sheds light on the scope of blockchain to improve security, transparency, and autonomy in educational operations. In a practical sense, more evaluation on how these can be applied and empirical case studies would provide a fuller implementation of blockchain in place within education.

A review as in a detailed analysis [3] highlights the importance of blockchain revolutionizing education. This article outlines some areas where blockchain is applied and considers the barriers to such integration within educational settings. This chapter offers critical insights into ways blockchain can enhance moats around data, operations, and security for education institutions. More specific applications and case studies could provide more insight into how blockchain can indeed transform education as we know it.

The article [4] talks about Blockchain's potential use cases in the education domain. In this special issue, it discusses the potential to improve security, transparency, and efficiency in educational processes as well as related challenges. This article provides important lessons for how blockchain could work in academic areas, such as innovative approaches towards verification of credentials, student records, and collaborations among research despite the lack of a demonstration. More research on practical applications and case studies related to blockchain will increase our knowledge of how it can potentially transform the future of education.

The chapter [5] investigates transforming Education in the Contemporary World as an exploration of blockchain and its evolution as a disruptive tool for contemporary education. These innovations concern credential and student data enablement, as well as developing an education platform that advances security, efficiency, and transparency in higher education. Although informative, deeper insights into applied case studies and intricate applications would better illustrate blockchain's position to foster Education 4.0.

The journal article [6] proposes blockchain and smart contract solutions in a university education process. The research looks into the potential of such technology to enhance transparency, simplify administrative processes (like admissions or course registration), and protect academic records. The essay contains critical findings about blockchain in higher education, including demonstrated efficiency gains and operational advantages. More empirical research and practical implementations on the impact of blockchain would be beneficial in establishing a broad-based understanding of how it affects various functions within a university.

The review [7] analysed the use of blockchain technology to authenticate academic and professional certifications. Its focus is on the promise of blockchain to improve security and trust in credential verification, demonstrating a way that could be used to deter fraud through transparency. The article is short and crisp, summarizing the transformative potential of blockchain for credential management in higher education and beyond. In conclusion, empirical evidence and more practical case studies could provide a better indication of how blockchain can preserve the credibility of credentials.

An extensive review [8] shows the use of blockchain in education which will change everything from digital diplomas to smarter schools. It provides an exhaustive review of how decentralisation affects Education. It covers several new inventions and results, paying particular focus to improvements in credentialing validation/adjudication processes, student data management systems for schools/universities, etc., and increased academic transparency arenas. The study explores blockchain in improving efficiency and trust within educational contexts. Although providing valuable lessons on blockchain application, more (especially empirical) research and implementation measures will be necessary to fully understand how transformative it could become in the education space.

The article [9] presents the uses of NFT for academic institutions focused on online payment systems. In other words, the technology is lauded as an effective approach to providing security, reducing transactional friction, and adding transparency in formal academic financial transactions. This paper includes an early vision and framework to integrate blockchain into educational financial processes. We need additional studies for real-world implementation and validation to evaluate the scalability of this model in practical education settings.

In the doctoral dissertation [10], the corresponding author explores the integration of blockchain to secure mobile payment systems in higher education. The research also features his ideas to use blockchain to securitise financial transactions and deliver transparency as well as alleviate fraud in educational settings. This research study highlights how the functionality of blockchain can be leveraged to enable universities to transactions through a secure and efficient mode. However, further empirical study and applications are needed for the scalability and practical efficiency of blockchain-enabled mobile payment systems in academic institutions.

Modern higher education presents all conditions to be replaced or transformed by blockchain technology. Blockchain solves all concerns by strengthening data security and streamlining administrative operations, making it easier to authenticate credentials, conduct research, and collaborate for the industry. It can be implemented to create an improved, verifiable, and transparent higher education ecosystem making the system efficient for students, teachers, and administrators. By enhancing data security, streamlining administrative processes, improving financial transparency, enabling easy credential verification, and supporting research and collaboration, blockchain addresses many of the challenges faced by educational institutions. Its implementation can lead to a more efficient, secure, and transparent higher education system, benefiting students, educators, and administrators alike.

3. Blockchain Technology in the Education Sector

From the systematic literature review, it was found that Blockchain technology can play a vital role in the education sector. The study progressed through an analysis of IEEE Xplore to identify the number of papers published on Blockchain Technology focusing on the education sector solely and found the following result as shown in Figure 2. The Graph shows the publications as stated above, that happened from 2018 to 2023 [13]. The increase in the publication count is evident to state that integrating Blockchain technology into the education system can provide improvement in a wide range of services.

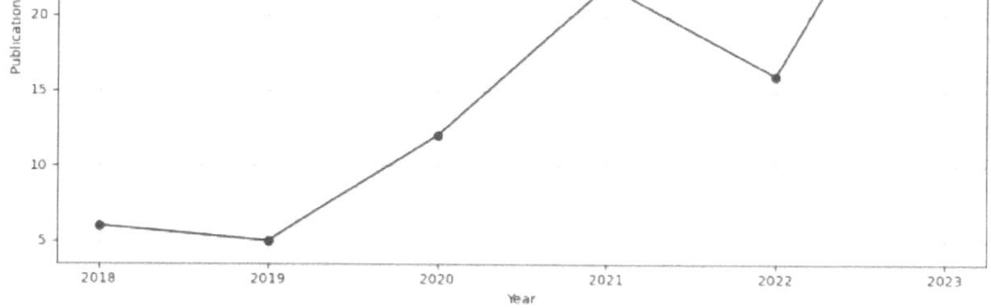

Figure 2. Publication rate over the last 6 years.

Blockchain technology can provide substantial services within the education sector. It can provide tamper-proof academic credentials verification, secured student records management, simplified admissions and enrolment processes, decentralized education resource storage and intellectual property protection, authorized Learning Management System, safe payment transactions, streamlined student and faculty identity management, immutable record keeping for accreditation and enhanced quality assurance activities, automated and distributes research and grants management, fair exams and proctoring systems, accurate alumni network and career service management, enhanced student governance and voting and many more. Figure 3 illustrates all these

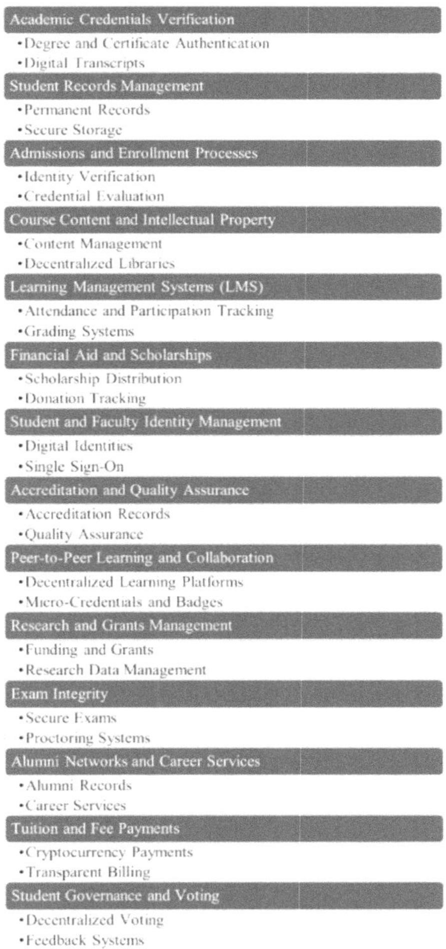

Figure 3. Blockchain services in the education sector.

features and services that can make the education system much stronger and more secure. By integrating blockchain technology into these various activities, educational institutions can enhance security, streamline processes, improve transparency, and foster trust among students, faculty, and stakeholders.

4. Proposed System

This work proposes a blockchain-based infrastructure for the Modern Higher Education System to improve its financial activities. The following diagram Figure 4 shows the working of the proposed system with the major entities such as the University, Student, Credential Verifier, Blockchain Platform, Smart Contracts, Registrar, and Financial Aid Office.

In student enrolment and registration, the student has to first apply for admission. The admission office will be verifying the academic credentials via a blockchain-based verification procedure. Blockchain will be recording the verified credentials securely. Similarly, for tuition and other fees payments, the student has to first select the courses and generate a fee invoice. The student will initiate the payment using blockchain-based cryptocurrency or related digital tokens. Here also blockchain will be recording the transaction securely as well as transparently. In the case of financial aid distribution which usually happens in a higher education system, a similar procedure will only be carried out. Here also the student will apply for financial aid or scholarships. Now the blockchain will verify the eligibility criteria. Once it gets verified, the funds will be disbursed directly to the student's account. The transactions will be recorded on the blockchain for transparency and auditability. In terms of credentialing as well as verification, the student will be earning credits while completing his courses and the blockchain will be recording the academic achievements based on which it will issue the corresponding digital certificates or diplomas. The interesting factor is that, now employers or other institutions can also verify the credentials through blockchain records. As research funding and grants are also important activities in higher educational institutions, we need to ensure security in these areas as well. For this, the faculty members or researchers should apply for grants or funding. The Blockchain will do the verification based on the proposal details after which it disburses the funds securely. The progress along with the outcomes for the funded projects can also be recorded on the blockchain for further procedures. In terms of administrative processes, the Blockchain can secure the storage and the sharing of credential documents such as contracts, agreements, etc. Here, the smart contracts can automate the agreement terms and conditions ensuring compliance and reducing disputes. During audit and compliance, verification by

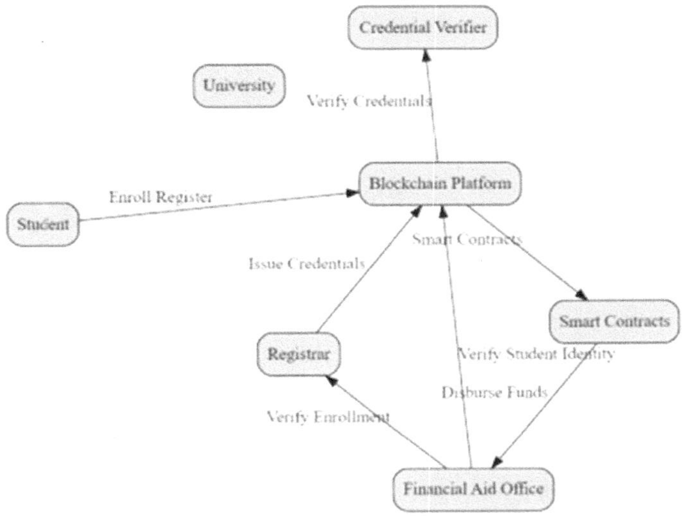

Figure 4. Flowchart showing the proposed system working.

the blockchain can deliver a transparent as well as tamper-proof record of financial transactions and academic credentials. This allows auditors and other regulatory bodies to conduct their verification of compliance easily. Last but not least, continuous monitoring and feedback can help improve all blockchain-based financial activities. Thus, an adaptation of blockchain technology can address all the emerging needs and challenges in the modern higher education system focusing on its financial activities.

As shown in the flow chart at its core is the Blockchain Platform, which serves as the distributed ledger maintaining transaction records securely across multiple nodes. Smart Contracts are programmable scripts deployed on the blockchain, facilitating automated and transparent execution of payment agreements. Users interact with the system through Wallets, and digital repositories for storing cryptocurrencies or tokens used in transactions. Payment Gateways act as interfaces between users' wallets and the blockchain platform, facilitating the initiation and verification of transactions. The system relies on Validators distributed across the blockchain network to verify and validate transactions, ensuring consensus and integrity of the ledger. Users engage with wallets and payment gateways bidirectionally, enabling seamless transaction flows between parties. Overall, this blockchain-based payment system offers enhanced security, transparency, and efficiency compared to traditional centralized payment systems.

5. Proposed System Architecture

The proposed system can be seen as having an architecture with nine major components and several subcomponents as shown in Figure 5. The component blockchain network consists of nodes and consensus protocol. The nodes are nothing but the participants in the network which can be universities, students, faculty members, administrators, etc. The consensus protocol is the mechanism used for validating the transactions by maintaining the blockchain integrity. The next major component is smart contracts which include automated contracts that are self-executing with predefined rules and conditions. The major functions of a smart contract handle processes like student enrolment, fee payments, credential issuance, and research funding.

As in any automated system, the proposed system also requires a set of user interfaces which are mainly web or mobile interfaces that can be used for the nodes in the blockchain system. Also, integration points between API and other nodes should be there. The data layer in the

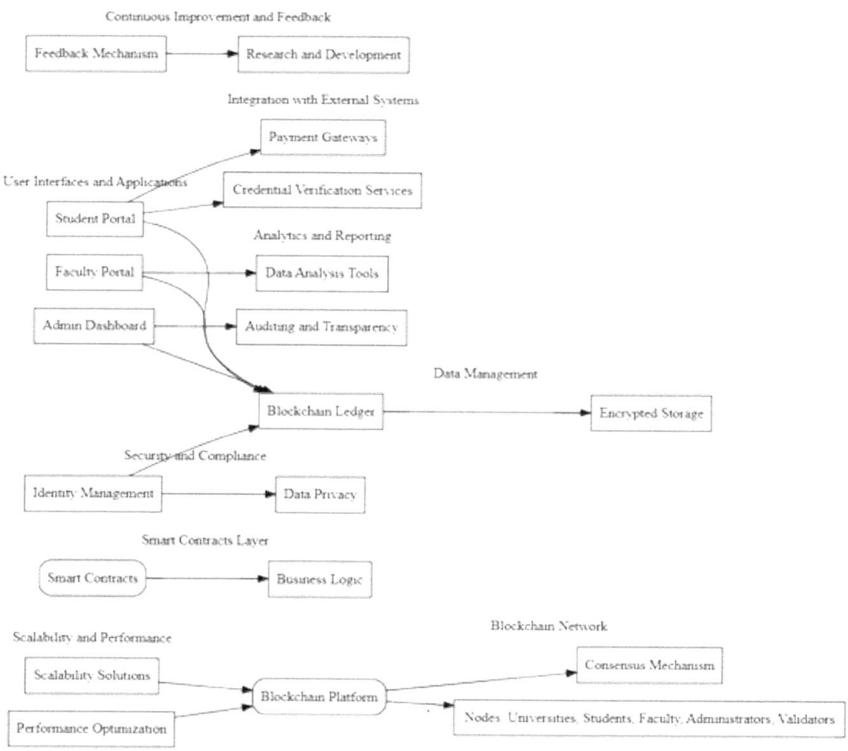

Figure 5. Proposed system architecture.

architecture consists of an immutable ledger wherein all the transactions and academic records are stored securely with the help of encryption which is done on student credentials, academic achievements, financial transactions, research data, and much more. Since the proposed system mainly focuses on financial activities, it needs payment gateways for the payments in Cryptocurrency or digital tokens. Third-party verification services are also needed for verifying the above-stated credentials and academic achievements. Concerning security, the proposed system uses data encryption in terms of compliance. The system should have adhered to data protection regulations and academic standards. Analyzing the blockchain data, the system can prepare the financial activities of students and faculty members or also their academic records and research findings based on its inherent understanding. The system helps in increasing operational efficiency and decision-making. Auditors get immense benefits as the system has records of transactions and interactions that are immutable. Moreover, the system is transparent by publishing all the transactions and keeping better confidentiality with only if needed. The platform is grounded on a feedback mechanism, allowing the stakeholders to provide their responses for making real-time improvements.

6. Challenges

Establishing a higher education financial model based on blockchain is fraught with technical, legal, operational, and adaptational challenges. Scalability is a major technological concern as blockchain networks commonly feature slow transaction times and low throughput, which may not be compatible with the high volume of transactions in place at large educational institutions. Moreover, the implementation of blockchain with traditional institutional systems such as student information and financial systems is difficult and expensive. Blockchain Technology is secure in itself, but it's a big challenge to handle these data as these are confidential student data along with financials, and both scenarios require privacy enabled. Additionally, smart contracts must be highly reliable because they are code-based and this type of reliability avoids mistakes or bugs to avoid financial losses and risks of compromised operability.

On the regulatory front, legalities relevant to data protection, financial transactions, and digital identities are challenges that need navigating. And, these regulations are what make the legal use of blockchain and cryptocurrency in education possible. In addition, to be used as verification or payment systems in the real-world states and accreditation bodies need to give blockchain-based credentials some kind of legal recognition. Technically that means implementing and maintaining the blockchain infrastructure is expensive when operationally speaking. Institutions are drawn to a large upfront cost of implementation (technology adoption costs + training) with most resource delivery solutions. Furthermore, moving from legacy systems to blockchain-based systems also demands elaborate change management strategies to manage the resistance among employees and stakeholders.

User acceptance - particularly among students, faculty, and administrative staff- is key to adoption; success in using new systems will require effective education and training. This creates a headache over what should be flawless and frictionless top-of-funnel experiences, but resistance to new technology is real. What also has to be considered, they added, is that the digital divide could limit students' and adults' ability to avail themselves of such technology in regions where access is not only professional but educational. Other than that, blockchain-based credentials and financial systems need a good ecosystem for widespread adoption and utilities with support coming from institutions like banks and human resources. Dealing with the transaction costs (there are more cost-effective payment methods), and the volatility of some cryptocurrencies could hinder their actual use as a means to pay. While blockchain may prevent some fraud, new risks arise from the technology- for example; phishing attacks that prey on private keys or sophisticated scamming and other forms of fraud stemming from smart contract vulnerabilities. These are the challenges we must solve to bring blockchain technology into higher educational financial activities. In any case, to fully leverage the capabilities of blockchain technology while managing its risks, a transition must be properly planned and executed.

7. Conclusion

A blockchain network developed in higher education has a lot to offer as a platform for financial services, improving academic security and transparency. The blockchain is decentralized and allows an organized way to reduce fraud and streamline administrative chores such as audits of transactions and financial records because every single transaction is in just one system. This can ease the process of utilizing smart contracts to automate and securely transact for services such as tuition payments, scholarships, grants, etc., without needing many intermediaries in between, thus reducing operational costs. But when it comes to deployment, this framework has multiple issues. Meeting the needs for technical scaling and interoperability, regulatory compliance, as well as cost-effective operation models and massive user adoption will be the most important jet contributors to blockchain implementation success. Reliable infrastructure, comprehensive training programs, and excellent change management processes can enable educational institutions to be migrated into blockchain-based systems. We also need to build an enabling ecosystem that will support achieving innovation while maintaining standards of quality and legal or ethical compliance by partnering with regulators, financial institutions (banks), and technology providers. By adequately responding to these challenges, universities will be able to fully benefit from the power of blockchain technology and have a safer, more transparent, and accessible financial system that supports an unblemished educational experience whilst also making operations efficient.

8. Future Research Directions

In concluding this chapter, we may identify a few potential future research directions by focusing on some critical areas to be considered as paramount for applying blockchain technology within higher education systems aiming at maximizing such opportunity in academia. One of the key things to research would be how transactions can scale, allowing blockchain platforms in higher education such as to process and manage huge transactional records each year. That may well involve creating better consensus mechanisms and layer-two solutions. Interoperability with the existing educational technology is also a key component. Standardized protocols and APIs that facilitate seamless university integration with student information systems, financial management platforms, or other institutional databases should be researched. When it comes to adopting blockchain in the education sector, privacy and security are keys. Further research is warranted to study stronger encrypted algorithms and develop data protection measures for offering privacy-preservation of student records, and financial activities. Exploring zero-knowledge proofs and secure multi-party computation might provide solutions that can keep transactions private whilst making sure all works on a transparent audit trail.

Another important axis lies in improving the reliability and security of smart contracts. The research needs to go into creating a kind of formal verification that can help find and avoid vulnerabilities in smart contracts. Adapting the programming languages and frameworks used to develop smart contracts can also have a positive impact on increasing the robustness (software quality) of error-free implementations. It is important to find solutions to the regulatory problems that arise in relation to blockchain technology for education. This means securing and a better understanding of the legal status of blockchain-enabled credentials in financial transactions to allow regulators to directly interact with these technologies; establishing contexts for compliance by various groups where data protection laws require a very different approach than banking ones. It will be important for this to involve working with stakeholders and regulators in helping establish conducive legislation. The success of our platform depends on user acceptance and adoption, so it is really important to understand what can impact users' decisions. Further research into best practices to train users, manage the change, and overcome resistance should be in focus. Finally, it is also important for unfettered access to blockchain technology so that no digital divides exist between different students and staff anywhere in the world where internet problems are few as well as technological facilities.

Thus, creating a vibrant ecosystem comprising educational institutions, technology providers, financial institutions and regulators is imperative to suggest research that could develop a partnership and collaboration framework to facilitate innovation and scalability of blockchain-based systems in higher education. The outcomes and cases summarized in this study indicate that blockchain could be effectively utilized to innovate higher education, improving its security of operations including information transparency and process efficiency if the research gaps discussed here are addressed.

References

[1] Mann, R.J. (2023). *Payment Systems and other Financial Transactions: Cases, Materials, and Problems*. Aspen Publishing.

[2] Alenizi, A., Mishra, S. and Baihan, A. (2024). Enhancing secure financial transactions through the synergy of blockchain and artificial intelligence. *Ain Shams Engineering Journal*, 15(6): 102733.

[3] Gowri, S. and Devi, P.M. (2024). Application of blockchain technology for secured financial and academic transactions in institutions. *Financial Technology and Modern Finance*, 25.

[4] Rani, P., Sachan, R.K. and Kukreja, S. (2024). A systematic study on blockchain technology in education: Initiatives, products, applications, benefits, challenges and research direction. *Computing*, 106(2): 405–447.

[5] Jameel, R., Wadhwa, B., Sikri, A., Singh, S. and Idrees, S.M. (2024). Transforming educational landscape with blockchain technology: Applications and challenges. *Blockchain Transformations: Navigating the Decentralized Protocols Era*, 197–209.

[6] Samala, A.D., Mhlanga, D., Bojic, L., Howard, N.J. and Coelho, D.P. (2024). Blockchain technology in education: Opportunities, challenges, and beyond. *International Journal of Interactive Mobile Technologies*, 18(1).

[7] Stal, J. and Put, D. (2024). Blockchain as a disruptive technology in Education 4.0. In *Supporting Higher Education 4.0 with Blockchain,* (pp. 37–61). Routledge.

[8] Alzahrani, A.M.M. (2024). Utilization of blockchain technology and smart contracts in the education procedure of universities. *International Journal of Intelligent Systems and Applications in Engineering*, 12(12s): 652–661.

[9] Rao, K.S., Shirisha, P., Navaneswar, M., Chaitanya, K. and Nithin, K.H. (2024). Blockchain based academic and professional credentials. *International Research Journal on Advanced Engineering Hub (IRJAEH)*, 2(05): 1383–1386.

[10] El Koshiry, A., Eliwa, E., Abd El-Hafeez, T. and Shams, M.Y. (2023). Unlocking the power of blockchain in education: An overview of innovations and outcomes. *Blockchain: Research and Applications*, 100165.

[11] Rani, P., Sachan, R.K. and Kukreja, S. (2023). Academic payment tokenization: An online payment system for academia utilizing non-fungible tokens and permissionless blockchain. *Procedia Computer Science*, 230: 347–356.

[12] Moonde, C. (2023). *Secure Mobile Payment System based on Blockchain Technology for Higher Learning Institutions* (Doctoral dissertation, The University of Zambia).

[13] https://ieeexplore.ieee.org/search/searchresult.jsp?queryText=blockchain%20 technology&highlight=true&returnFacets=ALL&returnType=SEARCH&matchPubs=true&searchWithin=education.

[14] Al-Filali, I.Y., Abdulaal, R.M., Alawi, S.M. and Makki, A.A. (2024). Modification of strategic planning tools for planning financial sustainability in higher education institutions. *Journal of Engineering Research*, 12(1): 192–203.

[15] Li, Q. (2024). Empowering financial management in educational institutions: A multi-objective decision-making system using intelligent fuzzy logic algorithm and digital marketing. *Computer-Aided Design & Applications*, 21: 198–210.

Index

I

K

L

M

P

R

S

T

About the Editors

Randhir Kumar has a Ph.D. from the Department of Information Technology, NIT Raipur, India. He completed his Postdoctoral from Department of Electrical Engineering, IIT Hyderabad, and is now an Assistant Professor, Department of Computer Science and Engineering, SRM University, AP, India. He has 7 years of teaching and 4 years of research experience. He has published his research articles in leading journal and conferences. His paper has been published in some of the high impact factor journals such as – IEEE Internet of Things, IEEE Transactions on Intelligent Transportation Systems, IEEE Transactions on Network Science and Engineering, IEEE Transactions on Green Communications and Networking, IEEE Transactions on Industrial Informatics, IEEE Intelligent Systems, IEEE Consumer Electronics Magazine, IEEE COMSNETs, IEEE ICC, MobiCom, GlobeCom, Computer Networks, JPDC, and Transactions on Emerging Telecommunications Technologies. His paper was recognized as most cited paper of year 2020–2021 in Transactions on Emerging Telecommunications Technologies. He received best paper presentation award in one of the reputed conferences, i.e., GLOBECOM in the year 2022. He has qualified UGC-NET in the year of 2018. He has been awarded as Best Engineer Trainee by Honeywell Technology, India in the year 2009. He is active reviewer of many of the reputed journals like IEEE TDSC, IEEE TGCN, IEEE TNSM, IEEE TII, IEEE Access, Journal of Super Computing, Journal of Ambient Intelligent and Humanized Computing, and International Journal of Information Security and Privacy, IGI global. His research interest includes Cryptographic Techniques, Information Security, Blockchain Technology, Digital Twin and Services, Machine Learning, and Web Mining. He is also a member of IEEE, IAENG.

Prabhat Kumar has a Ph.D. in Information Technology, NIT, Raipur, India, under the prestigious fellowship of Ministry of Human Resource and Development (MHRD) funded by the Government of India in 2022. Thereafter, he worked with Indian Institute of Technology Hyderabad, India, as a Postdoctoral Researcher under project "Development of Indian Telecommunication Security Assurance Requirements for IoT devices". He is currently working as Postdoctoral Researcher with the Department of Software Engineering, LUT School of Engineering Science, LUT University, Lappeenranta, Finland. He has several contributions in the area of Machine Learning, Deep Learning, Federated Learning, Big Data Analytics, Cybersecurity, Blockchain, Cloud Computing, Internet of Things, Digital Twin and Software Defined Networking. He has authored or co-authored over 28+ top-tier journal/conference articles, including 13+ IEEE Transactions/Magazine papers. One of his Ph.D. publications was recognized as a top cited article by WILEY in 2020–21. Some of his research findings are published in top cited journals and conferences, such as IEEE TII, IEEE TITS, IEEE TNSE, IEEE TGCN, IEEE IoT-J, IEEE Intelligent Systems, IEEE Consumer Electronics Magazine, IEEE MICRO, JSA (Elsevier), ComCom (Elsevier), Comnet (Elsevier), JPDC (Elsevier), ICDCN, IEEE ICC, ACM MobiCom and IEEE GLOBECOM. He is an Expert Evaluator of top scientific journals and conferences, including IEEE TII, IEEE TITS, IEEE TNSE, IEEE TGCN, IEEE JBHI, IEEE IoTJ, IEEE Network Magazine, IEEE IoT Magazine, IEEE Access, ACM TALLIP, ComCom and IEEE ICC. He is also an IEEE Member.

Sobin C.C. has vast expertise in studies of "Delay Tolerant Networks (DTNs)", "Wireless Networks", and "Internet of Things (IoT)". Dr Sobin's M. Tech and Ph.D. research from premier institutes in India, such as IIT Madras and IIT Roorkee enabled him to acquire in-depth knowledge in developing routing protocols for DTNs and designing IoT-based applications. Also, well-versed in building IoT applications over DTN in case of limited Internet connectivity. PI published articles relevant to his area of expertise in leading reputed journals in the specified field (Journal of Network and Computer Applications, Wireless Personal Communications, International Journal of Communication Systems, etc.).

N.P. Subheesh is the Chairperson, Educational Activities of IEEE Education Society, Kerala, India. He received his bachelor's degree in applied electronics and instrumentation engineering from the University of Calicut, India, in 2004, and master's degree in media and sound engineering from Indian Institute of Technology Kharagpur, in 2013. He is currently completing his Ph.D. degree in Engineering Education at the Indian Institute of Technology Madras, Chennai. He has authored or co-authored more than ten articles in peer-reviewed journals and international conferences. His research interests focus on Information and Communication Technology (ICT) in education, Technology-Enhanced Learning (TEL), Artificial Intelligence and Machine Learning (AI & ML) techniques in education, Engineering Education Research (EER), and assessment and evaluation in higher education. He is a member of the IEEE, IEEE Education Society, and the Portuguese Society for Engineering Education (SPEE).